A NEW CHRISTOLOGY

A NEW CHRISTOLOGY

Karl Rahner & Wilhelm Thüsing

A CROSSROAD BOOK · THE SEABURY PRESS · NEW YORK

1980
The Seabury Press
815 Second Avenue
New York, N.Y. 10017
Published originally as *Christologie—Systematisch und Exegetisch.*
Copyright © 1972 Verlag Herder, Freiburg-im-Breisgau,
Federal Republic of Germany.

Adapted by Karl Rahner.
New Material copyright © 1980 Karl Rahner

Translated from the German by David Smith & Verdant Green.
English translation copyright © 1980 Search Press Limited.

Printed in the United States of America

Library of Congress Catalog Card Number: 79-92336
ISBN: 0-8164-0211-6

Second printing

Contents

PART ONE

JESUS CHRIST AND CHRISTOLOGY

by Karl Rahner

1. Christology today

It is, I think, important to preface what I am going to say on the subject of Christology by a few preliminary remarks.

First, it is obvious that it would be impossible to exhaust the subject in the present work. The theme is, after all, concerned with the whole of Christianity and the whole of human and Christian existence and the inexhaustible mystery of that life in all its dimensions. Some of the most illustrious scholars in the Western world have lived, believed in, prayed and reflected about Christology for two thousand years. It is a theme which presupposes a whole anthropology and theology. It calls for the most detailed knowledge of the Bible and the history of dogma and it has always to be studied in the light of our present situation in the world of today. Bearing all this in mind, it is clear that only very few remarks can be made about such a subject in this space and that these will to some extent be chosen arbitrarily. This inevitably involves the risk of passing over in silence certain aspects of the subject that the reader might find more helpful than what is in fact said. These limitations have clearly to be taken into account at the beginning of any lecture on Christology.

Second, I would fail to do justice to the subject-matter if I did not appeal to the whole mystery of human existence and approached the question simply as one special object of man's curiosity alongside countless other objects of equal status. This question can only be discussed in the context of the whole of man with his ultimate mystery, God, and with the urgent questioning about salvation that he usually suppresses or allows to remain unanswered in his everyday life. Christology can only be discussed if the whole reality of man in his unity and free responsibility is taken fully into account, since it is above all an answer to the one, whole question about human existence. This does not necessarily mean that Christology has to be discussed in a meditative or edifying way or that the exertion of conceptual language has to be completely avoided. It is important, however, that the reader should be quite clear from the very beginning that he should have an attitude of free, conscious responsibility for his existence as a single whole if he is to understand what follows on the matter of Christology.

Third, it is possible to approach Christology today in many different ways. A theology of love of one's neighbour, a theology of death or a theology of the future are all possible points of departure and there are, of course, many more. All could lead to a questioning, searching Christology which would find its answer in the Church's confession of Jesus Christ as the victorious and unique Word in which God has made his promise known to man historically in a tangible and irreversible way. The basis of a real consent in faith to Christology should also be made even clearer by these and other more explicitly enunciated approaches to the subject. It is, however, necessary to simplify a little more and see the various approaches to Christology today, which can and should be differentiated from each other, as a whole.

Fourth, it would be impossible to delineate the whole of the Church's official Christology in all its fulness and many distinctions at a high theological or even at a traditional catechetical level within this framework. All that can be done is to try to indicate a point of departure for such a Christology in man today. It is possible to show that modern man is able to reflect the Church's Christology when what is hidden within him is developed and taken seriously only by means of an assurance that this point of departure contains what is proclaimed by the Church's official teaching about Jesus.

For this reason, then, we do not begin by saying that Jesus is God, the Word of the eternal God made flesh, existing with the Father from eternity. Nor do we begin by speaking of the hypostatic union of the divine and human natures in the one person of the divine Logos. Our point of departure is not the Christological formulations of Paul and John in the New Testament, providing a highly developed reflection about faith. We do not accept as a condition of our investigation that no questions can be asked about this 'late' New Testament Christology on the basis of more original and to some extent simpler experiences of faith with the historical Jesus, his message, death and having become definitively saved (his resurrection). We do not believe that it is bound to be certain and obvious in advance that orthodox faith in Jesus as the Christ can only and exclusively be expressed in the formulations of the classical Christology of the western Church, even though these formulations are undoubtedly normative for our faith today and in the future. The precise meaning of this fourth preliminary remark may not be clear at present, but it may perhaps emerge in the course of my exposition.

Let us therefore begin by examining what is meant by what might perhaps be called a searching Christology. In freedom and orientated towards definitiveness, man is concerned with himself as a single whole. It is true that he can let himself be driven along through the multiplicity of experience in his life and be preoccupied first with one and then with another detail of his life and his various possibilities. He should, however, allow the whole and the singleness of his existence to appear before him and be answerable for this in freedom. He should, in other words, be concerned for himself and for his 'salvation'. If he does this, he will, however, be placed in a peculiar and fundamental predicament. Since it is a question of the whole and the singleness of man's existence, this same whole would seem to be able to be significant in salvation only as a single whole. It would also seem that any particular detail of his life or his individual and collective history cannot be decisive for the whole and singleness of his existence. However much he may be a historical being in the rest of his existence, man would seem to be outside history in his salvation.

Man consequently tries again and again to present the whole and singleness of his existence to himself outside history. He may do this by presenting it to himself in a mystical state of recollection in the depth of his being, where everything seems to be one. He may, on the other hand, try, in a movement of metaphysical ascent, to seize hold of the eternal truth that hovers constantly above history and promises him his eternal being above the multiplicity of his historical experience. Again, he may attempt to discover the real truth of his existence by showing all truth, in a mood of sceptical resignation, to be historically and socially conditioned. All this is, however, of no real importance in the end, because man believes that he can discover himself only outside his authentic historical existence as a single whole and recognizes that history as such is apparently without salvation and is no more than the appearance that conceals man's true being in a thousand empty externals.

Man may, however, be convinced that he can only work out and experience his salvation within his history, because he can only come to himself and express his freedom in association with his environment and his fellow-men, in other words, in history. He may also at the same time believe that he can never really step outside his history even in metaphysics and mysticism. In that case, he will look for another person in whom — through God's free sovereign power — salvation has been really successful and can as such be experienced by him. In that other person too, salvation appears not only as an abstract possibility, but also as a real promise that hope will be fulfilled and this also applies to him because of his solidarity with that person. The man who is really looking for his salvation, then, in the knowledge that he is responsible for it in freedom, will inevitably look within the history of the one mankind to which he belongs for a person in whom this salvation does not simply happen as a promise made to him, but also becomes tangible as though it had been accomplished triumphantly through God's sovereign power, thus enabling him to have concrete hope for himself rather than a purely abstract possibility of hope.

Whether this successful and therefore also experienced event of salvation can only be sought in history or whether it can also really be found in history is a question that cannot be considered at this stage of our investigation. We can, however, call the person who is at least sought in this way (thus going forward rather quickly and erratically in our examination of the question) the absolute bringer of salvation, because it is, as we have seen, not simply a matter of one individual existence alone, but of an existence that promises *us* salvation as a firm hope and *our* salvation victoriously as coming from God. This of course presupposes that this person who is sought and who comes into salvation exists in absolute solidarity with us and that we are able to and in fact do extend the same solidarity to him.

This salvation that has really succeeded in the person sought can only be conceived in our human predicament as it is in fact as taking place in death, since it is only in death that history is completed, freedom becomes definitive and man definitively gives himself in freedom to the mystery of God, his transcendence entering the incomprehensibility of God and his history becoming definitively one. This death, in which man achieves salvation, must also — because it is a victorious promise of salvation for us, God's gift of himself to us and not simply the individual fate of this man — become tangible for us as something that is successful and enters God in an experience that is absolutely unique. In other words, the death of this man must be capable of being comprehended as entering what we call, in the traditional language of Christianity the resurrection of this person. In addition, of course, the life and self-understanding of this person (who is still sought) were of such a kind and are comprehended historically by us in such a way that we are able to believe that this life was saved: in other words, we can believe in this man's 'resurrection'. Subject to these conditions, however, a person of this kind, who has to some extent been projected *a priori* from our questioning about salvation, can certainly be regarded as the absolute bringer of salvation.

He can be seen simply as this man and not as salvation, since the latter can only be God himself, in the unlimited transcendence of man beyond all individuality and the radicalization of that transcendence by what we call grace. Salvation, then, can only be constituted by God's direct and definitive communication of himself. This person who is sought, however, is only the absolute bringer of salvation if his fulfilment through his death and resurrection in the power of God in solidarity with us is the irrevocable sign for the fact that God has promised himself to us as the fulfilment of our salvation.

As I said at the beginning, it is not possible within this space to demonstrate explicitly and exhaustively that this absolute bringer of salvation, who is sought, at least implicitly taught what is understood in the classical Christology of the Church as the hypostatic union, in other words, the incarnation of the eternal Word of God in the unity of one person and the unadulterated duality of a human and a divine reality. I am of the opinion, however, that it is certainly possible to demonstrate this and I presuppose it here. Wherever a man takes God's promise of salvation made to him *in* the individual fate of a man and *as* someone who has experienced salvation, he is practising Christology either thematically or unthematically. If he looks for such a person in his history, he is practising a searching Christology, either thematically or unthematically. Since, moreover, a man is guilty if he suppresses questioning his own salvation, this thematic or unthematic practice of a searching Christology is the presupposition today in transcendence and grace in all men that his mysterious Christology seeks and will eventually also find. We do not have to experience the classical Christology today simply as a strange myth that can no longer be grasped and understood.

We must now move from a searching Christology, which seeks to discover the absolute bringer of salvation in history, to a Christology which has really found this bringer of salvation in history. It is in this conviction that the bringer of salvation has been found that the very heart and substance of Christianity subsists. According to Christian teaching, then, we have found the absolute bringer of salvation, the Christ of God, the Son of God, in Jesus of Nazareth.

Have we sufficient reason and the right to make this claim today? It is certainly possible to state that Jesus of Nazareth is the event of salvation that has really succeeded, that this event is as much experienced in faith and that Jesus is the absolute bringer of salvation who guarantees our concrete hope of salvation in history. Seen from the purely human point of view, this statement about a unique, unrepeatable and historically remote event is full of difficulties. A man may experience in his own individual history that his actual existence is based not only on statements that can be verified in the sphere of the natural sciences, but also and even more decisively on historically unique experiences (despite the fact that the latter are always open to doubt). He may similarly experience that he must risk his existence again and again on such historical experiences (even if this only amounts to an unconditional trust in the love of a fellow man). For such a man, it is not possible to escape from the historical experience of this Jesus by adopting an attitude of reasonable scepticism, in the opinion that everything in history is obscure, uncertain and ambiguous. He knows that he must transcend the questionable nature of his historical experiences with regard to his fellow man courageously and come to a final decision. Why, then, should it not be possible and legitimate to do this with regard to Jesus?

It is not true to say that we no longer have any certain knowledge today of the historical Jesus or that we only know what is theologically in accordance with faith and therefore unimportant. It is also true that it has been demonstrated by historical and critical exegesis that we are concerned, even in the earliest documents in the New Testament relating to Jesus, with testimonies of faith in him as the Christ and not simply with historically neutral reports of his life on earth. It is also clear from modern biblical theology that there is a great and dramatic development within the New Testament between the preaching of the historical Jesus about the imminence of the Kingdom of God and his own understanding of himself on the one hand and the extremely developed Christology of Paul and John on the other. (The latter is very close to the later classical Christology of the Church.)

All this, which has become the common property not only of Protestant theology, but — a little later, it is true — of Catholic exegesis and theology, does not, however, imply that we know nothing today about the historical Jesus that is relevant to our Christology or that nothing can be proved with regard to the legitimacy of Jesus' historical self-understanding and its relevance to the Christology of Paul and John on the one hand and the Church on the other, especially if the Easter event is also taken into account. The historically tangible proclamation of Jesus and his self-understanding, which is implied in this, have a distinctive, unique and incomparable character which enables us to say that God's promise of himself as our salvation has become in Jesus a historical event in a unique and irreversible way. We can also say that this promise was definitely confirmed by Jesus' death, with the result that he has really become, in his proclamation and his death, the definitive Word of God for us in history. This is, however, something that cannot be discussed in detail here and, as I have already pointed out, it is equally impossible to develop here and now the classical Christology of Scripture and the Church that is implied in the historical Jesus' self-understanding. All that we can do is to point to the fact that Jesus did not simply proclaim a liberating image of God as the Father before whom all men, including sinners and the socially and politically underprivileged, stand with equal rights. He did not only proclaim a God who forgives men and sets them free and whose grace transcends man's helplessness. Jesus did all this and it is certainly a great deal. But if this were all that was contained in Jesus' proclamation, we might well ask whether this liberating knowledge of God as the Father could not have been obtained without Jesus, whether it really transcends the accumulation of prophetic teaching in the Old Testament and whether it could not also be grasped in hope without Jesus and therefore be ultimately separable from Jesus and his proclamation.

We do not have to answer this question here and now and can point to the fact that Jesus proclaimed much more than this, wonderful as it was for himself alone and pleasing and liberating as it is now in a modern Jesuanism of freedom and brotherly love between men. From the historical point of view, Jesus proclaimed something much more radical, which cannot be separated from his person and his proclamation. His proclamation contains a new turning of God towards man, a new coming of the Kingdom of God, since this coming is not simply an offer made to man in his historical freedom, with the result that it remains open for man to consent to or reject God's offer of himself, thus leaving the history itself of this offer open. What Jesus proclaimed was that this offer of himself by God, not as the judgment, but as the salvation of mankind, was made irreversibly victorious by his power and that it was also made historically tangible in its irreversibly victorious quality in him, in his proclamation and finally in his death. He also proclaimed that this was so even though individual men are not made exempt from the responsibility of their individual freedom by the reality and tangibility of God's victory in the history of mankind and that they are only able to comprehend this victory of God in hope.

We may ask, of course, how the man Jesus could have come to know of this victory of God that was given with him and his message in the sinful and unreconciled world in which he lived. We may also ask how he could have known that God's offer of himself to man not only provided his ultimate possibility of finding God directly, but also brought about the victory of this offer itself. In answer to these questions, we can only say that Jesus knew that he was indissolubly united with his God and that he was faithful to this unity throughout all the catastrophes that occurred in his life, including his death. We can also say that he was equally united, with such an unconditional solidarity of love, to all men, despite their wretchedness and guilt, with the result that he was not confronted by the dilemma of choosing between God and his fellow men, but understood his own salvation to be that of the whole of mankind.

It is, of course, possible to say, with regard to Jesus, that God's will to save, which unconditionally creates not only possibility, but reality, was undoubtedly at work and has always been at work throughout the whole of the history of mankind. We can, however, only say in faith and in the light of Jesus himself that he was not simply an offer of possibility, but was himself and in himself reality and that, as such, he became irreversible in his own history and historically tangible. Jesus himself said this in his message about the new and definitive coming of the Kingdom of God that was inseparable from his person and what he said was confirmed in his death. I may therefore conclude this part by saying that Jesus is the new and insurpassable Word of God's promise of himself to us, even if history continues and what is already established in Jesus' fate and in his message has to be supplemented and has to appear in the entire history of mankind until it comes to an end.

At this point in my outline of Christology today, I must discuss a little more explicitly a question that we have already touched on — the resurrection of Jesus. This event was the confirmation and appearance of what was given with Jesus' person and message. It was the historically visible victory of God's promise of himself to mankind. What is really meant by the resurrection of Jesus can only be grasped in faith if four aspects of its indissoluble unity of elements are apprehended.

I shall consider each of these aspects in turn.

The first is that it is necessary to understand correctly what is meant by resurrection. Resurrection contains a statement about the whole and the one man. It points to the definitively saved nature of the person and of the history of a man with God. It also indicates that there is no return to our spatio-temporal biological life. It is not a raising up from the dead in the sense of a return to our present corporeal existence as reported in the New Testament and the history of the saints. Our and the original witnesses' experience of the resurrection therefore has an absolute quality which cannot be compared with other experiences and which is consequently 'historical' in a very special way. It is historical because the definitive salvation of a history is experienced in it until that history ceases to exist.

The second aspect of resurrection that has to be taken into consideration is this. Man is only able to understand an experience of such a unique kind to the extent that he extends to it his own hope that he will *himself* be definitively saved in his own existence. If this does not happen, a man cannot be anything else but sceptical with regard to the report of Jesus' resurrection and he is bound to look at it as something that took place in the obscure past and ultimately does not concern him. Man can, however, have his own hope of resurrection and may not simply let human existence and history fall into the empty void of having been, both on his own account and in solidarity with the dead, without destroying himself. Man's faith in his own resurrection, which need not be localized at a 'later' period or point in time in the distant future, takes place where there is real love and hope, even if that loving and hoping man fails, through lack of ability or courage, to verbalize, thematize and objectivize his own hope of resurrection in the unreflected way in which he expresses his own existence.

Man can, on the other hand, give courageous expression to his own hope of resurrection. He can regard himself as called to the definitive expression of his own existence. He can also receive the message of Jesus' resurrection in the light of the claim of the life and death of Jesus with an absolute love for both God and his fellow men. If he does this, he can regard himself as entitled to seize hold of the resurrection of Jesus in faith. He is asked, moreover, whether he would not deny his own hope of resurrection in a final guilty act of despair, if he could not find the courage to believe, in view of *this* life and this death of this Jesus, that he was the one who was definitively saved and raised from the dead.

There is a third aspect of resurrection. It is this. We hope that we shall ourselves rise again and we receive the claim which Jesus' fate places on us. We also receive the message of resurrection brought by Jesus' disciples and encounter the faith of two thousand years of a history of Christian hope. We are bound, however, to ask whether it is really possible to refuse to consent to this message and this hope, since there must be faith here in the definitive, unpresentable and incomprehensible nature of God. Jesus' disciples bore witness to their experience of Easter: 'The Lord has risen indeed'. It is difficult for us to visualize the distinctive character of this experience clearly and to distinguish it from other apparently similar visionary and mystical phenomena, which cannot in the long run be compared with the experience of Jesus' resurrection. The New Testament contains reports of individual appearances of the risen Christ which ultimately cannot be fully harmonized with each other. These may be regarded as settings and interpretations of various aspects of the original experience of the resurrection on the part of the disciples.

This experience of the resurrection is not, however, removed from the world in this way. It was made by men who bore witness to it, although they were not particularly well disposed to do this because they were in despair about the catastrophe of Jesus' life. They were, however, certainly capable of distinguishing this experience from other apparently similar visionary and hallucinatory phenomena with which they were familiar. Why, then, should we not believe their testimony, on condition, of course, that we look forward to our own resurrection with a desire based on our own existential hope, that we receive the claim that Jesus' life and death places on us and that we do not let his unique life, led in unconditional love, fall into the empty void of having been? We are bound to be united with the dead and cannot simply dismiss them as having been and only useful in that they may make our own history possible.

The fourth aspect can be outlined in the following way. If our own transcendence is alive to the immediate presence of God in grace and freedom, and it takes place and comes to itself in history, and if we encounter Jesus of Nazareth with our searching Christology, then it will be possible for us to experience the risen Christ, even though that experience is also dependent on the testimony of the first disciples. The experience of our transcendence to the immediate presence of God in history reaches a unique climax in this. In grace, we experience an ultimate freedom which transcends all the powers and principalities of history, law, guilt and the tyranny of all human conditioning. This experience becomes tangible and is confirmed in history. This experience also looks for Jesus in the disciples' and the Church's experience of Easter, when they bore witness to the crucified and risen Christ. It finds in him the confirmation that it is seeking and also finds it precisely in this risen Christ, since such an offer cannot be found elsewhere in the religious history of mankind. There is an indissoluble unity between this experience of freedom in the immediate presence of God on the one hand and the encounter with the risen Christ on the other and they also condition one another. We hope absolutely for ourselves, because we receive Jesus' fate as the unique Word of God addressed to us. We also believe in the resurrection, because we hope in ultimate freedom for everything and for God in himself. This experience which is united in spirit and history is certainly an experience of the risen Christ in ourselves, even if we are only able to name it, by means of the testimony of the first disciples and the Church, with the name of Jesus (this experience would otherwise have remained to some extent anonymous).

These four aspects of the resurrection should therefore be understood clearly in faith and hope and as a unity. If they are, it should be possible for us to believe today in the resurrection of Jesus without at the same time believing that we are losing ourselves in a mythological interpretation of something that happened in the past and that simply resulted in a utopian hope which fell into an ultimate void. We should as Christians have the courage to believe in the resurrection because we can understand it in responsibility for the ultimate importance of our own existence. We dare to believe, in hope, in our own history and this enables us to believe in the resurrection of Jesus.

Many important points must inevitably be left out of these brief comments on Christology today and we must now pass on to consider an individual question within the whole, that of the individual Christian's personal relationship with Jesus. As the risen and exalted Christ, Jesus should not simply be a cypher for a personal relationship with the external God. He should not, as the exalted Christ, simply disappear into the nameless mystery that reigns inexpressibly and incomprehensibly above our existence and is called God. Jesus, as the saved man with his own real fate that has become definitive, is our guarantee that we too shall be able to reach God in the fulness of his life and freedom and in his light and love. This guarantee is, for this reason, the eternally valid and lasting communication of the immediacy of God in himself and that is why we can and should, as Christians, have a personal relationship of hope, trust and love with this Jesus, who has been saved, in the uniqueness of his human reality.

This is a real possibility and one that should be developed and cherished by the Christian. Why should it not be possible? We have the hope in our own hope of resurrection, in which we anticipate the definitive salvation of our own personal existence and our history, that such saved men, who have themselves become definitive, really exist. We have no right to dismiss the dead of history and those who have left our own circle and have entered the silent eternity of God and to behave as though they no longer concern us.

We will not, as Christians, try to enter into a relationship with the dead who are alive by spiritualistic or parapsychological means, because the conjuration of the dead was rejected in the Old Testament and such practices are contrary to the dignity of God himself and the mystery of the definitive salvation of the dead which is not available to us. This does not, however, mean that we Christians, who confess our faith in the communion of saints in our creed, should simply give up our loving relationship with the dead and act as though they were no longer alive in themselves or at least for us. If we were to do this and regard the Church's act of remembering all her members who have gone home as an empty ritual, this does not in any sense mean that we are acting correctly; it only points to the incomplete state and the partial emptiness of our own existence.

If this is correct in general, it is also correct when it is applied to the particular relationship that we can and ought to have with the living Jesus. He is saved and is the unique guarantee of our own existence and as such lives in himself and for us. We are able to hope in him, love him, call to him, rely on his love and faithfulness and reassure ourselves in meditation of his life and death on earth in the conviction that Jesus' fate was to be saved and that it was reserved for us as the eternal guarantee of our own hope. We can experience in his Spirit that he loves each of us in a unique way and that we also love him, again in a unique way, since each of us possesses this uniqueness in our human existence and history. It is in this love for Jesus in the eternity of God that the ultimate reconciliation between time and eternity on the one hand and history and God's transcendence of history on the other takes place. It is in and with Jesus that we can understand the blessed untouched nature of God in himself, since it is in him that God has given himself to time and history, with his infinite nature and his freedom, irrevocably for Jesus and, in him, also for us.

We are also able to grasp, in Jesus and our love for him, that neither he nor we in him, with our individuality and our history, perish when we approach the burning and unconditional immediacy of God, but that we will continue to exist and be definitively saved. In him and with him too, we can experience the unity that exists between God and the world without either one or the other perishing. Jesus is the unique and irrevocable seal of the ultimate reconciliation. That is why the individual Christian's loving and unique relationship with Jesus is not something that is bound to disappear into the nameless, silent and incomprehensible mystery of God's immediacy. On the contrary, it is an essential inner aspect of this immediate relation with God, by which our continued existence and definitive salvation is confirmed, even when God has become all in all and history has come to God and is saved. We have to enter Jesus' fate and give ourselves over in faith, hope and love to his unconditional love for his fellow men and his death. We have to live and die with him in the empty darkness of his death. We shall then learn in his Spirit how to associate with God himself beyond the reality of this world, how to fall without perishing into this inexpressibly mysterious God, whose judgments are so imcomprehensible, and how therefore to discover the ultimate and definitive reality beyond this life. If the Christian has a personal and direct love for Jesus and lets Jesus' life and fate become the inner form and entelechy of his own life, he will inevitably find that Jesus is the way, the truth and the life and that he will take him to the Father. He will also discover that he is able to call the incomprehensible God Father, even though he is nameless and that this God, who is without a name and a way, can still be his home and give him eternal life. Jesus, we may conclude, must be loved and his fate must be accepted in that love as the norm of the Christian's existence. If that existence is to be experienced as something that is redeemed, happy and cheerful.

On the other hand, it is also true to say that many people who reject the orthodox formulae of classical Christology (because they misunderstand them) are certainly able to believe authentically in the incarnation of the divine Word. It is possible to believe that the living God has said the last, decisive, irrevocable and all-embracing word in Jesus and his death on the cross. It is equally possible to believe that God has redeemed man in Jesus from the captivity and tyranny that are present in his narrow, guilty existence that is ultimately given over to death. Whoever accepts this is ultimately believing something that is

only true if Jesus is the one who is the object of the Christian confession of faith. Whether he knows it consciously or not, that person
believes in the incarnation of the divine Word.

This is not a refutation of the underlying meaning of the formula of
the creed, which is objectively correct as the ecclesio-sociological basis
of shared Christian thinking and believing. Only the heretic (not the
Catholic Christian), who makes no distinction between those who
sincerely believe the redeeming truth in their hearts and those who confess the orthodox formulae of the Church, can *a priori* deny that there
may still be faith in Christ if the orthodox formulae are rejected. It is
simply not possible for a man to adopt every position that is thinkable
in the expression of his existence. Consequently, the man who accepts
Jesus as the ultimate truth of his life and confesses that God is saying,
in Jesus and his death, the last word, the Word towards whom he is prepared to orientate his own life and death, will accept him precisely in
this as the Son of God, that is, as the Church confesses him, whatever
form the theoretical, unsuccessful and even wrong conceptual formulation of the expression of faith in his own existence may take.

We may go further and say that many people have in fact encountered Christ without knowing that they were in contact with the
one whose life and death was their own redeemed fate. They have encountered, although they did not know it, the one whom Christians
rightly call Jesus of Nazareth. The freedom of the creature is always
found in a venture into what cannot be clearly seen as a whole and,
whether we know it or not, this is always to be found in what we want
to see. What is purely unseen and what is simply different are not
appropriated by freedom, so long as they are only striving after a
definite and limited objective. But what is unexpressed and unformu-
lated is not necessarily what is unseen and unwanted. God's grace
(and Christ's) is, however, present in everything as the mysterious
essence of the whole of elective reality, with the result that it is not
easy to strive after something without being concerned in one way or
another with God (and Christ). A man may therefore accept his existence and his humanity (this is not easy to do) in silent patience and
perhaps without any verbal formulation which explicitly refers to the
Christian revelation), or better still in faith, hope and love (or whatever
he may call these virtues), as the mystery that is hidden in the mystery
of eternal love and gives birth to life in the womb of death. The man
who accepts his life in this way is in fact assenting to something to
which he entrusts himself as to what is immeasurable, because God has

filled it with what is immeasurable, in other words, with himself, in letting the Word become flesh. Even if he does not know it, that man is giving assent to Christ.

The man who lets go and leaps into the unknown falls into the depths and not simply to the extent to which he has plumbed them. Whoever accepts his humanity completely (and this is inexpressibly difficult to do; it is doubtful whether any of us really ever does it) has at the same time accepted the Son of Man, because God has accepted man in him. According to Scripture, he who loves his neighbour has fulfilled the law. This is the ultimate truth, because God himself has become this neighbour. In every neighbour, then, this one neighbour, who is most near and most far, is accepted and loved.

Man is a mystery. He is more than this. He is *the* mystery, not only because he is open to the mystery of the incomprehensible fulness of God, but also because God has expressed this mystery as his own. Assuming that God wanted to express himself in the empty void and that he wanted to call his Word into that void, how could he do anything other than create in man an inner hearing of his Word and express his Word in such a way that the self-expression of that Word and its being heard become one. The fact that this indeed happens is itself a mystery. The unexpected, incalculable element that is both astonishing and self-evident (it is only self-evident because the mystery in the last resort makes the conceptual aspect understandable and not *vice versa*) is also a mystery. God's becoming man, then, is the absolute mystery and it is also self-evident. It is almost possible to imagine that the strange, historically contingent and hard aspect is not the reality in itself, but is the fact that this absolute and self-evident mystery has taken place, then and now, in Jesus of Nazareth. Our longing for the absolute nearness of God, which is incomprehensible in itself, but which makes it possible for us to endure everything, may, however, make us aware that this nearness is not to be found in the claims of the spirit, but in the flesh and here on earth. In that case, we shall find that proximity of God in no other place but in Jesus of Nazareth, above whom God's star is placed and before whom we can have the courage to kneel and pray: 'The Word was made flesh and dwelt among us'.

2. The provenance of the Church in the history of salvation from the death and resurrection of Jesus

I would like to preface this chapter by making two simple comments. This text is a slight revised version of a lecture given by the author to the Philosophical and Theological Faculty of St Pölten. It has not been adapted or elaborated in any way, to transform it into a learned treatise. There is consequently no bibliography and there are no references to other works in footnotes. With regard to the version of the *ius divinum* in the Church's constitutional law that is used here, the reader should consult the essay which the author has published in his Theological Investigations, Vol.5. My first preliminary comment is this. In view of the great dimensions of this ecclesiological theme, despite the limitations already imposed on it, it is only possible to choose rather arbitrarily a number of points relating to this theme. A certain arbitrariness within the theme could not be avoided. Ecclesiology – the question of the provenance of the Church from Jesus of Nazareth, the crucified and risen Christ, and the question of the foundation of the Church by the same Jesus Christ – is such a great, difficult and complex subject that it would be absurd to imagine that all its aspects could be equally discussed in this space.

Let me conclude this introduction with a second remark. I am a systematic theologian, not an exegete, and I do not want to give the impression that I am one. It is extremely important to stress this at the beginning of this chapter, since, in view of the subject-matter itself, an exegete ought to be asked to speak about history, textual exegesis and biblical theology and their contribution to our understanding of the relationship between Jesus and the Church. Wilhelm Thüsing discusses these questions in Part II.

Let us now get down to the matter in hand. I should like to begin by saying one or two things about the whole question and in particular about the solution provided by the traditionally accepted Catholic scholastic theologians of the past few centuries and the problems to which this traditional solution — which has not been officially defined by the Church — has given rise. I would then like to show how the same question of the provenance of the Church from Jesus Christ can be seen and interpreted in a rather different way, with the result that this possible solution can be more easily reconciled with our present historical knowledge.

The question that I have to deal with here, as a systematic theologian with at my disposal an armoury of possibilities that is different from that of the exegete, is this: Can we really speak of the Church having been founded by Jesus? When this problem is posed today, we are bound to ask the preliminary question: Do you mean the historically tangible Jesus — or perhaps tangible only with great difficulty — of before the Easter event or do you mean the risen Christ?

This distinction has hardly ever been made in the traditional scholastic theology of the Church and particularly in its ecclesiology and fundamental theology. The traditional scholastic theologians did not worry very much whether Jesus made certain statements that referred to the Church according to the authors of the synoptic gospels or the fourth gospel before the Easter event or after the resurrection. Nowadays, however, this distinction has to be made when this question is asked. It will, moreover, be clear in the second part of this chapter that this question in itself also gives rise to another special problem in the direction of the solution that I shall at least try to indicate, again in the second part of my argument.

What, then, has this traditional scholastic ecclesiology to tell us? (I am referring here, of course, to the teaching about the Church that flourished in the post-Tridentine period above all under the aegis of that eminent doctor of the Church, Robert Bellarmine, with his particular concept of the Church. This is the ecclesiology that I myself learned forty or more years ago as a student of theology.)

To confine the problem to the question that concerns us directly here, we may perhaps say that the Church has been regarded in the classical scholastic theology as having been founded by Jesus (either before or after the Easter event), insofar as this foundation can be traced back to explicit, objective and to some extent juridically interpreted statements made by Jesus.

According to this traditional view, Jesus named Peter the first pope, gathered a group of apostles around him, which came to be known as the college of bishops, and gave this community, which may be called juridically constituted and which was based on the explicit words of foundation interpreted in this particular way, certain powers. (Jesus was able to grant these powers because he was the one whom Christian faith saw in Jesus of Nazareth.) The central notion of this scholastic ecclesiology is that these ideas about the foundation of the Church are to be found at an objective and juridical level as such. This understanding of the Church is based on the principle of the foundation of a specific community. According to Bellarmine's ecclesiology, which continued to be, if not the only and complete teaching, then certainly the leading and most influential teaching about the Church until the publication in 1943 of Pius XII's encyclical *Mystici Corporis*, the Church was regarded as a juridical organization based on the idea of a perfect society (*societas perfecta*). It was always recognized that this Church was different from a profane community, state or assembly of people. At the same time, however — and this brings us nearer to the heart of our problem — it cannot be denied that the foundation of this society by means of explicitly juridical statutes can only with difficulty be reconciled with the idea of Jesus as the crucified and risen redeemer.

I have already pointed out that it was not regarded as of fundamental importance in this traditional scholastic ecclesiology whether Jesus pronounced the words of foundation before the Easter event (nowadays we would say that Jesus did not take his failure on the cross into account before it happened), or whether he said them after the resurrection. There are, as we have seen, two conceptions of the Church. On the one hand, there is what may be called the idea of the Church according to fundamental theology: a social reality, constituted by Jesus' words of foundation interpreted in a juridical sense. On the other hand, there is the Pauline concept of the Church as the body of Christ. By extension, the Church can also be seen, in the Pauline tradition, as the fundamental sacrament of salvation or the continuing presence of the eschatological act of salvation brought about by Jesus Christ. The first of these ecclesiologies can be called the social concept of the Church based on fundamental theology and the second the soteriological, dogmatic ecclesiology. In the past, they were not separate, but existed side by side as two parallel ideas to which no thought or discussion had been devoted.

The ecclesiology based on fundamental theology which I have tried to describe very briefly contains certain very great difficulties. Whether we turn to Diekmann or to other fundamental theologians, we find that this idea of the Church was accepted almost without question in the classical fundamental theology of the Catholic Church until the nineteen-fifties. The problems inherent in this understanding of the foundation of the Church by Jesus were, however, raised sixty or seventy years ago by the Modernists. It is not surprising that the initial reaction to these problems in the Church was sharp, conservative and defensive and that it took some time, perhaps too long, before they were really seriously considered, discussed and dealt with. At a very modest and cautious estimate, we can, I think, say that it has taken the Catholic Church fully sixty or seventy years to deal to some extent with the ecclesiological problems raised by fundamental theology within the Catholic sphere (for practical reasons we are bound to leave Protestant theology out of account in this matter) and brought sharply into focus by the Modernist movement.

What, then, were these problems? One very great problem of fundamental theology which was, at the time of Pius X's *Lamentabili* and *Pascendi*, not brought to light and recognized was the imminent expectation of Jesus. Jesus, it was said, looked forward to the imminent coming of the definitive and eschatological Kingdom of God for his generation (although he did not give a precise date for this). In this imminent expectation, he could, it was claimed, not have founded a Church. If the world was to end in a few years' time, it was suggested, he would not have attempted to organize a Church, which, under the circumstances, would have had no real meaning or task. What was expected was the imminent coming of the last judgment, the Kingdom of God and perhaps the redeeming mercy of God. What in fact came, however, was the Church, because Jesus had been wrong in his expectation, but that Church did not come from Jesus. It was not, in other words, his intention to found a Church. On the contrary, the Modernists claimed that something emerged during the gradual historical process in which this imminent expectation was broken down, from the community of disciples who believed in Jesus as the risen Christ. This phenomenon came to be called the Church. Whether this process took a long or a short time is not an urgent problem for us here. The first problem raised by a historical and critical exegesis, to some extent following the Modernist tradition, and challenging the traditional scholastic understanding of the Church as founded by Jesus, then, is the problem of Jesus' imminent expectation of the end of time.

A second problem is one that I shall leave aside for the moment and only touch on here. It is that the Church of the Judaeo-Hellenistic New Testament period does not present us with the absolutely structured picture provided by the traditional ecclesiologists of the Church as founded by Jesus. It has therefore been claimed that there was in the early Church a Peter as well as a Paul, but no pope. It has also been asserted that the most diverse possibilities of community organization existed side by side in the Church at the time of Paul and that these were patterned on the various sociological data within the Jewish and the Hellenistic worlds. It has also been said that, according to Catholic teaching, the Church had an episcopal and papal structure which was unchangeable and permanent and instituted by Jesus Christ himself on the basis of God's law. All that can be found of this structure in the New Testament, however, is at the most a very modest beginning, perhaps nothing at all. We may therefore legitimately ask, in conclusion — and this is the heart of the problem — whether it is possible to say that Jesus 'founded' a Church at all.

Before we attempt to answer this question, however, I am bound to point out that there are, in my opinion, clear signs of an incipient social structure in the group formed by Jesus and the disciples who were gathered around him before the Easter event. Peter was also obviously given a position by Jesus that was in a sense privileged. Jesus' group of disciples, moreover, did not emerge from Israel and its covenant as a Church — it is evident that it had, in some sense, a social structure.

I do not wish to deny this or pass over it in silence in the second half of this chapter, but it is certainly more a matter for the exegete and the biblical theologian and neither of these are roles that I can or want to play. The problem of Jesus' imminent expectation and that posed by the New Testament image of the communities of the period certainly seem to suggest that Jesus did not found a Church. Despite the radical rejection of the Modernists' ecclesiology by the Catholic Church at the time of Pius X and afterwards, it is striking how frankly and sincerely a theologian of the calibre of Hans Küng can assert today that Jesus did not found a Church and, what is more, in saying this express a truth that can no longer be denied. The fact that Küng still regards the Church as meaningful and necessary is a different question, which should not be obscured by my reference to his statement that Jesus did not found a Church.

In what direction, then, should we look for a convincing solution to this question of the foundation of the Church? Here too, I can only make a number of suggestions. Although the subject attracts me very much, it is clear that I cannot deal fully with the question of Jesus' imminent expectation as such in this context. When Jesus spoke of a temporally imminent coming of the Kingdom of God, was he making a 'mistake' or is it possible to avoid this conclusion with regard to Jesus' teaching? Yet what is left of this imminent expectation of the eschatological reality in the concrete, especially as far as its correctness, importance and validity for us today are concerned, when we are bound to admit that two thousand years have passed since the time of Jesus and the world has still not been transformed, in the fire of God's wrath, into the eternal Kingdom of God?

I cannot go into this question in detail here. I believe, however, that we are bound to react differently from Catholic Christians at the time of Pius X and frankly, sincerely, soberly and clearly admit that there was a temporally imminent expectation present in the case of Jesus and that this expectation was not fulfilled in the way in which he presented it to himself and formulated it in words. Although I cannot discuss it in depth here, this does not in any sense mean that we have to believe that Jesus made a 'mistake' within his own sphere of understanding. It would not be heretical to say that he made a mistake, but only a wrong formulation and, what is more, one that can and should be avoided (without obscuring anything), because a formulation of this kind is basically an existentially mistaken concept of truth (I cannot, alas, go more deeply into this interesting question here, although I shall return to it later when I suggest a solution to the problem.) In the meantime, however, it is clear that it is very important to recognize the absolutely essential content of Jesus' imminent expectation and its absolute significance for us in the matter of faith today. And now I must return to the real subject and try to answer the question: How can we speak of a foundation of the Church by Jesus or a provenance of the Church from Jesus, if (and although) Jesus himself proclaimed the nearness of the Kingdom of God?

Although my colleague Hans Küng would possibly reproach me for the careless arrangement of my argument, I would like now to ask whether it is possible for me to dispense with the word 'foundation' here and employ instead another concept, 'provenance'? The essential meaning of the former, traditional word might not only be preserved in accordance with faith, but also emerge more completely and irreplaceably if the latter term were used. If 'foundation' is understood in its full range of meanings and if it is at the same time borne in mind that it can also be used analogously, this concept is not necessarily synonymous with that of the verbally juridical organization of society. Despite this, however, it has to be admitted that, when we say that Jesus 'founded' the Church, we almost always involuntarily think of a foundation of a kind that cannot be justified in the face of the criticism that comes from scholars specializing in historical biblical studies. It should therefore be possible to keep to what the Church has always said and taught ('the Church was founded by Jesus') if we interpret (I would rather not speak of replacement in this context) the concept of 'foundation' as 'provenance'.

If something comes from something else in an intelligibly active way or if reality B is necessarily given by reality A (this is, of course, something that has to be demonstrated), we can say either that B is 'founded' by A or, more usually, that B 'comes' in an unequivocal way 'from' A. This is no more than a preliminary remark to do with terminology ('provenance' is, of course, 'coming forth from'), but it is quite important.

I must now consider the question raised by the title of this paper: the Church comes from the death and resurrection of Jesus as an aspect of the lasting eschatological value of the crucified and risen Christ. Let me examine this statement and its implications.

The eschatological significance within the history of salvation of Jesus' death and resurrection is, of course, intimately connected with a theme that in itself is extremely difficult, mysterious and differentiated, so much so that I can only indicate one or two aspects of it here. I cannot, for example, deal here with such questions as whether Jesus really rose from the dead or how the historical Jesus interpreted his own death. All that I shall attempt to do here is to consider the provenance of the Church from the crucified and risen Jesus, presupposing in this consideration the Catholic dogma (and New Testament conviction) of the universal eschatological significance of Jesus Christ within the history of salvation.

How is it possible to formulate very briefly and with this particular consideration in mind what took place in the death and resurrection of Jesus? I would like to suggest that through the crucified and risen Jesus Christ God's victorious, eschatological and definitive self-communication finally appeared.

God has always loved the world despite all human sin and has loved it from the beginning. At all times and places in the history of man, he is the inner dynamic force or entelechy of the world and with his grace he has always impelled human history, which is possibly two million years old, towards his immediate presence, which we call the beatific vision. This is something which was not so clearly known before the time of Jesus, but which was even then the inner dynamic force and structure of the world. God has always given himself, as himself with his own glory, to the world as power, origin and goal in the mode of an offer to the freedom of that world. His relationship with the world is not simply that of the creator who has, as it were, inserted something that is different from himself into the empty void extending around himself and who keeps this different element at an absolute distance from himself. On the contrary, in his grace, he takes this different world that he has created into his own glory. He does not simply give us, his creatures, what he has created as something that is different from himself. He gives himself to man, his creature, or at least offers himself as a gift to the freedom of that creature and to the whole history of mankind.

Seen from the perspective of God's offer of himself to man's freedom and the ambivalence of all freedom in the case of creatures, man's fate and the end of his history are bound, in the concrete, to remain open and questionable. It is also an absolutely open question as to whether this stupendous offer, in which God gives, not something, but himself, is accepted or rejected. The fearful history of man and Augustine's sensitivity, for example, with regard to the *massa damnata* of mankind would not seem to suggest that this stupendous, ultimate and unsurpassable peak in human history, which is saturated with the glory of God himself, has in fact been reached as a single whole by man.

What, then, is the situation with regard to Jesus Christ in this context? Paul speaks of justification by faith and not by the works of the law. There is also the synoptic sermon on the Kingdom of God and the fourth gospel refers to the descent of the light into the darkness of this world. All these biblical statements mean basically that, through the death and resurrection of Jesus, the history of man's salvation, which is in itself ambivalent, will in fact end well in the acceptance or rejection of God's offer of himself.

Nothing is said here that is quite unambiguous about the fate of each individual, but what is clear is that, in accordance with the freedom of God and man that is quite unprecedented and cannot be taken for granted this human history, which is indeed fearful and appears always to be plunging into the abyss of guilt and death, will, through the power of God's grace, really end positively and well.

Jesus was, on the one hand, unequivocally at one with God, whom he called his Father, and, on the other hand, he was equally unequivocally at one with men, including the sinners and the lost. Because of this, he was in a certain sense unable to avoid (even though he sustained his conviction through his own failure) rejecting in advance making a decision either in favour of God or in favour of man. What he said in other words was: No, wretched though it is, mankind is not simply victorious in the mode of God's offer. It is also victorious and saved by God in the mode of real success and authentically loved by God in his glory.

What we call the resurrection of Jesus confirmed and set the seal on this. The crucified and risen Jesus is therefore God's lasting promise made to the world, not simply as an offer, but as a definitive victory. Jesus can only be this insofar as this victorious offer of God is always present in the world.

Because of this, it is possible for us to say, with Willi Marxsen, in a positive, though not exclusive sense that Jesus had to rise again in the faith of those who believed in him. This cannot, however, be claimed in the sense that Jesus would only exist in that faith. On the other hand, if there were no community of faith until the end of time consisting of those who believed in Jesus as the crucified and risen Christ, the saved Son of God and the unique, definitive and eschatological prophet (however this may be formulated), there would be no permanent presence of God in the world and Jesus would not be present as God's promise of himself.

The Church, as the eschatologically definitive, yet historical and united community of believers, is the lasting presence of God's eschatological and eschatologically victorious promise of himself to the world in Jesus Christ. If Jesus were not the one he claimed to be, this community of believers in the world would not be the permanent presence that makes it possible for him to remain historical as the eschatological promise of himself made by God to the world. In how many numbers the Church will continue to exist is quite a different question. We may, however, say with conviction that the Church, as the sacrament of the world's salvation or the baptism of the world as a whole, is not in the last resort dependent on social power or the numbers of those who belong to it.

These are, of course, no more than indications, but they do at least enable us to understand the provenance from the crucified and risen Jesus of a Church that is, as a community of believers, constitutive of the reality of Jesus himself and therefore necessary in itself. Jesus would not have been Jesus, if there had not been such a Church. His proclamation of the irreversible presence in the world of God's salvation would not exist if the Church were not present as the permanent community sustaining this proclamation in the world. Jesus can, of course, be reduced to the level of a preacher whose moral pronouncements can be understood and approved, even if they cannot be easily carried out without him. He can also be regarded simply as a kind of revivalist, preaching about human freedom and choice. On the other hand, however, we can avoid thinking of him in this way. At the same time, we can also, in our faith in God, be convinced that, in his absolute, incomprehensible mystery, he has promised himself definitively to the world as its ultimate salvation. In that case, it should be clear to us that that promise of salvation took place in the crucified and risen Jesus and that the Church is the lasting presence of that historically tangible promise, given in an eschatologically irreversible way.

It is, however, quite possible to say that both Catholic and Protestant Christians would certainly be in agreement with what I have just said, but that I have not really revealed the actual structure of this eschatologically lasting community of faith. It is also possible to say that there must have been a community of faith if God's promise of himself was made visible in history in the crucified and risen Christ. It is, of course, quite a different question when the way in which the Church is organized is considered. A possible conclusion to this consideration is that there should be no episcopate or papacy in the Church. It may be suggested according to the New Testament, there were many different social organizations of the community of faith, and that the claim made by the Roman Catholic Church that it is the only legitimate organization of this community of faith has to be rejected.

Despite all that I have said about the provenance of the community of faith from the crucified and risen Jesus, this remains a very difficult problem that cannot be solved now as it was by those who practised the traditional fundamental theology. According to the latter ecclesiology, Jesus initiated the episcopate when he chose the twelve apostles and appointed the first pope when he gave preference to Peter. This has resulted in the problem as to how this same Peter, who appears in certain texts in the New Testament to some extent with a certain theological importance, yet played practically no part at all in the Pauline communities, came to be regarded as the first pope. It is similarly possible to ask why James, as a kind of caliph in the community of the disciples, was not chosen. Why, also, was this arrangement, which can be seen first in Ignatius of Antioch and later, in the third century for example, in Cyprian, something that cannot only be, but also must be. Why, again, to use the traditional ecclesiological formulation, should these structures, which came about at a later period in the community of believers, really have been *iuris divini*, a matter of divine right, and founded by Jesus Christ himself?

As I have already indicated, there are also several factors which would seem to be against this. Despite this, however, there is in my opinion a divine right that is developing or that may develop. What, then, does the traditional teaching about the *ius divinum* of papal primacy and the episcopal structure of the Church, in other words, the divine right of the monarchical episcopate, a teaching that is also to be found in the Constitution on the Church, *Lumen gentium*, of Vatican II, have to tell us?

It tells us above all that this structure cannot be dispensed with. It is obligatory for the Church of today and tomorrow. This is the basis of the practical teaching about the *ius divinum*. We can, however, legitimately ask: *must* there always have been a *ius divinum* of *this* kind present in this way, *unambiguously* and irreversibly and obligatorily *tangible* in the apostolic era? In answer to this question, I would say that this is not necessary. In denying the necessity of this explicit and formal tangible presence of *this* kind of *ius divinum*, I am not denying that the structures of the Church as they exist today became gradually tangible (this can be seen in I Clement and the ecclesiology of Ignatius of Antioch at the turn of the first century), then became more and more clearly reflected in the later history of the Church until they came to be regarded as obligatory for the Church.

I should like to clarify this by saying that the same reality always follows the same direction and may be either collective or individual in its history. In both of these cases, it can be seen from the human point of view that, in any history of this kind, decisions are involved both in the individual and in the collective reality (which is essentially a closed and constantly united society). These decisions cannot be revoked and remain obligatory in the future. The concept of a historically free decision does not necessarily imply that a freely taken decision can always be revoked at will and can therefore remain open to the free availability of the factor responsible for this decision. The history of freedom has one single direction and creates an obligation that can only be eliminated if freedom is denied in the world (a situation that involves guilt). This is because freedom consists not in deciding at will, but in deciding what is irrevocable. This is not necessarily bound to be so always and in every case, but it forms an essential part of any history of freedom.

Marriage, for example, may permit divorce, but this does not change the fact that two people were married to each other and that their marriage had an obligatory, lasting reality with eternal dimensions. If I have a particular profession that I have practised for forty years, it is simply impossible for me to reconsider this freely taken decision of forty years ago in such a way that I can begin again at the point where I stood at that time. In other words, history moves in a single direction and in it decisions that are historically irreversible are taken again and again. We cannot go in the opposite direction in this one-way street of history that is formed of free decisions. We cannot go back and then go in a different direction from that earlier point. This can certainly not be done if it is presupposed that such decisions are not necessarily obligatorily based on the earlier situation, but are in accordance with the beginning, which is the constant law of the whole way.

On the basis of this simple outline, I would say that certain initial historical decisions, which were in accordance with the theological interpretation of the essential being of the Church at the time, were taken by the Church during the apostolic era. This may not, however, have been obligatory with regard to the Church's social structure and were not reversible in a backwards direction. They could only be developed in a forward direction, towards the future. It was also impossible to cancel them out (and thus enable the Church to go back, as it were, to an earlier point in its history). These decisions,with their bearing on the Church's concrete social structure could, however, be regarded as irreversible at least in conformity with their beginning as the *ius divinum* (Whether or not free decisions were taken that were *iuris divini* after the apostolic era is, however, a question that we must leave open).

In the apostolic era, the Church had the duty, derived from its origin, to organize itself in a more concrete social form. At the end of the apostolic era, the structure which is now described as Catholic *iuris divini* and which, it is now claimed, cannot be changed was already tangibly present, at least in its beginnings. This does not necessarily imply that this decision to give a certain structure to the Church in the apostolic era went back to an explicit formulation on Jesus' part, expressing his will to found the Church. This is something that cannot be proved and any attempt on our part to postulate any such words of foundation would be of little use to us from the point of view of fundamental theology. On the other hand, these free decisions made in the apostolic era (which should, incidentally, not be thought of as very short in duration, as the formation of the canon, including its later texts, shows) can and should be seen, explained and retained as of divine right, without being traced back to Jesus' explicit will to found a Church. Such irreversible decisions which are meaningfully in accordance with the essential being of the Church and are derived from the origin of the Church and are derived from the origin of the Church as the community of those who believe in Jesus cannot be traced back juridically to define historically tangible words spoken by Jesus. They do not have to be — they can still be regarded as constituting the structures of the Church which were, in the sense in which I have described them, of divine right. They were in accordance with the origin or the foundation of the Church and they were justified as historical decisions by the concrete historical situations which the Church was bound to enter.

The Church seems to me to have a completely open future. Divine right in the Church and the structures which are ultimately correctly traced back to Jesus have a real history. The Church lives in this history and has to make decisions on the basis of this history. We may assume that this history will continue. It is therefore clear that the Church as such has an open and unpredictable future in its actual form, although this does not necessarily cancel out the divine right that is attributable to it or obscure or deny its provenance from the crucified and risen Jesus.

We do not know what the Church will look like in the year 2000 or 2500. Will there still be a pope in Rome or elsewhere? Will the Church still possess the great Roman bureaucracy that we recognize and perhaps endure with sighs today. Perhaps there will be many other things which we cannot even imagine today. The Church may by then have learnt, for example, that women can be admitted to the priestly office and that an academic training — however much I, as one who has spent his working life providing it, value this — is perhaps not so necessary for candidates for the priesthood as we think it is now. It may even have become obvious by 2000 or 2500 that sacramental sanction can and should be given to charismatically gifted and called leaders of basic Christian communities. There are, of course, many other possibilites, too many to enumerate here, but these must remain open questions and we should be on our guard against expecting an answer to them either exclusively deduced from theological principles or else drawn exclusively from the early tradition of the Church.

In all these things, however, we can expect everything possible from the Church, which is a historical reality and which has a *ius divinum* that is also subject to history. Some Christians find that events move too slowly, while others think that they move too quickly in such transitional periods in the history of the Church. Often too, many aspects seem to be obscure or uncertain, causing certain Christians to complain. These and similar experiences are not necessarily wrong or absurd. They are the result of transitional phenomena and are inevitable in any authentic history.

Enormous historical developments and changes have taken place in the Church since the time of the crucified and risen Jesus. They should be frankly admitted. We should not imagine, for instance, that Peter believed (Mt 16. 13-20) that he was the first pope and that several hundred other popes would follow him in Rome, where a complex curia would surround them. Such a thought clearly did not come within Peter's vision. It is obvious that he did not worry whether he would leave behind an individual or a small group of leaders. The pastoral letters reflected a later period.

The Church has always been in history, which has moved in one direction, but within which the Church has never lost its own legitimate past. It also comes, in this obscure, unpredictable and often suffering history, from the crucified and risen Jesus. Whatever may be the form of its social organization, this Church has always borne witness to the fact that God loves the world and that God's love does not fail because of our guilt. This same Church has also always testified to the fact that the God of the grace that comes, not from us, but from him has constantly prevailed in the world, at least when the whole of mankind is considered.

This simple message is at the same time the most mysterious and enormous. We can only know, by looking at the risen Christ, that God himself is the ultimate content, power and aim of this wretched and finite creature, man, not only in his origin, but in the end result. The fundamental message of Christianity is that God's salvation will prevail through him and the Church is present in the world so that this message may always remain present. Without the Church, this message would not be definitive. Despite its historical character and the historical nature of its divine right, the Church therefore really comes from the crucified and risen Jesus Christ.

3. The death of Jesus and the finality of revelation

Christian revelation, in so far as it is 'publicly' and 'officially' directed to all men and women in a binding way, closed with the death of the last apostle. That is a venerable axiom of Catholic theology. Hence the history of revelation proper has come to an end, even though the history of the understanding of revelation, revelation's history of faith, and the history of theology continue. Therefore the Second Vatican Council in *Dei Verbum* (4) says: 'Hence the Christian dispensation, as the new and definitive covenant, is insurpassable, and no further public revelation is to be expected before the coming of our Lord Jesus Christ in glory' The Council grounded this axiom of the finality of public divine revelation by referring to Jesus Christ, the Word of God made flesh; he has fully accomplished the work of salvation, and the Father is revealed in his entire life, death, resurrection, and sending of the Spirit. There was no express reference to the apostles (or to the ending of the apostolic age with the death of the last apostle) in this declaration by the Second Vatican Council on the definitive character of Christian revelation. Since the conciliar text was not concerned so much to establish the exact time of the end, as to offer the foundation for that end, the Council did not discard the traditional statement that revelation ended with the death of the last apostle.

That does not mean, of course, that the statement is clear and easily stands up to all the critical questions that can be asked about it. Cardinal Bea, working from the traditional formulation of this axiom, concluded that all the canonical writings of the New Testament must have been written before the death of the last apostle; otherwise, no one among the original bearers of revelation could have been the inspired author of the latest New Testament writings. But if we set the origin of the latest inspired writings of the New Testament *after* the death of the last apostle, and if we take the inspiration and the knowledge of the inspired nature of those writings in the traditional sense (which is not wholly compelling), then we must say that Christian revelation closed with the apostolic age, even though we can easily extend that era to the time when the last writings of the New Testament were written. Nevertheless, just as we can always determine the era of Jesus and his apostles more exactly in time, the period of the Church in formation, in contrast to the fully established Church, might also be more precisely located in time. But the axiom's basic meaning is clear: namely, that the revelation of God in Jesus Christ occurred as a unique historical event. Its time in history is definite and circumscribed; therefore it is insurpassable. It is valid for all subsequent ages; nothing more that is truly 'new' can happen in the history of revelation.

Although we could offer a more finely-nuanced formulation which would be inappropriate here, this axiom (which we have to look on as Christian and Catholic dogma, in view of the teaching of the new and eternal covenant in Jesus Christ) is not easily accommodated by the modern mind. Ratzinger in his commentary on *Dei Verbum* reminds us how difficult people find this axiom nowadays. I cannot go further into this problem or its solution here but, because it is important for our question, which concerns the connection between Jesus' death and the fulness of revelation. I shall make some comments on it.

Today man sees himself as existing in a history which is open without restriction to the future. He does not think of his essence as something given beforehand, as something to which history would make mere accidental alterations; then that statically understood essence would not be historical in the true sense. Man nowadays does not see the necessity of freely becoming himself as a stigma of his finitude. Instead it is the sign of his freedom which, as he transcends himself towards the future, will come about in ways that are always new and surprising. Hence modern man will see the history of religion as always being open to an unknown future, inasmuch as he understands that history as something more than an outdated and obsolete period of the history of his emancipation. History is always salvation history; and salvation history without faith (and, therefore, without revelation) is not possible. If a contemporary Christian always sees revelation history at work in this history of religion (at least of the past) he finds the statement about the finality of revelation history very difficult to understand, to say the least. The idea seems to rob history of its ultimate profundity; its dignity disappears if the history of revelation is in fact at an end.

If we try to solve the problem by saying that the Spirit of God always guides the Church towards the whole truth, and that the history of the reception of revelation and the history of its transmission to generation after generation (the history of faith) goes on, theology has to work out more clearly at least than before the unity and history of revelation (ended) and the history of faith (continuing); it must in some way relativize more clearly and legitimately the caesura established by the axiom. If we argue that the axiom teaches an insurpassability of revelation in Jesus Christ rather than an 'ending', then modern man is helped — terminologically at least — to understand the axiom. He sees that there can be an historical event fixed in time that can be decisive for all succeeding time, but directed towards a real future; and he understands that more easily than the idea that an historical occurrence itself could merely be finished, so that it does not happen again, and yet claim a meaning for subsequent ages. If we understand the axiom in the sense of historical insurpassability, this idea should be more precisely explained in terms of the philosophy of history and the theology of history. But of course this has not been done adequately as yet.

Of course, we would have to demonstrate the precise *content* of the insurpassability of revelation in the Christ-event. Here much has already been done in theology and in the proceedings of Vatican II, where revelation is no longer seen simply as the enunciation of propositions, as happened before, but as history (to which propositions also apply). The question of the insurpassability of Christian revelation has become the question of the insurpassability of the Christ-event. We can of course say that after Jesus Christ nothing new is to be said, because everything has been said already. Everything was given in the Son of Love; for him God and the world became one. We may say that God irreversibly promised himself to the world in Jesus Christ in an historically tangible way: as its victorious salvation in self-communication of the absolute God himself; as the absolute future of the world which is coming about victoriously and irreversibly because of God. We may say that that promise is insurpassable because it is the personal promise of the absolute God in himself to the world; and that it is not concluded in any real sense, but is open to an unending future; in that sense, it is insurpassable. History stays open in all its dimensions, even in those of grace and revelation; it proceeds in that openness in the historically extended promise of absolute salvation: a promise which by God's victory successfully cancels the ambivalence of the world's freedom to salvation and damnation.

I do not intend here to reconcile the axiom in question in detail and from every viewpoint with modern man's self-understanding. To do that a more extended treatment would be needed. I restrict myself above all to the question of whether and how the *death* of Jesus as such relates to the insurpassability of the revelation-event in Jesus Christ, and how from that point we can eventually reconcile the new spirit of an open future with the dogma of insurpassability and the 'finality' of Christian revelation. The latest church formulation of the axiom (by the Second Vatican Council) refers to the death and resurrection of Jesus in the sentences before the conciliar formula. But it is not clear whether this reference to the death and the resurrection of Jesus is made only because they could not very well be omitted from the account of the last original bearer of revelation; or whether the death *as such* completed in the resurrection) has an essential and unique meaning in regard to the insurpassability of Christian revelation.

My thesis is indicated by the second of these points. We might put it thus: only by the cross of Christ as such can the insurpassability of the Christian revelation be constituted, and only thus is it constituted. The theology of the cross is an intrinsic constitutive element of the insurpassability of Christian revelation as a whole. I do not say that the theology of the cross is exhausted in this regard; but I do say that the 'end' of revelation history in the reality of a mankind presented with this revelation, and in a continuing history, can be offered only in the death of the man who is the bearer of revelation and the revelation-event at one and the same time. The theology of the cross also has this aspect and serves this function, even if not exhaustively.

We shall suppose that history as the history of man's freedom continues, and that salvation history continues too. Broadly, then (that is, implying the history of faith), history remains the history of revelation; otherwise the history of man as a history *complete* in all its dimensions would not continue. It follows that the 'finality' and 'insurpassability' of a revelation-event in continuing history can occur only in the historical appearance of the absolute self-promise of God as such, and as the end or goal of history itself. Every other 'word' of God which is not God himself is finite and therefore essentially and always provisional; open to other possible new words of God which replace the former word (even though in some way 'sublated', or cancelled and transcended at the same time, in the Hegelian sense). Otherwise such a word with its finite content would have to do with a merely declaratory explanation. It would be the last word only by an arbitrary divine decision, although (speaking absolutely) completely new words of revelation could follow. But that viewpoint would not only negate the open history of mankind, as now understood, but would reduce revelation to a myth no one today could believe. It would conceive of an arbitrary divinity who suddenly stops being a partner of the very history into which he had previously allowed himself to enter. We would also say, if we approved of this phrasing: A *prophetic* word of revelation is always essentially provisional. The *eschatological* word of revelation can consist only in the self-promise of God as the absolute future of the world. The question here can stay open whether or not every prophetic word, if it is to be a personal 'supernatural' revelation-word, must hold its own reference to the future and openness *to* the eschatological Word of God, if it is to be a truly genuine Word of God in the Christian sense. The (only) eschatological Word of the self-promise of God as such (as the absolute goal of history and as the absolute future) implies another characteristic. This eschatological Word of God offers God not merely as the highest and insurpassable possibility of freedom and the history of human freedom, so that it is always an open question how the history of human freedom as a whole will react to this preferred possibility; rather, the offer of God as that *possibility* is in itself the history of human freedom as it is in reality. But even then there would be no event in revelation history through which this possibility could enter in an enduring, insurpassable and even an eschatological way.

The eschatological Word of God's self-promise of God to the world must be the irreversible victoriousness of this offering by God himself of God to the world. This Word must to some degree be a proclamation not merely of *gratia sufficiens* but of *gratia efficax* for the world and its entire history: if, of course (as the doctrine of the co-existence of God's efficient grace and human freedom implies) the freedom of human history is not cancelled, and if with this proclamation of the victory of God's self-offering no theoretical assertion is made in favour of the individual about the fate of that individual in history. God himself promises himself to the world in the eschatological Word not only as the final and insurpassable possibility but as the fulfilment, actually effected by him, of that possibility. That is, I believe, the sense of the message of Jesus: that in him now a victorious presence of the Kingdom of God is given which was not given before. Therefore it cannot consist merely in the possibility of freedom to decide for God, in the freedom always ready at hand, even if that is a graced possibility.

How is this to be conceived of as an eschatological and insurpassable word of revelation? Let us for simplicity's sake presuppose the statement of Vatican II (*Dei Verbum*, 2); that 'this design of revelation is realized by deeds and words with an inner unity'. We also presuppose that the history of mankind comes from God and has in itself a unity and solidarity of its individual events so that one event is that history has meaning and 'speaks' for all others. The question is how, in view of these presuppositions, the eschatological Word of God, the irreversible victoriousness, and the divine self-promise are to be conceived, if this victorious self-promise of God is to appear historically and in a continuing history. On the foregoing presuppositions, we can say that the divine self-promise, if it is to be not merely words but deeds, can be given only in one man who has accepted that self-promise freely and definitively. Only thus can the victoriousness of God's self-promise appear historically as deeds and not only words. Of course the free, definitive acceptance of this divine self-offering must become historically tangible for us through one man.

Before I continue on this point, I must protect myself from any suspicion of heterodoxy. My task at this point is not to develop a Christology equally in all its dimensions and show that the absolute bringer of salvation (that is, the reality and the bearer of the absolute, irreversible, and victorious self-promise of God to the world in an historically tangible form) is necessarily the one man presented in the classical Christology of the hypostatic union. We shall presuppose that here, of course. For our question only one thing is important: namely, that this historically evident self-promise of God to the world (if it is to be eschatological, therefore not merely an offer, but the offer of God made victoriously by God himself) must necessarily occur in a man who accepts that self-promise freely and definitively, and in such a way that that acceptance becomes tangible for us as a definitively historical action.

That seems self-evident. A mere word, in which the self-promise of God would be thought of as having occurred, would be a mere offer to those addressed by that word — to the freedom of man. It would be an offer whose definitive acceptance would still be in question. If we said that that Word of God also assured us that it would really be accepted and actually succeed, we could nevertheless ask where that happened. Has this acceptance already occurred or is it still to come in history? Or has that acceptance, whether past or still to come (if it is not already the deliverance of the world in its entirety, and therefore the end of history), already taken place, so that through a single historical event the successful outcome of the whole of history is established irreversibly? The Word of God as such, guaranteed by God eschatologically as the real and triumphant goal of history, must therefore happen through an historical event; that can occur only in the actual, definitive acceptance of God's self-offering to the world: acceptance by a man who must be so conceived in his own constitution that *his* acceptance of the definitive establishment of that self-offering in obedient freedom guarantees the salvation of the whole world. This would be the starting-point for the classical Christology of the hypostatic union, something which must be more thoroughly and precisely explicated by a theology that would have to explain the solidarity of this God-man with all mankind and its history.

But here I examine only one question: How can we accurately and actually conceive this free and definitive acceptance of the self-offering of God as the absolute future of all history; an acceptance through which the offer of God is established above all as the eschatologically definitive Word of God to mankind?

My question must be answered thus: That free, definitive acceptance of God's self-offering, which makes the Word of God to the world eschatological and predestines the world's history to salvation, can take place only through the *death* of the man who freely accepts this offer. Then that death must be understood more exactly as redeeming and as redeemed. And with that death we include what is known as Jesus' resurrection. The *death* of Jesus in this sense is a constitutive inward aspect of God's eschatological self-promise to the world.

This is not the place for a precise, detailed theology of death in general, even though that is the presupposition of the basic thesis under consideration. There are many standard studies of the theology of death in general which fit the bill. It is enough for our purpose to say that death, which is continually lived throughout life until its very end, is understood in a wholly human as well as a theological way, and not merely as a biological event that ends life, or as a medical expiration. It is the one act of self-realization of freedom as a human being in which man disposes of himself entirely and irrevocably (either for God or against him) in that final creaturely impotence which finds its most external realization and manifestation in what we commonly experience as and call death. In the Christian idea of freedom the one free act in human life which is ultimately decisive occurs only through actual death and not independently of it, even though from an empirical viewpoint the last free act in which a man definitively posits his own being is not necessarily the precise moment of his medical and biological exit.

There is no conclusive self-realization of freedom in the Christian view of man which could be said to occur either independently of death, somewhere within life (in some mystical act that would not extend to death), or only after death. Fundamentally, therefore, the way in which a man's death occurs is irrelevant. Acceptance of the actual way in which death finally and uncontrollably occurs is also part of the successful, decisive act of freedom that we call death. No theologian is forbidden (even if he is not encouraged) to reflect on why and how the actuality of Jesus' death (its power as against political and religious forces, its utter God-forsakenness, and so on) is still essential and significant for the salvific meaning of that death for Jesus himself, and above all for us. It is decisive that death, which for Jesus too is basic in the sense of being the highest act of freedom in radical impotence, should be seen as ultimately definitive in its orientation.

If the final and ultimate acceptance of the self-disclosure of God takes place in Jesus, and if he is thus the eschatologically triumphant Word of God to the world, that can happen only in and through his death. It occurs in such a way that we can also grasp in faith the successful outcome of this acceptance in the impotence of death, and can therefore understand it in conjunction with Jesus' resurrection.

The death of Jesus and accordingly his entire passion form an essential constitutive element of the eschatological Word of the self-promise of God to the world as its absolute future. This Word of God is insurpassable, and only this Word is God's ever-insurpassable revelation.

That revelation is final. At the same time it opens up the restricted incomprehensibility of God himself; it makes a continuing history possible and legitimate, because that history already has an infinite goal which is being realized victoriously. It can and must be said that the death of Jesus compromises the open-ended nature of the finality of revelation, and that without the death of Jesus that ending of revelation is inconceivable. Properly understood, the cross of Jesus marks the end of public revelation. Although textbook theology usually says that the public revelation ended with the death of the last apostle, it would be better and more exact to say that revelation closed with the successful death of Jesus, the crucified and risen one; it ended, therefore, with the cross: because in that God pledged himself irrevocably to history. Beyond that final Word of God, God can say nothing more, even though history continues within this final Word. It continues as divine revelation of God, as the history we usually call ecclesiastical or faith history: the history, in other words, of that final Word of God. In the right sense, it may always be called the history of revelation. The end of revelation must be said to occur in the successful death of Jesus on the cross, and in the resurrection. That is not to deny but implicitly to state that the constitution of the Church, as the historical and institutional (because public) tangible sphere where faith seizes the crucified and the risen one, has to do with that cross as the victory of divine self-promise of God to the world. Without that faith, God's self-pledge to the world in Jesus would not be victorious at all.

We can also say that the public Christian revelation ended with the apostolic age, if only we understand that 'ending' in the sense that the apostolic age was centred on the cross of Christ, which is not only an event in that phase of history, but its gnoseological axis. In Jesus' cross, man's transcendental and historical dimensions are reconciled finally and irrevocably. Man's absolute orientation to the mystery of God's self-communication becomes an historical event in the successful death of Jesus. Without Jesus' death that reconciliation would not have been possible. Man's transcendence towards God in his unmediated reality is definitively successful through God's own act; it carries man above all categorical particulars and temporal limitations. That is the substance of the Christian revelation in the event of the cross of Jesus and in Jesus himself. Hence the cross is the fulfilment of Christian revelation.

I shall look now from a different viewpoint at the complex of problems I cited at the start of this chapter. Those problems concern the incompatibility of the modern notion of the human impulse and desire to attain an unlimited future and of the doctrine of the finality of public revelation which is the ultimate content of history itself. I cannot treat all aspects of the problem adequately here. But if modern man wishes not only to exist as the same kind of man as his forebears (even though under somewhat different conditions), but really to establish a new future in creative freedom (individually and collectively, within the limitations of both those dimensions), then that will of men today is continually refused and thwarted by death, which takes on a new unique and radical quality through its opposition to this novel will of man. This fatal contradiction between the radical will of man to unrestricted freedom and his subjection to the sentence of death is quite understandable, even though all contemporary ideologies ignore it. But that contradiction is not resolved (as far as man who exists for all time is concerned) by conceiving it as a succession of generations continuing into an indefinite future even though at the same time it is marked out for death. That deadly contradiction is not permitted by the thought that man goes on forever, and that every generation is only a base on which the monument of the next generation is set; and that new generation, in spite of its victory, will perish in its turn. Every man has a responsibility not only for his successors but for the dead who lived before him; and he is responsible not only for his own life but for his death. In all truth, the modern idea of an unconditional orientation to the future must acknowledge that it is frustrated by death. If a reconciliation of this crucifixion of all history through death is to be conceived and hoped for, that is possible only if death itself is not the annihilating end of history but the event in which history itself is saved through God's action in God's unrestricted freedom. The experience of a Christian's faith in the cross of Jesus is that death can be this saving event; that as such it has already proved successful; and that as such it is a pledge to our own death.

PART TWO

NEW TESTAMENT APPROACHES TO A TRANSCENDENTAL CHRISTOLOGY

by Wilhelm Thüsing

1. The relevance of the Bible for modern theology and the problem of co-operation between dogmatic theology and exegesis

I. The Problem

1. Posing the Question

It is not possible nowadays to give an automatic answer to the question as to whether exegesis is really necessary for theology and especially as to how it can have any place in a lecture on dogmatic theology. This question has to be taken back to an earlier one: what is the relevance of the Bible for modern theology?

It would certainly be possible to find an easy answer by going back to the Constitution on Revelation of Vatican II. According to Chapter V, Art. 24, 'Sacred theology rests on the written word of God, together with sacred tradition, as its primary and perpetual foundation. By scrutinizing in the light of faith all truth stored up in the mystery of Christ, theology is most powerfully strengthened and constantly rejuvenated by that word. For the sacred Scriptures contain the word of God and, since they are inspired, really are the word of God; and so the study of the sacred page is, as it were, the soul of sacred theology'. In this case, work would be done subject to the classical solution, in other words, the traditional doctrine of inspiration, which has proved to be easily misunderstood (because of its objectivization, which is too little reflected, and its closeness to mythology) and which does not take fully into account the content as it is known to exegetes today.

The mutual relationship between exegesis and dogmatic theology is, moreover, not so automatically accepted as it was in 1961, at the time of Karl Rahner's essay on exegesis and dogmatic theology and the publication of his work on inspiration (1958). What was assumed in Rahner's work of that period as unquestionably accepted by Christian theologians would no longer be accepted, at least consciously, by many theologians today.

It is therefore impossible to justify a policy of burying one's head in the sand and behaving as though the problem had not become an acute one today. Only an open discussion of the whole question can throw light on it and lead to an authentic decision.

It is, of course, true that many of those concerned will, in the meantime, already have found a personal solution, namely more or less to ignore the Bible. On reflection, however, this easy way out cannot be accepted.

2. The phenomenon of lack of interest in exegesis and questioning the relevance of the Bible for theology

In this section, a few possible reasons for this phenomenon will be considered. No claim is made to completeness and the emphasis is on calling into question.

a. One major reason for this lack of interest would seem to be found in the way in which exegesis — both research into the subject and teaching — has developed in recent years and the way in which it is often practised nowadays. There is a widespread impression that specialized exegesis as a science and, even more so, tradition-historical research into the New Testament consist of very disparate theological projects and a multiplicity of theologoumena that cannot be reconciled with each other and can only be explained with reference to the history of comparative religion. A general tendency to stress discontinuity and not to look for continuity and unity in multiplicity is reinforced by a strong interest, which is understandable in itself, in individual events. Even in tradition-historical research, which, if it is comprehensive enough, can act as a positive corrective, it is often decided to isolate one particular level and to ignore structural interconnections that might show that the question of continuity was meaningful. One also has the impression that a great deal of ostentatious effort is made in biblical studies to produce a relatively small result.

b. A too abstract version of the assumption of a hermeneutic communication between the historical situation of the text or its authors and our own historical situation will also result in a form of relativization. This tendency will become more acute if a form of philosophical and theological hermeneutics emerges that is too abstract and is based on the individual events of exegetical study which are seen in isolation and as discontinuous and which may even be only apparent. This may give the impression of historical relativization or simply that the theological statements found in the New Testament about who Jesus really was go back to the theology of a community.

This is is particularly likely to happen when it is no longer recognized that there is a special case of the so-called hermeneutical circle in the New Testament. It must be clearly understood that the text of the New Testament together with its historically conditioned sphere of ideas was not the sphere of God's revelation itself and cannot therefore be identified with our contemporary sphere of ideas. In other words, the New Testament text is not the same as a breakthrough of God's transcendence into the immanence of our world. If, however, we do not at the same time recognize that the text is linked with God's revelation in a very special way that does not exist in the case of other religious texts, we shall relativize the whole question.

c. There is another tendency, which apparently runs counter to the one mentioned above under b, but which is in fact closely connected with the question as a whole, and that is to see the reasons for our contemporary activities as existing outside history. The view that different texts are required for the tasks that have to be carried out today is also connected with this.

It is also important to mention in this context the tendency to see no possibility of communication and only a contradiction between tolerance, which is nowadays almost universally approved, and the claim to absoluteness (which has characterized the New Testament and Christianity as a whole). Also connected with this is the relationship between experience and the verbalization of that experience and the question as to whether this verbalization has an obligatory character.

We are bound to ask whether — and how — the obligatory and demanding character of the New Testament message with regard to this hermeneutical situation can be demonstrated — through the way of thinking that is inevitable nowadays because we have inherited it from the Enlightenment. (Rahner's transcendental approach is a very good example of this.)

3. The problem in 1961 and now (assuming that the Bible is relevant for theology)

a. The real problem today is not simply — and perhaps no longer — the relationship between exegesis and dogmatic theology working within the sphere of fundamental theology. What is above all called into question is the relationship between the biblical theology that emerges from the texts as a result of historical research into the traditions and above all the editing of the New Testament on the one hand and the dogmatic theology that is derived from the sphere of modern philosophical and theological thinking on the other. When Rahner published his article on exegesis and dogmatic theology in 1961, historical research into the editing of the New Testament had hardly been introduced into Catholic biblical studies.

The question now is quite different. It is concerned with exegesis as it is in fact practised today and a dogmatic theology that is in a process of change. Exegesis is at present at least implicitly a task of biblical theology, in the sense of an elaboration of the theological tendency on the part of the individual New Testament author to make statements, even when it is carried out in the form of verse by verse analysis of the text. Dogmatic theology, on the other hand, is frequently no longer scholastic. It is often open to contemporary philosophical assumptions.

This is why the problem of the relationship between exegesis based on the principles of fundamental theology and 'scholastic' dogmatic theology — the problem to which Rahner drew attention in his essay of 1961 — cannot be simply set aside. It is still important. I agree therefore with what Rahner has said, for example, about the theology of the life and death of Jesus and the experience of the resurrection, but this does not mean that the whole problem as such has been completely understood. It would be a very difficult task to deal in a sufficiently comprehensive way with this problem, but the task has to be attempted.

When Rahner says that the exegete is the representative of scientific reflection about the historical experience, he is only defining that part of the exegete's task that is concerned with fundamental theology, not the other, more important part. The exegete is above all the interpreter of the new interpretations of the fundamental kerygma of the New Testament that are closest to the origin. He is, in other words, the representative of reflection about the theological projects which, at the beginning, fairly adequately revealed the origin and the basic pattern of life in the Christian Church and which were, as such 'constitutive' for the Church, insofar as they prove to be legitimate in their reference to the historical Jesus and the early post-paschal theology of the Church.

b. In Rahner's essay, 'Theology in the New Testament',[1] we find the fully justified and helpful claim that it ought to be fundamentally possible to have an approximate idea as to how the dividing line runs, at least approximately, between the content of the original statement about revelation and the New Testament theology of revelation. This, of course, raises the question as to how we should understand the normativity of the late New Testament theologies, as explicitly accepted by Rahner himself.

In this context, we are also bound to ask to what extent the earlier pattern of the *dicta probantia* still influences Rahner, despite his removal to a new state of reflection, with the result that a real dialogue between dogmatic theologians and these 'late' New Testament theologies in all their diversity may be made difficult. It is, after all, necessary for the relevance of these theologies to be recognized if this dialogue is to be possible.

II. Ways towards Recognizing the Relevance of Scripture for Theology

1. A preliminary remark on the importance of method
One cannot avoid being strangely impressed by the way in which a too abstract philosophical and theological form of hermeneutics on the one hand and a too detailed way of working with the New Testament on the other can lead to relativization and uncertainty. These apparently so dissimilar, even contradictory ways of working to some extent pass the ball to each other. On the other hand, there is always the chance of reaching much more positive judgments if an attempt is made to avoid the mistakes to which we have drawn attention. In detailed exegetical work, the whole should not be forgotten. At the same time judgments that are too abstract and cannot be verified should be avoided in the practice of philosophical and theological hermeneutics and contact should be maintained with the text itself and with what it is saying as a whole.

2. Scripture as a special case of hermeneutics
The New Testament provides us with a special case of the hermeneutical pre-understanding that is universally necessary for literature. It is necessary, even in pre-understanding, to bear in mind the possibility of a breakthrough of the inexpressible mystery that we call God into the apparently so closed, but in reality – in our transcendental understanding – so open anthropological context of this world. This breakthrough should not, of course, be understood in the sense of a *deus ex machina* or a cancelling out of the physical laws of nature, but rather be thought of as God's communication of himself.[2]

3. The connection between Scripture and ecclesiology
The most important way towards a solution of our problem was indi-

cated in Rahner's book on the inspiration of Scripture.[3] In this, he says that the early Church was not simply the first period in the Church from the point of view of time; it is also the lasting foundation and constant norm for everything that was to come and the law governing the whole course of the Church's history. It was this precisely because of Scripture. The Church, Rahner says, made its paradosis, faith and self-expression concrete in written form. By doing this, in other words, by forming Scripture in itself, it turned as the normative early Church towards its own future. The opposite also happened. By appearing as the normative law and constituting itself as such for the future, it also formed Scripture.

4. The connection between Scripture and Christology

In the introduction to this chapter, we drew attention to the fact that the relationship between exegesis and dogmatic theology or between the Bible and our contemporary understanding of faith has become indistinct or even problematical for many people today. The danger has moreover to be recognized that the problem may be solved in a negative way either in unreflecting practice or by constructing an 'ideological superstructure'. On the other hand, however, we are bound to stress that, in dealing with this question of the relevance of the Bible for theology, we are not really moving away from our theme of Christology. This relevance, after all (obviously in the case of the New Testament and also, in the Christian understanding, in the case of the Old Testament as the foundation of the New) has a Christological basis. Otherwise, this relevance cannot exist. An elimination of the Bible, in whatever form, ultimately leads, if not to an elimination, then at least to a relativization or diminution of faith in Jesus and Christology.[4]

Christology is unthinkable without its ecclesiological implications. Because the Church was constituted by Scripture,[5] it is also unthinkable without its biblical and hermeneutical implications and its significance for our understanding of Scripture.[6]

The Bible is relevant when what is affirmed in the doctrines about the significance of Jesus is true. In that case, it is extremely relevant.

It is not possible to escape from the hermeneutical circle that exists between the early Church's understanding of faith and our understanding today. The existence of this circle implies a binding force, if a pre-understanding of faith can be introduced into it in which the causal connection of this world can really be made open in a transcendentally anthropological and theological sense. In other words, God's irreversible self-communication in Jesus has to be made open without calling the world as such into question.

This can only take place if Jesus, in accordance with this understanding of faith, is the one who has been raised from the dead and is now living and has his (transformed) function for the community of disciples and the world. The New Testament (and also the Old Testament in the sense in which it is related to the New as well as the New Testament in the sense in which it is understood in the light of the Old) can, moreover, only be relevant for theology if Jesus was not simply a rabbi or a prophet who lived once and is now dead. It makes sense if he was, perhaps not in a sense that can be verbalized, and certainly not in the sense of knowledge based on the natural sciences, but in the real sense, that he is alive and that he is living with God in the midst of his own and that this fact constitutes the Church and that the function of the New Testament as constitutive of the Church (and therefore its relevance for theology) is dependent on this.

III. An Attempt to regard Biblical Theology (including Exegesis as Detailed Work on the Text) in such a way that it is orientated towards Dialogue with Dogmatic Theology

1. A preliminary remark

There are several possible ways of carrying out exegesis. The emphasis can quite legitimately be changed within the hermeneutical circle of detailed exegetical work on the one hand and the elaboration of views of the whole and structures on the other. This has to be stressed so that there should be no suspicion that the view expressed in this section is an absolute one. The elaboration of the New Testament sphere of understanding, fundamental theology in the narrow sense of the word and detailed exegesis as a prelude and precondition for biblical and dogmatic theology and historical research into the tradition and editing of the New Testament are essential tasks requiring a full programme of work on the part of those who carry them out. It is not without reason that a New Testament scholar should spend the whole of his working time on a study of the editing of the synoptic tradition or even of one gospel.

There are two main preconditions for the justification of all views of exegetical work. The first is that the text should be central in all forms of exegesis. The second is that there should be no deep division between then and now, giving a purely relative value to the past as pure past. We may note in passing that this problem is different in the case of teaching and in the case of research.

The real function of New Testament theology is, in my opinion, frequently neglected, but it can, as I see it, be defined under the following four headings.[7]

2. As far as exegesis of individual Scriptures is concerned:
Here I would place the emphasis on the view of the whole or objective structures. Detailed work on the text should never be neglected, but it should be carried out in such a way that, at least initially, the whole should remain in view.

3. As far as the task within the New Testament as a whole is concerned:
Here I regard my main task as elucidating the question of the late Scriptures and their orientation towards Jesus. This question is basically the same as the question of 'continuity in discontinuity' in the New Testament theologies or that of the legitimacy of the late theological projects within the New Testament.

This question can also be expressed in another way: To what extent can the constant Christological conviction in the New Testament of the central function that the risen and living Jesus had for his community and the world be justified by investigating the early post-paschal theology of the New Testament and the question of the historical Jesus?

What I am asserting here, then, is that it is of decisive importance to go back to the question of the historical Jesus and that of the continuity of the New Testament theologies. Why is this so? To answer this question, we must consider the analogy that is found in dogmatic theology, where it is also necessary to go back to Jesus himself. Despite all the narrowing down and distortion of the New Testament that takes place in dogmatic formulations, the fact remains that dogma is constructed on the basis of the late New Testament theological projects, such as the Gospel of John. The relevance of the task facing us in this section for a re-interpretation of dogma in continuity with the Church's teaching tradition and based both on our contemporary understanding and on the Bible can be recognized in this perspective.

4. As far as the relationship between the New Testament and systematic theology is concerned:
The most important task, in my opinion, is to emphasize a systematic

theology the superabundance contained in the New Testament theological ideas that is valuable to dogma and a scientific, dogmatic interpretation, even if this interpretation is done using contemporary philosophical and theological ways of thinking. In other words, what is necessary is to give recognition to the source which nourishes dogmatic theology and is ultimately God himself, acting in Jesus through the Old and New Testaments.

The most important theological projects in the New Testament provide a superabundance of this kind, that is, a number of dogmatic formulations contained in the New Testament which can be utilized by the exegete in the discourse structure that is so closely connected with the content. These are not simply discourses about Jesus Christ. They also have above all the structure of dialogues as God's initiative through Jesus and our response to and orientation towards God through Jesus.

We cannot deal at any greater length in this chapter with the material content of the contribution that can be made by exegesis to systematic theology.[8] All that we can do is to point, in the following paragraph, to an aspect of the question, in order to show that our contemporary way of thinking has to be involved in the relationship between exegesis and systematic theology.

It must become clear from the central points outlined above that the New Testament and its message of the crucified Christ (if it is properly understood) are not, as they are frequently claimed to be, an obstacle to social development, but an impetus.[9] We do not have to bring the New Testament up to date by adding contemporary thought to it. We must rather elucidate the texts objectively in order to demonstrate how the testimony borne by the early Church can motivate Christian life today and to reveal the breadth and freedom that emanates from early Christianity and the openness to the future that is one of the most essential aspects of that testimony.

5. The aim of theological work on the New Testament

Our aim should be to do exegetical and theological work on the New Testament in such a way that the New Testament and our contemporary ways of thinking can merge together. If New Testament exegesis is to be relevant for the contemporary Christian, it should not be confined to the purely New Testament sphere, nor should it leave this task of merging together the two spheres of thought to other disciplines. It should carry out this task itself so that the demanding character of the New Testament message is visible to contemporary thought.

Even when it is used in this way, exegesis should certainly not be regarded as a substitute for dogmatic theology. Here I am bound to disagree with F.J. Schierse, who suggested that the exegete was a 'theologian *kat' exochen'*.[10] The exegete may, however, think of his work as a form of total theology that can be carried out on the initiative provided by the textual basis of the New Testament. An elucidation of the Letter to the Romans in this sense can, for example, be understood as a project of a contemporary total theology of the textual basis of this Pauline document if this task of merging together spheres of thought is really understood and practised.

It should not be forgotten that many of the Church Fathers did their best 'dogmatic' work in commentaries on books of Scripture. A good example of this is Augustine's treatises on the Gospel of John, which can be regarded as a total theology, even though it is not systematized.

Unlike the Church Fathers, however, we can, I believe, only practise exegesis in dialogue with dogmatic theology and contemporary philosophical thought if our exegesis is to be meaningful. What is more, it can only be done meaningfully if it leads to teamwork with systematic theologians. The 'theologian *kat' exochen'* of today can be neither a dogmatic theologian nor an exegete. The task facing us today is one that has to be carried out, at least approximately, in co-operation between both disciplines.[11]

In view of this, the exegete has not only to understand his own trade – he has also to be able to think 'systematically', that is, from within the sphere of contemporary understanding of faith and the world. On the one hand, the text must always remain central and, on the other, exegesis must not be made absolute, but must be placed in confrontation with present-day thinking.

It is only when exegesis is in this way fundamentally open to systematic theology that a meaningful bridgehead can be made between the two disciplines.

IV. The Relationship between Exegesis and Dogmatic Theology within the Framework of a Reform of Studies

1. The need to look for the unity of theology

a. The question of the unity of theology is not simply linked to the question of meaning – the two questions are identical. It is only when theology – or faith, as the object of the theologian's reflection – is seen as a unity that theology and faith can be regarded as meaningful.

b. This intensive search for the unity of theology is necessary in order to go counter to the possible danger of fragmentation and loss of effectiveness. It is only in this way that illegitimate processes of selection, such as the attempt to make the contemporary sphere of thought absolute in a selection process that may be conscious or unconscious and in this way to neglect or even to eliminate altogether the biblical way of thinking, can be countered.

c. A concern for the unity of theology is also necessary because of the task itself. It is only what is regarded as a unity that can be expressed as testimony and be understood by those who hear this testimony.

2. Concrete points in the reform of theological studies

a. All the material used in teaching must be checked to see if it expresses the unity of dogmatic theology and exegesis.

b. This second point is concerned with what is perhaps the most difficult task of all if a unity of theological thinking is ever achieved. The two different ways of thinking − the historical and critical thought of exegesis and the philosophical and systematic thought of dogmatic theology − should not be left standing side by side. They have to be reconciled as closely as possible.

The co-operation between dogmatic theology and exegesis cannot be allowed to remain at the stage of simply pointing to differences. The task consists rather of aiming at as complete a communication as possible between the two disciplines. It has, however, to be recognized that this unity has to be sought. It is not already given and it is important to avoid any false attempts to reconcile or harmonize dogmatic theology and exegesis. This co-operation can only be relevant if the exegete and the dogmatic theologian help each other to do their own work better.

The old conflict between exegesis and dogmatic theology can only re-emerge in the sharp form that characterized it in the past if both the exegete and the dogmatic theologian remain immersed in their own specialized sphere and do not communicate with each other. It will emerge again − or continue − if the exegete concentrates rigidly on the details of the tradition and editing of the New Testament texts and is no longer concerned with connecting lines and structures and if the dogmatic theologian practises scholastic theology of a kind that accords no place for biblical thought.

c. In the light of what I have said so far, it will be clear that I can only strongly recommend the basic course suggested by Karl Rahner for the first time or more of theological study,[12] especially to exegetes. It would be good to know whether it is possible to have a corresponding basic course in biblical theology for dogmatic theologians or whether a methodological and exegetical introduction to the Bible would be better. In any case, the openness of the Bible and biblical theology to systematic theology and the relevance of the Bible to theology as such must be made visible.

Close co-operation between dogmatic theology and exegesis can begin in earnest at a more advanced stage of study (perhaps the third year). The theological conception of a basic course might provide a model for a nuclear course at this stage. The task should not, in my opinion, be carried out even at this level simply by holding occasional joint seminars. There should rather be public discussions or public co-operation at the level of lectures.

d. Rahner has said in *Sacramentum Mundi* that what may perhaps be developed in the course of the Church's reform of theological studies is a special subject in which biblical theology will not function either simply as a continuation of normal exegesis or merely as an aspect of dogmatic theology, but will, as a scientific study in its own right, provide a suitable communication between exegesis and dogmatic theology.[13]

The task that I have in mind here cannot, however, be performed by the emergence of a new subject that is added to the already existing theological disciplines. It can only be carried out by exegetes who have the time and freedom to participate in dialogue with systematic theologians. Systematic theology will have the leading part to play in this and for this reason co-operation will have to take place within the framework of lectures on systematic theology or at least within an orientation towards such lectures. It will, in other words, certainly have to occur outside the normal framework of the exegete's work. This problem will not be solved by the creation of a new subject or discipline alongside the existing ones. Those practising this new subject might well work according to their own ideas and take little notice of what their colleagues were doing in the related disciplines of exegesis and dogmatic theology. Indeed, the establishment of such a new, independent branch of theological study would probably only lead to a false sense of security.

We can add one final comment to the leading question contained in this chapter on the relevance of the Bible for modern theology. This comment forms a link between the question itself and human experience.

Whether exegesis is necessary to systematic theology or not can only be experienced by allowing the texts to have their effect on us and by opening oneself to the ideas of Paul, for example, with the same intensity as one consents to important contemporary theological ideas.

V. Instead of a Summary

It is not really a return to the Bible, Martin Buber once said, but rather a question of living in a unity that is close to the Bible with the whole of our being that is so involved with time. We have to live, he suggested, with the whole weight of our late multiplicity on our souls and in the presence of the unchangeable matter of this particular moment of history. We have to remain firm in dialogue and responsibility, open in a faith that is true to the Bible to our present situation.

Buber went on to ask whether he was referring to a book here and replied: no, we mean the voice. Do we mean that we ought to learn how to read? No, he replied, we have to learn how to hear. We cannot go back. We have to turn round on our own axis until we are not on a part of our own way that we have been on before, but are on the way where we can hear the voice.[14]

Is what Buber is correctly asking for here obscured in the New Testament, as he — wrongly, in my opinion, believed? If not, how can we hear the voice? How can we practise Christian theology and its central teaching, Christology, in such a way that the voice of the one whom Jesus called his Father can be heard? How can Jesus, the risen Christ who is now living, help us through is Spirit to turn round so completely that we can hear the voice anew, respond to it and pass its message on in such a way that it can play its part in saving the world?

How can it be demonstrated, then, that the kerygma of Christ enables us and is indeed necessary especially for those of us who are called and sent to hear the voice within the contemporary sphere of life and help others to hear it?

2. Questions and notes on transcendental Christology

I. Attempts to build up a Transcendental Christology from a Biblical Way of Thinking

Preliminary remark: A precondition of the attempts that follow is that a fundamental distinction should be preserved between pre- and post-Cartesian thought. Despite this, these attempts are based on the assumption that it is meaningful to try to find ways of justifying a transcendental Christology on the basis of biblical theology, even though transcendental thinking can only be given implicitly and initially in these biblical phenomena.

1. A reflection about the relationship between creation and redemption (or the Old and New Testaments) as an analogy with transcendental and Christological thinking

This transcendental Christology ought to measure up to modern thinking about man and show that creation (in the centre of which man must figure) and redemption are in harmony with each other. In other words, it must show that they fit in with each other without any illegal, mythological ancillary structures. The relationship between creation and redemption, that between the history of man and the history of his election (which is also present within the Old Testament itself) and finally that between the Old and New Testaments are all analogous with the relationship between transcendental Christology and a Christology *a posteriori*. It is possible to say that the problem of the relationship between the Old and the New Testaments is 'varied' and in this way re-interpreted — in the gnoseological form that is necessary today — in transcendental Christology. What we have here, in other words, is the question as to why the New Testament (as the kerygma of Jesus as the mediator and absolute bringer of salvation) had to be added to the Old, with its wealth of theological and anthropological meaning.

If this question is thought of as a question about the relationship between *faith* in the Old and New Testaments, the transcendental or gnoseological element is contained in it, even if that element could not be expressed in precisely that way at that time and the point of departure during that period was explicitly 'God' and only implicitly man.

One result of attempting to communicate a transcendental Christology on the basis of the biblical datum is that our reflection should not be confined exclusively to the New Testament — it has to take the Old Testament constantly into account as the 'root' (see Rom 11, 16-18). This is particularly important, for example, if we want to give real meaning to the abstract concept 'bringer of salvation'. It is simply not possible to do this without presupposing, on the basis of the Old Testament and its relationship with the New, a personal dialogue between the God of the Old Testament who takes the initiative and man in the same Old Testament who responds to that initiative on the one hand and the definitive action undertaken by Jesus in the New Testament to make this relationship radical and powerful on the other.

2. *The protological statements about Christ in the New Testament as equivalent to an attempt to build up a transcendental Christology*

The following statements are 'protological': Christ as the 'first-born of all creation' (Col 1. 15); the statements about Jesus' mediation of creation, which are fitted into Jesus' function in connection with the event of salvation (in Paul generally and especially in 1 Cor 8. 6); the idea of *eikon* in the Pauline and Deutero-Pauline letters; the statements in Paul in which a parallel is drawn between Adam and Christ (Rom 5. 12-21; 1 Cor 15. 21 f); the Logos statements (Jn 1.1 f[1]) and finally the inclusion in the New Testament of Old Testament themes of a pre-existing wisdom.

Christology is linked in these protological statements with a view of the whole of mankind within creation and of man's origin and ultimate expectations. This link is fundamental to any transcendental Christology. The protological statements must therefore have been, at the time that they were made, a form of quasi-transcendental Christology. They must have been equivalent to an attempt to build up such a Christology and to recognize the unique and contingent event of Christ not only as absolute, but also in its universally contingent dimension.

3. Pneuma – in the Bible and especially in Paul – as the way of making openness to God possible

Openness to the absolute mystery that we call God is, of course, a striking characteristic of Rahner's attempt to achieve a transcendental Christology. If we go further and try to link this approach to the biblical way of thinking, then the biblical concept that is above all connected with what we know now as openness to God, namely the concept of pneuma,[2] suggests itself at once. It is especially in the writings of Paul that pneuma is used in this sense.[3] In our present context, two factors are important. In the first place, the dynamic power by which God realizes creation and man as its ultimate meaning – in other words, the pneuma – is also the power by which man is made open to the absolute mystery of God. In the second place, this dynamic power of the pneuma is also intimately connected with Christ the Kyrious[6] (2 Cor 3. 17: 'the Kyrios is the Pneuma'; 1 Cor 15. 45: 'The last Adam became a life-giving Pneuma').

What is clearly present here is the situation outlined above in section 1. On the basis of the Pauline statements mentioned in the immediately preceding section, a transcendental Christology is even more clearly justified as an *a posteriori* conclusion.

According to Gal 4. 6 ('God has sent the Pneuma of his Son into our hearts, crying, "Abba ! Father !"'), the Pneuma makes itself known as 'the medium of the encounter between God and man' (see Rom 8.15),[4] but it can only be this by being, first and fundamentally, the medium of the communication between God and Christ. The exalted Kyrios lives through the Pneuma in a constant state of openness to the Father and it is precisely this Pneuma of the Son of God which makes it possible for the latter's brothers to be turned towards God himself (see Rom 8. 29).[5]

It is on the basis of Paul's Pneuma-Christology that an anthropology can be directed towards the absolute bringer of salvation. On this basis too, it should be clear that this anthropological approach to the absolute mystery that we call God, an approach that we must try to find in post-Cartesian thinking, is in no way contradictory to the theocentric approach that predominates in the Bible itself. To take man as our point of departure does not imply an order of priority in which man is placed first and God second. On the contrary, this transcendental approach implies that the sanctification of the name of God, the first petition of the Our Father, which would appear to reflect the primary intention of Jesus himself, is not made secondary, with the consequence that it might be eventually forgotten and eliminated.

4. The gnoseology of the First Epistle of John as an example of a biblical analogy of the transcendental approach to the event of Christ

a. The gnoseological element is expressed exceptionally strongly in this epistle. It would be possible to quote a number of texts from 1 Jn as 'formulae of knowledge', but for the sake of example, we will cite only one: 'We know that we have passed out of death into life, because we love the brethren' (3. 14).

In these formulae of knowledge, which often make explicit use of the verb 'to know' (*ginoskein*; see 1 Jn 2. 3,5,19; 3. 19,24; 4. 2,7,13,16; 5.2), the object of knowledge is community with God. This is not simply expressed, as it is in 1 Jn 1. 3 (cf. 1. 7), by the word *koinonia*, but is rendered above all by such Johannine phrases as 'to be in the truth', 'to be in the light', 'to have passed out of death into life', 'to have known him' and so on.

The subject of this knowledge is always the believing and thinking Christ who is addressed in the letter. The way of knowledge is, throughout the letter, either brotherly love or else the Pneuma that makes that love possible.

This gnoseological way of thinking and form of expression leads to the central content of knowledge that has to be communicated in this letter. It is, of course, the central theological idea of the author, namely that God is love. God reveals himself as love to the whole world in his Son's death and self-surrender. He also implants his love in the individual believer by means of his Spirit so that whoever has received that love can hand it on in a brotherly love that has been made normal and possible in Jesus' self-surrender in death.[6]

b. The author of the letter comes to this view in two ways. On the one hand, he takes as his point of departure the fundamental kerygma of the early Church and its basis in the proclamation of Jesus of God's mercy in his own death 'for' the world, the disciples' experience of the Pneuma and the consequence of a demand for fundamental brotherly love. On the other hand, his point of departure is his own gnoseological intention, which moves from the other, that is, the anthropological side to the theological side, in other words, to the central message that God is love, insofar as he has revealed himself through Jesus Christ.

Here too, the aspect of faith implies and leads to an anthropological and gnoseological approach. The most significant expression of this is: 'So we know and believe the love God has for us' (4. 16).[7]

It is important to note in the context of 1 Jn – as in the Old Testament – that *ginoskein* means a loving knowledge and a knowing love and implies a movement towards the highest form of personal community. *Ginoskein* is therefore directed towards the object of knowledge, that is, community with God.

c. The following questions arise as a result of these reflections. Are views, such as those expressed in the first epistle of John the consequence of an interaction between an approach that is knowable and made *a posteriori* (through faith and bearing witness) and a quasi-transcendental (and implicit) approach? Are the New Testament interpretations of Jesus' saving significance and his death in any way analogous to the claims of a transcendental Chirstology? It is certainly permissible to presume that such approaches to the event of Christ exist in the New Testament and it is legitimate to look for them, since human thought cannot manage without them.

The first letter of John undoubtedly contains the most striking New Testament equivalent of Rahner's central concept of God's communication of himself. This is clear, for example, from 1 Jn 4. 8, 16: 'God is love'. This love is the love that communicates itself in Jesus and in the Pneuma and at the same time is handed on by man.[8]

Is it, then, possible to interpret Jesus' death as the author of the epistle does (God is love in the sense of self-communication) without transcendental thinking somehow influencing this interpretation? It is certainly important to observe that we have, here in the first letter of John as well as in the Bible as a whole, an authentic theocentric approach in the pre-Cartesian sense. This indirect or rather implicit theocentric character of the transcendental approach – insofar as man is regarded as a being open to the absolute mystery of God – is essentially the same and should therefore not be underestimated, despite the predominantly implicit possibility of expressing it that is provided by the transcendental approach by its very nature. We would stress once again that it ought to make an attitude such as that found in the first petition of the Our Father possible, even in this way of thinking.

It is possible to cite further examples of gnoseological thinking in the New Testament, without discussing them in detail: 1 Pet 3. 15 ('calling to account for the hope that is in you'); the 'knowledge of the mystery' in Col and Eph and the reflection in the fourth gospel about the possibility and the necessity of an absolute bringer of salvation. This reflection is expressed in the objections raised in the fourth gospel by the opponents of Jesus. It is clear from this reflection that the author of the gospel did not accept the existence of such an absolute bringer of salvation simply as a matter of course and that he believed that this bringer of salvation was given in Jesus of Nazareth.

II. Questions asked of a Transcendental Christology by the Bible

Preliminary remark: In the section that follows, I am not trying to point out possible defects in Rahner's argument as a whole. All that I am attempting to do is to ask whether the emphasis that is revealed within the central approach or that emerges from it ought perhaps to be viewed in certain respects in a different light or filled with a different content and meaning. In other words, ought this strongly formalized view to be given a different and perhaps also a new emphasis by being given a content and meaning from the Bible?

What follows takes the form of corrections that are preconditioned by the view and the formulation of the approaches outlined in preceding 'Questions and Notes'.

1. Is the Old Testament, together with its abundance of promises and its personal dialogue with Yahweh, adequately expressed in a transcendental Christology?

We must now consider two essential Old Testament data which do not appear to play as important a part as they should in Rahner's project. Is this really a defect in the transcendental approach?

a. It is clear that the Old Testament contains an abundance of promises which go beyond the fulfilment in Christ, taken within the whole framework of the thought in the Bible. Rahner seems to have given hardly any attention to this fact.[9] Is this an effect of the transcendental approach that is in no way inevitable, but nonetheless factual? If attention is concentrated on the analogy between man's transcendent openness to God's communication of himself and the highest point of this self-communication that is reached in the absolute bringer of salvation, may this not mean that the factual realization of this absolute bringer of salvation in Jesus is already seen, to a much too great extent, as fulfilment? We are therefore bound to ask whether the continuity between the Old and the New Testaments and the tension in the latter between present and future eschatology that is so closely related to this continuity can be sufficiently guaranteed without explicit correctives. Because Rahner's approach is so open, however, there would be no difficulty in including such correctives.[10]

It is possible to say that Christ was, according to Paul, the 'end of the law' (Rom 10. 4), but not that the 'promises given to the patriarchs' were simply fulfilled in Christ, as a wrong or at least inaccessible translation of Rom 15. 8 has it.[11] These promises were rather made effective; in other words, both they and man's openness to the future and of time became irreversible.[12] According to Paul, what we have in the Pneuma-Christ is earnest-money and an offering of the first fruits. This does not mean that man's present salvation is devalued. On the contrary, it orientates it here and now towards the future.

b. At the beginning of the previous main section, we said that the Old Testament should be assessed according to its lasting content and meaning and especially according to the personal dialogue between Yahweh and man that is fundamental to its structure and not according to its function as a preparation for the event of Christ. This need is only partly satisfied in Rahner's article on the Old Testament in *Sacramentum Mundi*. Is this because of the abstract nature of transcendental thinking generally and its consequent failure to do full justice to the concrete historical reality of the personal dialogue between God and his people that is presented in the Old Testament?

Going beyond what Rahner says in *Sacramentum Mundi*, it is fundamentally a question — however much we stress the fact that the event of Christ is a new element that cannot be deduced from the Old Testament — of elaborating and considering structural analogies.[13]

In the history of Israel, God not only prepared his salvation as a historical event concerning the people of Israel and their development — he also planned its content and structure in such a way that it would take place definitively, validly and finally in Jesus Christ. The preparation of the event of Christ in the Old Covenant (and in creation, according to the Old Testament understanding of this event) takes place through the concept 'the God of hope', but not through that of the bringer of salvation.[14]

The difficulties confronting a transcendental Christology are inevitably connected with this undervaluation of the central theological content of the Old Testament. These difficulties are discussed in greater detail below.

2. Is Rahner's statement that the categorical quality of God's irreversible promise of himself can only *be a man possibly not conditioned by a definite* a posteriori *Christological model, in other words, the classical model, which is then made an objective in the attempt to find a trans-*

cendental Christology?

a. There can be no doubt that Rahner's existing version of Christological teaching is conditioned by the classical Christology of descendence, in which the connection between divinity and humanity is stressed. Rahner's statement is very obvious when this is borne in mind.

Seen from the point of view of the Bible, however, a potentially much richer Christology can be developed. The classical Christology which emphasized the union of divinity and humanity is, if this is done, not simply safeguarded by the fourth gospel, since the Johannine Christology is not identical with the classical Christology. It is rather given a greater content by this biblical way of thinking.

With this biblical climate of thought in mind, then, should Rahner's statement, in which he says that God's promise of himself *can only* — or must — be a man, not be reformulated? I would suggest: 'If God's communication of himself took place through a man (who did this and was what Rahner defined as the absolute bringer of salvation), then what we have here is the highest form of what can be apprehended in the transcendental anthropological sense of the highest level at which man can be considered in the open sense and in a transcendental way of thinking.'

In any attempt to achieve a collaboration between dogmatic theology and exegesis, the concept of the absolute bringer of salvation must, as we have already pointed out, be given a concrete content and meaning from the Bible, because it is too abstract in the transcendental approach and yet indispensable to this approach because it is abstract.

b. What has been said so far comes down to this rather highly concentrated question: Rahner's claim that God's absolute communication of himself can only be carried out by a man may perhaps not be contrary to the idea of God's freedom as such, but is it not in contradiction to the concept, so radically expressed in the Old and New Testaments, of the sovereign and free God, with which any transcendental anthropological approach must of necessity be confronted? Could God not have conceived his communication of himself in a different way? Could he not have brought it about in continuity with Hosea's proclamation of the radical and unfathomable love of Yahweh as an unmediated gift, that is, as a gift not mediated by a God-man? Is it not possible to think of God's communcation of himself as Buber did (namely that God commits himself to his people and the world immediately, that is, without mediation, and in this way completes the line that was begun by Hosea and the other prophets) and therefore have a transcendental view of that self-communication as a possible way in which God's freedom might have been realized?

The only valid argument that can be used against Buber's claim is that God's self-communication presupposes the overcoming of suffering and death and at the same time the absolute and unique man who leads us, through our sharing in the community of his suffering (the *sumpaschein* of Rom 8. 17) to a glory that can only be found in community with him. This brings us to the next question.

3. Is Jesus' cross and the stumbling-block that it forms as central to this transcendental Christology as the New Testament kerygma would suggest?

This question can also be expressed in the following way: Is it possible to regard the cross, within a transcendental Christology, as the object towards which the incarnation (in Johannine theology) and God's plan (in Paul's theology) are orientated?

A question with basically the same meaning is: Does Rahner's Christological approach give rise to a soteriology that really measures up to the New Testament datum, which is so much richer than the classical Christology and soteriology, and does this soteriology exist not simply alongside the central approach, but within it?

a. We should perhaps, in the context of this question, which is possibly the most important with which criticism can be concerned, not ask whether a transcendental approach as such is possible, legitimate and necessary, but whether such an approach, which results in a definite model of Christology and remains firmly tied to that model, despite all attempts to re-interpret it, is worth developing. Criticism can best begin with the observation that, on the basis of the theological ideas contained in the New Testament, it is possible to develop other Christologies into which the cross, the social implications of man's relationship with Jesus (the Church or the community) and eschatology can be integrated more adequately and given a more central position.

A working hypothesis can be formulated on this basis: Rahner's transcendental approach is determined by a previously given *a posteriori* understanding of Christology and, as a result of this, by the secretly, but legitimately envisaged aim. If this aim (in Rahner's assumed version of classical Christology) is not denied, but differently conceived, to include the greater wealth and fulness of New Testament projects, it will have a marked effect on the nature of this transcendental approach.

This approach is, after all, independent of the development of the Church's official classical Christology, even though the form that Rahner has given to it has been influenced by this development. We are bound to look for transcendental approaches to authentically New Testament Christologies simply because the contents of these approaches and the aims of these attempts are more all-embracing and pluriform than those of the classical Christology.

b. It is true that there are no fewer difficulties standing in our way today to the late New Testament Christologies than there were in the past to the classical Christology. As soon as the hurdle of the strange language and ideas has been removed, however, it becomes clear that the New Testament Christologies are immeasurably closer than the classical Christology to the real Jesus (or rather, to the crucified and risen Jesus in his identity). They are re-interpretations of a wealth that has not yet been fully recovered. We can express this idea figuratively: the New Testament Christologies bring us to the source itself, while the classical Christology is the stone construction built around the source (to prevent it from drying up in the desert sand). New beginnings may be revealed in considerable numbers from the originality and wealth found in the Bible as it comes into view from the vantage point of the classical Christology, even if this is conveyed to us by Rahner.

Paul's re-interpretation and synthesis of the relationship between Christology and soteriology and that between the present and the future eschatology within this Christology or soteriology have, in my opinion, not yet been fully explored.

In the case of the Johannine theology, we may also claim that the incarnation is more powerfully directed towards the cross here than it is in the more abstract classical Christology.

c. In looking for a transcendental approach to the cross of Jesus (or to Paul's proclamation of Christ as the crucified one), we must also ask whether the new interpretation of the doctrine of mortal sin, which is so necessary today, is not relevant to this. If the *lapsus* is not seen any longer as a single historical event, but as something that permeates the whole history of man,[15] then the problem arises as to whether it is at all possible to think in a 'supralapsarian' way in the Scotist sense or whether an 'infralapsarian' way of thinking has not to be presupposed in the case of a transcendental approach.

d. Finally, we must also ask whether Rahner's very important reflections about the death of man, the death of God and so on, which are abstract, but sufficiently all-embracing or at least open,[16] are not in need of a more comprehensive and intensive biblical amplification or foundation if they are to be used to give support to this transcendental approach to the real bringer of salvation or at least to make this approach to the bringer of salvation, who is none other than the crucified Christ, possible in an effective way.

4. The problem of openness to God within the transcendental approach[17]

We must first ask a preliminary question: Is it really possible for modern man to know that he is dependent on God and the absolute bringer of salvation in the sense in which this has been defined above? In other words, does the transcendent way of thinking provide access in this sense to modern man and under what conditions does his way of thinking have the opportunity to lead modern man to God in this sense?

Another fundamental question in this context is: If there is a successful communication between transcendental Christology and biblical thought, should the former not be more powerfully orientated towards the theocentric aspect of the contents of the Old and New Testaments as an aim?

It would seem to be particularly important to provide, from the vantage point of a transcendental approach, not only a Christology from below, but also the possibility of a theocentric approach in an ascending line and its communication by an absolute bringer of salvation. The claim of a Christological pneumatology on the basis of the Christ-Pneuma theology of Paul also has its place in this context.

Above all, however, it is important to consider the problem that is undeniably central to our whole thesis, namely how the biblical aspect of personal dialogue can be linked to this transcendental Christology.[18]

5. The connection between Christology and eschatology

One of Rahner's most characteristic expressions of transcendental thinking is to be found in his article on Christology within an evolutionary view of the world.[19] This connection between transcendental Christology and evolution is one of the most problematic of all forms of transcendental thinking. Ought this transcendental Christology really to be regarded as an evolutionary Christology? Seen from the point of view of the transcendental approach, this would seem to be almost a necessity. Seen from the point of view of the New Testament, it is not necessary, but it is capable of being communicated.[20]

Is it not possible that a one-sided evolutionary Christology might make it difficult to integrate the message of the cross? Does the New Testament not leave other possibilities open which should not simply be dismissed without a second thought? Or are such possibilities insinuated by the New Testament? It is very important to give consideration here to the preferences and difficulties that are contained in the idea of a Christology within an evolutionary view of the world seen from the standpoint of the biblical way of thinking and above all the problem of a Christology that is conceived predominantly for the present time, although from a transcendental approach.

6. The connection between Christology and ecclesiology

Ought we not to look for a transcendental approach to the New Testament idea of the Church as Jesus' community of disciples and its function in the world? Another factor that has to be taken into consideration is that the Church only has its function in the world in community with the Jesus who died and lives 'for the many' (see, for example, 1 Pet 2. 5, 9).

This problem also points to the possibility of checking, on the basis of the New Testament, whether this transcendental approach is sufficiently open to sociological implications.

3. The relationship between the late New Testament Christology and the classical theology

Some critical comments on Rahner's theology of Jesus' death and resurrection and his teaching about the classical Christology and soteriology of the Church and some preliminary work on the theme of a contemporary Christology based on the New Testament.

I. The Object of our criticism

The following criticism is not directed against Rahner's expressed intention, but rather against his belief that the so-called late New Testament Christologies can be subsumed under the model of the classical Christology.[1] This belief may well be at least a partial obstacle to our achieving a late New Testament Christology.

We are bound to recognize that Rahner is expressing, in his theology of Jesus' death and resurrection, an intention that is necessary nowadays. It is the decisive question concerning the earliest Christology.

II. Late and Early New Testament Christology

What is meant by early Christology — which is the counterpart to a late New Testament Christology, although it is not defined as such — in Rahner's teaching is really a Christology of Jesus himself and of the Christian community that came into being immediately after the Easter event. In other words, it is a Christology of the earliest stages of the Christian tradition insofar as these can be discovered.

What is meant by late New Testament Christology, on the other hand, is the Christological teaching of all the authors of New Testament texts in our possession, including, of course, the epistles of Paul, which are the earliest known New Testament writings.

III. The Meaning of the Late New Testament Christologies

The strong emphasis that Rahner places on early Christology in his teaching is fully justified because it is an extremely valuable aid in our quest for a Christology in which mythological and monophysitic mis-understandings can be avoided. It is also true that the continuity be-tween these Christologies and the historical Jesus presents us with a New Testament analogy for the problem of how to justify the classical Christology of the Jesus of history and of the earliest Christology.

1. It is only if these late New Testament Christological interpretations give us access to the historical Jesus that this access can exist at all Jesus' original and Christologically relevant intention cannot be known to us by a process of subtraction in which the existing New Testament texts are dissected. We can only know it through a knowledge of those texts and the theology that they contain, because there is no dividing line within the texts themselves that might make a process of subtrac-tion or dissection possible. We should rather try to find out the extent to which each text as a whole, taken in conjunction with its kerygmatic content as presented at the time when it was written, can provide us with information leading to knowledge of the Jesus of history.

We can also obtain such information from the texts that were modi-fied at a later stage. Without the data provided by these touched up texts, we would certainly have insufficient knowledge of the original tendencies expressed in the earliest texts, both in their individual pas-sages and in their central structures.

The tendencies of the late New Testament writings to provide a theo-logical interpretation therefore have a potentially heuristic function — they can help us to find out what was the early theology of Jesus him-self and of the earliest Christian community that came into existence after the Easter event, especially as far as the objective structures of that theology are concerned. These interpretative tendencies have this potentially heuristic function only insofar as they are not simply his-torically conditioned or determined by the 'Sitz im Leben' of each late New Testament community, but are rather legitimate re-interpretations of material that has its 'Sitz im Leben' in the life of Jesus himself.

2. It is only if it can be proved that the late New Testament Christol-ogies, as re-interpretations of the fundamental kerygma made in the second half of the first century, a period during which the Church was

*still being constituted, are more original, structurally closer to the early
Christology and richer in theological content than the classical Christ-
ology that they can help us to begin to formulate a new orthodox
Christology*

Rahner certainly provides a number of points of departure for a more
emphatic appreciation of the late New Testament Christology and
soteriology, but they are, in my opinion, not powerful enough, within
the framework of the whole of his teaching, to achieve the aim that
they are intended to reach. If, however, as Rahner says, the circle between the original experience and the later interpretation is not to be
discontinued, but if possible remade in a more intelligible way, then
even the late interpretation made by the New Testament authors must
be taken more fully into account than Rahner has in fact done.

IV. The Apparently Close Mutual Proximity existing between the Later New Testament Christology and Soteriology and the Classical Teaching

Rahner has called the classical Christology of the Church a Christology
of descendance. Among the most important elements of New Testament theology in any Christology are, in his view, the theology of the
Logos, the doctrine of Christ's pre-existence, the Johannine statements
attributed to Jesus ('I . . .'), the statements about God's sovereignty and
various explicit soteriologies found in the New Testament. He regards
these elements as proof of the close proximity that exists between the
late New Testament Christologies and the classical Christology of the
Church, at least in one respect, namely in that the latter is a Christology
of descendance. The late New Testament Christologies are, in Rahner's
opinion, so close to the classical Christology that they can be regarded
as being already present in the latter.

In fact, however, this far-reaching similarity is really only apparent.
The New Testament Christologies contain not only elements of a
Christology of ascendance alongside and subordinate to a descendance
Christology of primary importance, but also an abundance of teaching,
in comparison with which the classical Christology, with its teaching
about the hypostatic union, seems formal and narrow.

V. A Terminological Distinction: Descendance and Ascendance Christologies – Descending and Ascending Lines in Christological Theocentricity

1. Before going on to consider the following comments and especially the chapter on the Christologically determined theology of the New Testament, the two concepts – descendance Christology and ascendance Christology – must be explained.

These two terms are used in the methodological or epistemological sense and are determined by the distinction between 'ontic' and 'ontological'. The Christology of descendance is primarily ontic (although it can be transferred to ontology), whereas the Christology of ascendance is primarily an ontological concept. What is meant by the term 'ascendance Christology' or 'Christology from below', then, is fundamentally a Christology conceived on the basis of a transcendental (or gnoseological) anthropology. What is not primarily implied in this term is the aspect of openness to God (and the communication of this openness to God by the absolute mediator of salvation) that necessarily occurs in this Christology.

If we are to include the New Testament statements legitimately within the circle of our understanding, we are bound to make another distinction at a different level – the level of objectivization. We must, in other words, distinguish between the descending and the ascending lines in Christological theocentricity.

In the descending line, God is seen as the origin of salvation or as the one who takes the initiative to save and who gives. In the ascending line in theocentricity, he is seen rather as the goal or end towards which everything is orientated or as the one to whose gift of love a response is made.

2. These two related concepts are applicable to Jesus and, what is more, they apply above all to him. They are therefore Christological and soteriological. In other words, they apply to the question as to the part played by Jesus in this relationship.

We have first of all to establish whether the distinction that we have made at the level of objectivization between the descending and ascending lines in theocentricity and Rahner's distinction between a Christology of descendance and a Christology of ascendance intersect at any point or whether they are neither opposed to each other nor identical with each other. We may say that they do in fact intersect, but that they are not, because of the different levels at which they operate, antithetic or identical. I am of the opinion that neither the epistemological nor the objectivizing statements in the New Testament, which are in any case never without gnoseological implications in the New Testament, should lose their place in the hermeneutical circle, if what is said in the New Testament is to be interpreted properly.

3. The individual distinctions between the two sets of concepts

The descending line in Christological theocentricity includes not only a descendance Christology in the sense of 'God (or his Logos) became man', but also certain aspects of a Christology of ascendance (insofar as ontological and 'objectivizing' statements cannot be separated in that Christology). For example, the exaltation of Jesus is seen as a gift of the Father, the Father being the one who raised Jesus from the dead and exalted him.

Rahner appears to see this *descendere* and *ascendere* primarily and one-sidedly, in relationship to the New Testament, from the vantage point of Christ. In other words, it is for him predominantly Christocentric or transcendentally anthropocentric. *Descendere* and *ascendere* are not seen in such a consistently theocentric light as they should be if Jesus were a real man, even when he had been raised from the dead, in other words, if the theocentric implication of the transcendental approach — openness to God — were taken really seriously.[2] The Christological theocentricity of the New Testament in the descending line is — if we may be allowed to simplify here — primarily not ontic, but dynamic.

The ascending line of theocentricity on the one hand includes only part of the ascendance Christology. On the other hand, however, it goes beyond this (it is clear from this that the two sets of concepts intersect here), at least insofar as it includes an affirmation of the descending line, that is, the gift coming from God. As such, the theocentricity of the ascending line has a content of its own that cannot be indicated in Rahner's teaching or can at the most only be pointed out in an initial approach. It can, in other words, only be indicated as that which is a transformation of the theocentricity of the earthly Jesus and to which the risen Christ can soteriologically give a share.

VI. The 'Plus' of the New Testament Christologies as contrasted with the Classical Christology

1. The late New Testament Christologies are not only from the point of view of time, but also from that of their content – as re-interpretations of the fundamental kerygma – much more close to Jesus himself. The objective structures of the Christology of Jesus himself are maintained in a more original way than they have been in the classical Christology of the Church.

2. The Christological theocentricity of the ascending line found in the New Testament Christologies can be regarded as the most important New Testament corrective to the classical Christology and at the same time, to express it positively, the most important contribution that the New Testament can make to this attempt to find new approaches to an orthodox Christology.

As far as their content is concerned, we may mention a few examples here. There is, for instance, Jesus' *pistis*, which is expressed from time to time in the New Testament. This represents Jesus' attitude of trust towards his Father. In the letter to the Hebrews, it is a theocentrically expressed attitude of standing firm in a situation of contestation with eschatological fulfilment in view. Other examples are Jesus' temptations (*peirasmoi*), his *diakonia* and his obedience. Finally, there is his relationship with his Father, expressed particularly in the address 'Abba'.

What is especially important in this context is this theocentricity of Jesus is maintained in a whole series of important New Testament writings referring to the risen and exalted Lord. The fact that there is, despite the idea of pre-existence and comparable theologoumena, no danger that monophysitism arising as a result of adequately understood New Testament Christologies shows at least that they cannot, at this level, be simply subsumed under the classical Christology. The New Testament Christologies can be used not only to justify, but also to intensify radical thinking to the end about the doctrine of the hypostatic union.

We can outline the function of Christological theocentricity, that is, the theocentricity of the living Jesus himself and that of the community with him ('Christocentricity'), as found especially in the late New Testament Christologies, in the following way. It is, within the framework of our particular problem at least, initially the necessary communication between, on the one hand, what is justified in the descendance Christology and, on the other, the Christology of Jesus himself and the essential and original experience of Jesus as the Christ in the early Christian community or, as Rahner also calls it, the irreducible first revelation of Christian Christology.

Because of this function to communicate, it can also provide us with a valid approach to soteriology. The abstract notion of the absolute bringer of salvation, which is more strongly and one-sidedly Christocentric rather than theocentric, can also be given a suitable content by stressing the concept of the absolute mediator of salvation. This latter concept is present throughout the New Testament, although it is only occasionally mentioned explicitly.

Both the ecclesiological implications of the New Testament Christology and soteriology and their eschatological implications are connected with this and we shall draw attention to both these implications later in this work.

4.   The theology of the death and resurrection of Jesus

I. New Testament Approaches to the Heart of the Original Experience of Jesus as the Christ, which is the Irreducible First Revelation of Christian Christology[1]

1. The importance of the expectation of the parousia in the earliest post-paschal Christology

Within the then current Jewish ways of thinking and on the basis of the historical Jesus' way of speaking and acting, it was obvious and indeed inevitable for the early post-paschal Christian community to interpret the experience of Jesus' resurrection, together with the experience of the giving of the Holy Spirit, as the beginning of the last things, the *eschata*. One of the earliest, if not the very earliest of the Christological interpretations of the event of Jesus' resurrection must have been to identify Jesus with the 'Son of Man' who was to come.

2. Approaches to a rudimentary and implicit idea of exaltation in the early post-paschal Christian community

This idea of exaltation, in the sense of faith in the Christologically determined presence of the fulfilment of salvation, is always implicit rather than explicit in the New Testament, in accordance with the possibilities of kerygmatic and theological expression available to the earliest Christian community. We therefore have to make use of a whole series of arguments if we are to show that it probably existed.

We can only briefly indicate these arguments here. We can first of all arrive at a certain degree of probability regarding the presence of this idea of Jesus' exaltation by drawing an *a posteriori* conclusion Paul's writings and the early New Testament confessions of faith. Secondly, we can obtain a relatively greater certainty if we evaluate a series of facts that existed within the earliest community. The evidence of Jesus' resurrection appearances points clearly to the fact that it was possible for the risen Lord to communicate with his community. There is also the fact that, despite the danger, this early community of believers was formed in Jerusalem itself. This fact can only be satisfactorily explained as a consequence of the appearances of the risen Lord. What is more, the fact that the community gathered in Jerusalem implies that Jesus, who appeared to the community, determined the present life of that community. We can only really understand the community's prayer to Jesus, in the petition *maranatha*, for the *parousia* if he is seen as the one who are present among them and face to face with them.

We are also bound to consider in this context the evidence of the effects experienced in that earliest community on receiving the Holy Spirit. As far as the members of that community, who, since Jesus' appearances among them, were consciously subject to the demands made on them by the risen Jesus, were concerned these effects were surely also effects of this 'exalted' Jesus. Finally, we have also to mention the healings carried out by members of that earliest community 'in Jesus' name', their proclamation of the name of Jesus, their baptisms, their proclamation of the forgiveness of sins and their shared Eucharist.

It is possible to find in the New Testament a great number of traces of a transformation after the Easter event of Jesus' proclamation and above all of the proclamation of the community that had been with him before the Easter event. These traces also provide, together with the other data mentioned above, the most convincing evidence of the presence of a rudimentary idea of exaltation in the earliest community. To this can be added the Christologically relevant use of Old Testament and later Jewish ideas, especially that idea of 'humiliation and exaltation'.

3. The connection between the expectation of the parousia *and the idea of exaltation in the earliest post-paschal Christology based on the experience of the resurrection*

a. The first experience of the members of the Christian community in this early period immediately following the Easter event of the effects of the exalted Lord impelled them powerfully in the direction of the end of time and Jesus' *parousia*. What is inherent in their idea of exaltation is the coming of the Son of Man and, what is more, they were so conscious of the second coming that they were unable to look away from it, however much they experienced the effects of the exalted Jesus present among them. They were so powerfully carried along by this dynamic orientation of effects of the exalted Lord towards the *parousia* that it was only possible for a theologically independent and explicit statement about the exaltation to emerge gradually and with difficulty. This can be expressed in another way and perhaps more simply: the notion of exaltation is implicit in the earliest community's orientation towards the coming of the Son of Man in power.

b. How was this total view of Jesus both as the one who had risen from the dead and who was living and active and as the Son of Man and judge expressed in the theology of the earliest Christian community? Two aspects must clearly have predominated in this early teaching. The first is contained in the statement which was originally very simple, but which gradually gained in theological depth: 'he is risen; we have seen him'. The second is a theological consequence of this. It is a proclamation which had to express the fact that God had declared his faith in the crucified Jesus and had asserted his message and power in him. This proclamation also reaffirmed the two principal aspects of Jesus' message as contained in Mk 1. 15. The first of these aspects was, of course, the proclamation of the imminent coming of the kingdom of God. This was consistently and increasingly concentrated in the Christology of the first Christian community into a proclamation of the coming of Jesus as the Son of Man and judge. The second aspect was the call to conversion or *metanoia*.

This call to conversion was given a clearer and deeper meaning by such central words of the Lord as those of the earliest form of the Sermon on the Mount. The demand expressed in Mk 1. 15 had also to be Christologically defined by statements that insisted on the essential aspect of man's attitude towards Jesus if he is to be saved from final judgement. The proclamation of the forgiveness of sins made possible through the resurrection of Jesus and the sending of the Holy Spirit is also connected with this call to conversion.

The elucidation of the earliest and very simple apostolic proclamation of Jesus' resurrection in the further proclamation of a basic supply of the Lord's words and in a continuing process of making those words present must presumably have existed in the original form of the logia.

These, then, were presumably the dominant aspects of the proclamation of the Christian message that immediately followed the Easter event. Proclaimed alongside these elements, however, and no less important were the earliest attempts to formulate a kerygma of Christ's passion, as something that was inseparable from his resurrection.

II. Resurrection as Exaltation

1. In this section we shall contrast what Rahner has called the 'original theology of Jesus' resurrection as the beginning of Christology' with the early and late New Testament Christologies.

2. It is obvious that Rahner's emphatic declaration that the claim made by Jesus while he was still on earth was 'experienced as permanently valid and accepted by God' in the early Christian community because of the experience of the resurrection is extremely important, even from the point of view of the New Testament itself. We should in this context point to the epaphax ('once and for all') found in Paul and the letter to the Hebrews. This relates both to Jesus' death on the cross and to his life on earth and is indissolubly associated with the New Testament statements about his exaltation. It is hardly possible to over-emphasize the connection between the risen Lord and his real historical life on earth.

We are, however, bound to criticize and amplify Rahner's statement. We would ask, for example, whether the various forms of the New Testament idea of exaltation — in other words, the different expressions of the New Testament conviction that Jesus, who was then living with God, was still active in his community — were no more than models providing variants of the basic model of the 'lasting claim that Jesus made in his life on earth', as Rahner has called it. If we are to do justice to Rahner here, we must remember that this is a consciously provisional formulation made in the course of gradual process of thought in which he was deliberately avoiding mythologization. It is, however, perhaps not superfluous to point out, in the context of this gradual process of thought, that the most important aspect of the New Testament kerygma of the resurrection is either not expressed or else is only implicit in Rahner's statement. In this kerygma, it is, after all, not simply a question of reaffirming an event and a claim belonging to the past — it is also a question of affirming the result of the event of the resurrection. This result can be expressed in the following way. Not only was the claim made by the last prophets affirmed — the man, Jesus of Nazareth, was living as the one through whom God would bring about the fulfilment of his plan and who was already actively orientated towards that fulfilment, the kingdom of God.

Another of Rahner's statements is less ambiguous. He has elsewhere called the resurrection of Jesus the 'valid permanence of his person and cause'. Finally, the full solution, which can be verified in the New Testament, can be found in a third statement by Rahner: 'the risen Jesus is, with his concrete claim, the unrepeatable and unsurpassable existence of God himself with us'.

3. This formulation, which is in itself sufficient, must, however, be given a deeper meaning on the basis of the New Testament and be protected from the possibility of misunderstanding mentioned above. If this is to be done, we must first add to this formulation by using the New Testament statements about the function of the risen Lord. An example of this would be the statements about his advocating the cause (entugehanein) of Christians (Heb 7. 25; Rom 8. 34 par.). Secondly, the key concept of 'transformation', which has so far only been used once or twice, should be introduced here. This transformation is a counterpart to a mere preservation of the image of Jesus which the disciples had from his earthly life. This mere preservation was simply not possible because of the completely new situation that had come about as a result of the resurrection and the sending of the Spirit. The pre-paschal image of Jesus (or the pre-paschal Christology) had to be transformed by the disciples because of the resurrection of Jesus and the gift of the Spirit. This question of the post-paschal transformation or transposition of the image and message of Jesus that existed before the Easter event is of decisive importance for the problem as to whether there was any continuity between the Jesus of history and the post-paschal kerygma of the kind that would justify the post-paschal and late New Testament testimony to Christ. Both Jesus' claim and his history or life were transformed.

4. This datum presupposes what is in my opinion an original identification of resurrection and exaltation. In view of the present theological situation, we cannot avoid asking whether this view of a function of the exalted Christ (and the New Testament theologies, such as Paul's theology of Christ and Pneuma, which attempt to interpret that function) is no more than an illegitimate mythology. This suspicion is in striking contrast to the extremely emphatic statement that the reality and the real history of the historical Jesus was experienced as permanently valid and accepted by God in the resurrection.

We are bound to reiterate that this permanence of the real history of Jesus implies that his person was also lasting. It can, however, only have been so if the resurrection brought about a transformation of the pre-paschal function into a real function carried out by Jesus in the present with his community and the world in mind.

III. The Connection between Christology and Soteriology

Although what Rahner says about the theology of the death of Jesus in the light of the resurrection can be applauded by the New Testament scholar, his observations can be criticized on two accounts. In the first place, the New Testament soteriologies, which work with categories of 'sacrifice', are not sufficiently understood. In the second place, they bear evidence of a soteriological aim that has not been sufficiently liberated from the narrow confines of a classical Church soteriology. This limitation can be overcome if the New Testament soteriologies are used.

1. The conceptuality and objectivity of the New Testament soteriologies

The conceptuality of the New Testament soteriologies is not simply concerned with isolated interpretations that have been brought forward from outside. On the contrary, the concepts that have been developed here were connected with a legitimate re-interpretation of the original datum, although this re-interpretation is expressed in a language that is remote from our own. Although the terminology of these New Testament interpretations of the death of Jesus is historically conditioned, they should not simply be reduced to the level of later New Testament interpretations.

In Hebrews, Paul, 1 John and so on, the cultic concepts of the period are not used with their original meaning. They are used rather to help to erect an entire interpretative structure which is quite alien — and indeed theologically opposed — to the Jewish and pagan ideas of sacrifice of the same period and which, even though it gives the superficial impression of being related to those ideas, has in fact much less to do with them (and theologically nothing at all to do with them) and much more to do with the essential and original experience of Jesus as the Christ. In other words, they are used as a legitimate interpretation in continuity with the event of Jesus.

We have, however, to ask one fundamental question: to what extent can these ideas be traced back to the basic meaning of the New Testament 'for'. There is also another, related question: to what extent does 'atonement' have the same meaning as 'remission of sins' as 'reconciliation' (= restoration of community with God, see 1 Cor 5. 18 ff).

2. The event of crucifixion in the past and the function of the risen Jesus in the present

In the classical soteriology, our gaze is narrowly fixed on Jesus' cruci-fixion as an event in the past. Although there is great emphasis on the cross in the New Testament, especially in Paul's intensive theology of the cross, attention is not focussed on the past there. Rom 8. 34 is a good example. Here Paul insists that the one through whom God saves and justifies man is the crucified and risen Jesus in his identity. In this important statement, Paul places much more emphasis on Jesus' life and resurrection and his sitting 'at the right hand of God' than on his death on the cross ('Christ Jesus, who died, yes, who was raised from the dead . . . ').

Here, then, we have to go back to what we said above in Section II about the function of the risen Jesus. It is necessary to do this if we are to overcome this narrow focus. Although the classical Christology and its theology of the incarnation is not able to provide us with an ade-quate soteriology, the New Testament can do this. Indeed, we can go further and say that the specific New Testament expressions of faith in Jesus as living in the present and in his function are the presupposition for a satisfactory soteriology. This is clear from the easily misunder-stood New Testament statements about the 'blood' of Jesus. According to Hebrews, Paul and the gospel and first epistle of John, this 'blood' saves, not as the blood of Jesus shed in the past on Golgotha, but rather as the community with Jesus living in the present, insofar as he is the crucified and risen one in his identity.

The gospel of John and the epistle to the Hebrews show this com-munity with Jesus as that which saves, insofar as Jesus, according to John, still bears the wounds of his death on the cross and, according to the epistle, is theocentrically orientated towards the Father in the definitive permanence of his offering of himself on the cross. According to the model provided by Hebrews, Jesus takes his transfigured blood, which points to the permanence of his offering of himself, into the 'heavenly' sanctuary to the Father and thus intercedes for us as our advocate. It is clear from Paul, Hebrews and John, then, that Jesus can give us community and through this can provide us with a saving orien-tation towards God.

It is also clear from all this that we cannot do without the pre-understanding that comes from the later soteriological projects. These can clearly help us to understand the soteriology contained in the essential and original experience of Jesus as the Christ.

3. The absolute bringer and the mediator of salvation

There is a distinct possibility of giving (and indeed a need to give) content and meaning, on the basis of what we have said above, to the abstract concept of the absolute bringer of salvation, which points too clearly in the direction of transcendental Christology, and to refashion it in terms of the concept of a mediator of salvation. The idea of mediator rather than bringer does not complicate man's relationship with God (which is, after all, salvation in the widest sense of the word, including interhuman relationships as well), but tends rather to make that relationship between God and man possible and immediate.

4. The continuity between the late New Testament soteriologies and a pre-paschal theology of the passion

A theology of the passion (in a rudimentary form, of course) is present when a connection is made between Jesus' acceptance of death and the radical demand for succession. It can be established with fair certainty that such a rudimentary theology of the passion existed in the earliest Christian traditions. It has the same structure as theologies that were developed later in the New Testament, in that in both the decisive element is the community with Jesus who has accepted his death and has been, through his death, taken up into glory (see Jn 12. 24 ff; cf. Jn 12. 32; Rom 8. 17; 2 Cor 5. 14 ff; Rom 6, 10 ff; 8. 29).

Rahner's statement that Jesus 'belongs to us' should be expressed, in the light of the New Testament, which generally has a tendency that is not transcendentally anthropological, as 'to whom we belong' (see, for example, Rom. 14. 8) or as 'who (that is, Jesus) draws us into his community' (see John 12. 32).

These formulations can, however, also be expressed more emphatically, in accordance with the transcendentally anthropological tendency, in the following way: 'this man who is conscious of his function to form a community and who belongs to us by being there for us'.

The question of the words of the Lord's Supper and their relevance to the 'relationship between the pre-paschal Jesus and his death' should be considered here, but, because of its complexitiy, must be left aside.

As far as the early post-paschal soteriology is concerned, the idea of the forgiveness of sins should strictly speaking be developed in connection with a theology of baptism.

5. Christology and theology: the Christologically determined theology of the New Testament

I. The Programme of a Christology based on Theo-logy

1. The approach

a. Two Ways in Christology

Since the event of Christ, it has not been possible to separate theo-logy and Christo-logy. As Walter Pannenberg has observed, it is the aim both of theology and Christology to develop the connection between them.[2] Almost always Jesus has been the point of departure in Christology, with the aim of finding God in him, the idea of God being historically and objectively presupposed.

There, is however, another way in Christology. Pannenberg has referred to this other way, but it has not been followed by most other authors writing about the same subject. In this other way, the idea of God is the point of departure. Pannenberg said that, in this second way in Christology, Jesus is only considered from the point of view of his significance for the idea of God. What has to be said about Jesus must be presupposed as otherwise already known[3] Is there, however, anything that can or must be said otherwise, apart from his significance for the idea of God?[4]

The Christology of the New Testament is, of course, based on the thought of the Old Testament and has to deal with the problem as to how faith in Christ can be reconciled with monotheism. If this Christology is to be understood, it is certainly advisable to take the idea of God as one's point of departure and guideline. It is only in this way that the New Testament Christology, which is so much more closely linked to soteriology than to the classical Christology, can be adequately represented, since Jesus is always regarded in the New Testament as the one who made it possible for the believer to be in a situation of community with God in the present and the future and, what is more, to have that relationship by virtue of the sending of the Spirit of

God. Without this point of reference, God, there is no New Testament Christology.

Even today, the idea of God cannot simply be presupposed, as it has been in the classical Christology. It would, of course, be quite wrong to exclude the question of God from Christology, especially in view of the apparent crisis of that question — greater than that in which Christology and faith in Jesus find themselves at present. The idea of God is really the presupposition, without which Christology is meaningless.[5] There can be no Christology that is not constantly being confronted by the question of God.

We may therefore ask whether Rahner's Christology is not to some extent Christocentric, in that he gives less emphasis in fact to theocentricity than the New Testament does in its Christological ideas. This may well be because he tries to reach a Christology — quite legitimately — through a transcendental anthropology. He tends, after all, to think in terms of the absolute bringer of salvation, a concept which is open to the absolute mystery, but is not as such explicitly theocentric.

b. The intention of this attempt

The real intention of the attempt that follows, to outline a theo-logical Christology, is to do full justice, in the light of the data provided by the New Testament, to Jesus' own theocentricity and also to ensure that a Christology of the New Testament will fulfil the demands placed on it by its being based on the Old Testament and make a theo-logy possible. It ought to be possible, in other words, for a Christological theology, that is, a connection between theo-logy and Christo-logy, to be regarded, on the basis of the New Testament, as the essence of dogmatic theology.

2. The central problem

How can experience of God be communicated Christologically or at least made possible? For us, this problem is probably not brought to light most clearly by Jesus' idea of God, even though it is certainly presented very sharply indeed there. We, however, tend to misunderstand Jesus' idea of God today and to place it at the same level as the Jewish idea of God generally at the time of Jesus. We can therefore get a clearer impression of Jesus' concept of God from the New Testament data, which are post-paschal.

a. The heart of the problem, seen in the light of the New Testament Christologies

Can New Testament faith in Christ be reconciled with Old Testament monotheism? (The earliest and possibly most striking example of this faith in Christ is, of course, Paul's.) We can ask this question in a different way. Does New Testament Christocentricity lead to a complication and therefore also to a weakening and a reduction of the Old Testament faith in Yahweh, the one God? Or does it provide a final radicalization, making it possible to come into direct contact with God, by transposing faith on to a new level? Is direct contact with God, in other words, made impossible by the mediation of the figure of Christ, because the latter comes between God and the believer? Or is that direct contact made final and radically possible as a really direct relationship?[6]

b. The central concept in the relationship between Christology and theo-logy: faith

The early Christians' faith in Christ, as it emerges clearly in the New Testament, is continuous with the Old Testament faith in God that was accepted and made radical by Jesus. This continuity must also, as Schäfer has said, run over the identity of faith in God.[7]

Gerhard Ebeling has also suggested that faith is nothing but an agreeing with God.[8] The continuity between the Old Testament and Jesus' relationship with God on the one hand and the New Testament, post-paschal relationship with God on the other may, if Ebeling's definition of faith is correct, exist in an even more complete sense than Ebeling himself intended. As the one who 'bore witness to faith', that is, who testified to 'what it meant to agree with God and, what is more, to agree with him not only in life, but also in death', Jesus became the 'ground of faith' (through his resurrection), with the result that, in community with Jesus, 'agreeing with God takes place in fact again and again'.

Martin Buber has questioned this continuity in his work on 'two ways of faith'.[9] According to this author, there are only two ways of believing, which he calls 'emunah and pistis. The first expresses an attitude of trust, faith in the other or 'thou faith'. The second implies a relationship of recognition, according to which a datum or situation is recognized as true. It is 'believing that . . . ' The distinction between 'emunah and pistis points to the difference or even the contrast between the faith of the Old Testament and that of the New. Jesus, Buber believed, clearly had an Old Testament faith. 'The simple, concrete and situational dialogue of biblical man' in the Old Testament became, in the New, 'the most sublime of all theologies'.[10]

Our problem is expressed in the sharpest possible way in Buber's contrast between 'emunah and pistis. We may therefore ask whether the *pistis* of the early Church was contrasted to the *'emunah* of the Old Testament or whether it was on the side of the latter.[11] Continuity between the two may perhaps be possible despite the transposition resulting from the experience of the resurrection and the theological reflection ensuing from that event. It may even be possible because of that transposition.

3. The concept of 'theo-logy'

In this section, we shall attempt to define what is meant by theo-logy, understanding of God, the concept of God, faith in God and so on. In answering this question — what is theo-logy? — we have first of all to protect this concept against objectivizing misunderstandings. Secondly, we have to include within our definition the aspect of personal dialogue between God and man that is present in the Old Testament. We can indeed take as our point of departure the conviction that the extremely anthropomorphic form of many Old Testament pronouncements expressing this personal relationship of dialogue between God and man goes to the very heart of the matter. To express this more precisely, it goes relatively or more or less approximately, but nonetheless really to the heart of the matter, whereas, if this aspect of personal dialogue is neglected, the heart of the matter, with which the Old and indeed the New Testaments are concerned, is not touched.

Thirdly, this relationship with God in the biblical sense does not exclude fellow humanity, but includes it. This is particularly clear if we take the clarification of the New Testament understanding of God as given in the statements in 1 Jn 4. 8, 16 as our point of departure: 'God is love'. If God is indeed love, communicating itself in the radical Jesus and Pneuma event, then a relationship with the absolute mystery expressed in this particular way is only possible if the dynamism of that mystery which is impelled to communicate itself in love is expressed in handing on of that divine love that is normalized by Jesus' offering of himself and made possible by community with him. We obviously need to remove such objectivizing misunderstandings or, to express it more graphically, to smash all the images of God that we have made ourselves. This is clear from the fact that we can, as Schäfer has pointed out, only know God by bringing him into our world. In other words, all our knowledge is objectivizing, both that which is creative and that which is gained through encounter.[12]

There is an almost inevitable danger, especially in the present situation, that the idea of antiquity can no longer be expressed by a creative personality or figure who is orientated towards his own image of the world. In this dangerous situation, there is instead a tendency for theology to become indistinguishable from a teaching about fellow-humanity. In view of this danger, Schäfer has suggested that our capacity to understand should be extended and that we should investigate the nature of the 'transmoral content' of our faith in God.[13] If this attempt is not made, Schäfer believes, we shall not be able to understand either Judaism, which was not simply a moral doctrine, but also a religion, or the radicalization of the Old Testament faith in God that resulted from Jesus' attack against the contemporary Jewish understanding of God.

II. Pre-conditions for a Christian theology of later New Testament Ideas based on the Heart of the Original Experience of Jesus as the Christ

1. The contrary argument
a. The tendency in this chapter (5)
In the sections that follow (5. II 2 and 3), an attempt is made to criticize Rahner's structural approaches very briefly, in order to find the conditions for outlining the next sections (5. III and IV), in which the real argument takes place.

The New Testament scholar has, of course, to take the texts of Scripture as his point of departure. In the section that immediately follows, then (5. II), we shall discuss the understanding of God found in these New Testament theological ideas and indicate the way in which they are determined by Christology.

This will bring us to the main argument in Section IV. In this argument, we shall go back, through the New Testament texts, to Jesus and do this moreover in a more detailed way than in the present section (5. II), by using the New Testament kerygma.

Whereas Rahner moved in his argument from the historical Jesus to the Christ of the Church's faith, we shall here follow a different tendency, proceeding backwards from the New Testament data and in this way amplifying and deepening what Rahner has said on the subject.[14]
b. The two arguments are not mutually exclusive
Both the line from the historical Jesus to the interpretation of the phenomenon of Jesus implied in the resurrection and the function carried out by the risen Jesus as well as the contrary tendency (both are based on the New Testament, although the second is more emphatically

so) are legitimate and both are necessary to understanding.

Neither the early Church's interpretation of the original experience (the event of the historical Jesus as well as the resurrection, including the function of the risen Jesus) nor that aspect of the original experience known as the event of the 'historical Jesus' alone can be regarded as absolute. It is certainly relevant to see both these ways of thinking in the mutual relationship and to follow both of them. On the other hand, any ideas that might exclude one or other of these two points of reference (the New Testament interpretation based on the event of the resurrection and the historical Jesus) and therefore make the 'contrary' relationship between these two ways impossible are bound to be unjustified.

One question relating to what follows can be asked now. It is this. If Jesus was primarily related to God, in that he received from and responded to God and handed on God's love, should the person who comes into contact with Jesus not be drawn into this relationship with God, quite apart from the fact that he might be conscious of it or not?

We are bound to stress once again that this relationship with God should be seen as all embracing in that it includes a radicalized fellow-humanity, since the latter is based on the dynamism of the *thelema* or saving will of God.

2. *Structural conditions based on the Jesus of history*

In this section, we are particularly concerned with the humanity of Jesus, based partly on the deep consciousness of mission (or 'unity with God') that was present in Jesus in a way that cannot be found in other men, including the prophets. As Rahner has pointed out, Jesus was, in his human consciousness of himself, distant from and placed over and against God in freedom, obedience and adoration, as all men who are conscious of themselves are contrasted with God. Jesus' radical theocentricity is, in my opinion, of great structural importance for the transposition that took place after the Easter event. Jesus after all did not proclaim himself – he proclaimed the kingdom of God. Rahner has called Jesus the culminating point or the exemplary and original case of a man who was totally orientated towards the mystery that reveals both the action and the object of God and is God himself.

He was, as Rahner has also said, the man for others[15] because he was also the man for God: 'He was conscious of his closeness to God. For him, God was not a cipher for the meaning of man. He was completely at one with the social and religious outcasts because these were the men who were loved by his "Father" ... The man Jesus was purely and simply man because he forgot himself through God and his fellowmen who were in need of salvation and existed only in this forgetfulness of self'. Jesus' function, then, was extremely relevant. His very being was revealed in it.

Finally, we should mention another structural line – Jesus' attitude before the Easter event to his death. He freely accepted this fate, experienced it as the consequence of his mission and consented to it in a connection, which could perhaps not be verbalized, with that mission and with the content of his message of the kingdom of God that was already present in his own age. We may conclude with Rahner's words about Jesus' attitude towards his fate: 'Jesus went forward freely to meet death and regarded it ... at least as the fate of a prophet. In that fate, he knew that he was secure in God's intention to be close to and to forgive the world'.

3. The original theology of Jesus' resurrection and death as the beginning of the Christological theo-logy of the late New Testament

The resurrection event or experience brought about an entirely new situation with regard to all later interpretation, since the resurrection put the process of transposing the pre-paschal data into motion and obliged men to reflect about this transposition.

Jesus' claim, made during his life, is experienced as valid in the event of the resurrection, with the result that this at least initially meant the same as the (transposed) 'valid permanence of his person and function', that is, the function of the crucified and risen Jesus in his identity.

In the light of Jesus' resurrection as the fulfilment of 'God's eschatological promise', his death, which summed up and completed his life, can be regarded, like his life, as theocentric in a very radical sense. This is so, Rahner claims, because 'his death only becomes historically tangible for us and is only completed by the resurrection, at least as a death which was endured in complete obedience and in which life was given completely over to God'. The soteriological significance of Jesus' death – what followed from the 'for God' 'for the many' – can also be recognized in the light of the resurrection.

III. The Image of God of the New Testament – inseparably connected
with the Function of the risen Jesus ('through Christ') which makes
man's Relationship with God possible

1. A preliminary remark
For reasons of space, we shall confine ourselves here to Paul, the gospel
and first letter of John and Hebrews. We must, however, emphasize that
most of the other New Testament writings are also important in this
context, especially the theology of the synoptic gospels.

It would, however, take too much space to deal with the synoptic
gospels here. They bear witness to faith in Jesus after the Easter event
and also allow us to go back, because of the traditions that they incorporate, and question the Jesus of history. This twofold function of the
synoptic gospels should certainly be outlined separately, but that
would not be possible here. Below, in Section IV, the traditions that
can be distinguished in the synoptic gospels are considered within the
framework of what they have to say to us about the historical Jesus and
as arguments which incorporate the results of recent scholarship.

2. The argument
The ascending line of theocentricity is of decisive importance if we are
to demonstrate the function that Jesus had with regard to our understanding of God as presented in the New Testament. The ascending line
of theocentricity is important both as far as the objectivizing datum of
the New Testament and with regard to the possibility of experiencing
God that is present in the New Testament message.

We therefore assume that a theocentricity in an ascending line was
not only expressed by the Jesus of history, but also by the risen Jesus.
This is a fact that is often overlooked. It is, however, rooted in the New
Testament datum.

In the New Testament, the risen Jesus is still regarded as really man.
In other words, he is seen (in a transcendental understanding) as the
one who was open to the absolute mystery and as the one who received
from the absolute mystery what he had to hand on to others. This
vision does not contradict the understanding of Jesus' unity with God
(his 'divinity'), which was raised to a new level by the experience of his
resurrection.

In other words, in the New Testament, the risen Jesus is seen as
related to God in a singular and original personal dialogue. He completes, according to the New Testament authors, that relationship of

personal dialogue with God that is fundamental to the Old Testament.

3. The objectivizing datum: the risen Jesus as the one who lived orientated towards the Father and who orientated his own life towards the Father (the theocentricity of Christocentricity)

a. A preliminary remark

In what follows, I shall consider — in accordance with the plan for the argument outlined above in Section III 2 — the dialogue structure resulting from the exalted Jesus' relationship with God together with the constantly soteriological direction of his 'life for God'.

b. Paul

According to Buber, the situation of dialogue or the 'over and against' is replaced in Paul by a 'mystical situation' or an 'interplay'.[16] It would seem that Buber was influenced in this case by arguments which had been suggested early this century by specialists in the sphere of comparative religion and which have since been superseded. In fact, Paul's thinking is not predominantly Hellenistic or mystic.[17] His thinking is clearly dominated by the old Testament relationship of personal dialogue and it is not difficult to prove this.[18]

i. In Rom 6. 10, Paul makes a statement that is, in the light of most other previous or contemporary theological thinking, quite unexpected, namely that the risen Jesus — according to the context, it can only be he — 'lives for God'. This statement is fully in accordance with what Rahner has called the 'permanence' of Jesus' obedience on the cross together with the 'permanence' of his earthly life and his claim, which led him to death on the cross (see the *ephapax* of Rom 6. 10a). It is also in accordance with the 'permanence' of Jesus' real life in the present 'for' God (in the sense of a personal orientation towards God).

The term 'life for God' can be understood as serving God by keeping his commandments, doing his will in order to prepare the way for the coming of his kingdom and glorifying God despite challenges. This term was also understood at the time as an orientation towards the contemporary situation in which life on this earth was placed and as implying an aspect of dialogue. Rom 6. 10 is not the only place in which Paul speaks in this way. He says, for instance in 1 or 3. 23, that 'Christ is God's' and, in 1 Cor 11. 3, that the 'head of Christ is God'. This does not express a 'mystical situation'. It is clearly a case of a real situation of being 'over and against' that was not statically objectivized, but, in the Old Testament sense, determined by the dynamic situation of dialogue, precisely as Buber has defined it.[19]

Rom 15. 7 provides us with a statement about the glorification of God through the risen Jesus. There is no implication of a 'mystical situation' in that text or in the Pauline expression 'through Christ', which points to Christ's function as a mediator. Here too, the situation is one of personal dialogue. According to Paul, Christians could glorify God 'through Christ' or pray to him 'through Christ' and this was only possible because the risen Jesus was, both before and after the resurrection, 'over and against' God, for whom he 'lived'

ii. There are two data above all which demonstrate the relationship of dialogue in which Jesus was, according to Paul, placed after the Easter event. According to Gal 4. 6, the 'Spirit of the Son of God' was sent into the hearts of believers crying 'Abba! Father!'[20] This implies the permanence of Jesus' relationship with God, expressed by the Jesus of history in his address 'Abba'.

This 'over and against', which kept the risen Jesus in unity with God is above all expressed in such statements as that made in 1 Cor 15. 28, which point to the eschatological future and emphasize the subjection of the exalted Jesus, who has until this time ruled, to God. Paul says in this text that the aim of this subjection is that 'God may be everything to everyone', but this does not mean that this basic situation of dialogue no longer exists. That situation can certainly be reconciled with the theocentricity that is, according to 1 Cor 15. 28, complete — and is furthermore the fulfilment of what was commenced in the revelation of Yahweh in the Old Testament — and it is also constitutive for that theocentricity.

If, then, the idea of sonship that is applied to the risen Jesus, points, as we have already seen from Gal 4. 6, not only to the dignity of the Father, but also to Jesus' relationship with the Father, this aspect will also clearly be fulfilled eschatologically (see Rom 8. 29). According to the latter text, the risen Jesus was to become, as the 'Son', the 'firstborn among many brethren! In other words, the many were to be raised and therefore be joined, as brothers, to the one who had been raised first. This means that Jesus had a soteriological function, which is here linked to the *eschaton*, since Paul's thought was always orientated towards the end of time. It is important to note, however, that this soteriological function is not simply to be carried out in the eschatological future. It is also exercised in the present, in that the relationship between the 'sons' and the Father is already made possible by the one 'Son' (see Rom 8. 14 ff).

iii. We have, of course, to recognize here, as in many other places in

Paul's letters, the existence of the decisive link which makes it possible for the relationship between the risen Jesus and God to be extended to that between Christians and God. This link is the Pneuma. What is important in this context is Paul's dynamic identification of the risen Jesus with the Pneuma. We can give two examples of this identification here. In 1 Cor 15. 45, Paul says that 'the last Adam (= Jesus) became (through the resurrection) a life-giving spirit'. In 2 Cor 3. 17, he says that 'the Lord is the Spirit' ('the Kyrios is the Pneuma').[21]

iv. Paul's soteriology is theocentric, because his Christology is. The line from his theocentric Christology to the corresponding soteriology (salvation through orientation towards God) can be recognized in the connection between Rom 6. 10 and 11.[22] It can also be seen in passages such as Rom 5. 1 ff, according to which believers have, through the risen Jesus Christ, 'peace towards God' and a 'leading towards[23] the grace' of this relationship with God. Finally, it is important in this context to mention the 'intercession' of Christ Jesus, who was the dead and risen Jesus in his identity, but more the risen Jesus (Rom 8. 34).

c. The Gospel of John

i. The permanence of Jesus' relationship with the Father can also be recognized at the stage of the glorification in the fourth gospel.[24] According to Jn 17. 1, the aim of the glorified Jesus is to glorify the Father. (To glorify the Father, in Johannine terminology, is to 'reveal' him; revelation here has to be understood in an all embracing sense.) According to the most probable interpretation of Jn 6. 57, the earthly and risen Jesus lives 'because of the Father', in other words, in order to glorify him. We can also take the example of Jn 14. 31, where the author speaks of Jesus' love for the Father. This love enables him to take the way that leads to death. The permanence of this love can be seen in the Johannine statements about the glorification of the Father by the risen and glorified Jesus. An example of this is Jn 17. 26: 'that the love with which thou hast loved me (that is, the love which is made possible by and included in Jesus' love in response to that of the Father) may be in them, and I in them'.

ii. Jesus' relationship of dialogue with God — and, in accordance with the whole intention of the fourth gospel, this includes the relationship of the earthly Jesus that acquires permanence in the existence of the glorified Jesus — is well expressed in Jn 5. 17 ff. According to this passage, the Father 'shows' the Son the works that he ought to do and the Son 'does' the works that the Father shows him. It is clear from this (because of a connection between the ideas expressed in Jn 5. 20 and those of 14. 12 that can be justified exegetically and is indeed, in my opinion, necessary) that what we have here is a 'work' or 'works' done by the exalted Jesus' disciples at the time of the Paraclete.

iii. The most characteristic text for the soteriological aspect of John's thoroughly theocentric Christology is Jn 12. 32: 'When I am lifted up from the earth (= exalted, on the cross and, in connection with this, above all in glorification), I will draw all men to myself'. This clearly means that Jesus will draw all men first to the cross and then, through this, to glorification.

c. The Epistle to the Hebrews

i. According to Heb 12. 2a, Jesus — here too the earthly and the risen Jesus in his identity[25] — is the 'pioneer and perfecter of faith'. In Hebrews too, *pistis* is applied above all to the earthly Jesus and this *pistis* is standing firm[26] and continuing in the relationship with God. This *pistis* of the earthly Jesus as a continuing orientation towards the God of the promise even in the midst of challenges, being put to the test and in death is also transposed, not only in Heb 12. 1ff, but also in a number of other passages, to the level of the risen Jesus. According to Heb 9. 24, for example, Jesus, who is characterized by the author of the letter as the earthly and exalted one in his identity, passed through death and resurrection 'into heaven itself', in order to 'appear in the presence of God on our behalf'. It is clear from the passage that follows that the author is concerned with the permanence of Jesus' unique offering of himself on the cross.

ii. What emerges even more from Hebrews than from the other New Testament texts is the soteriological aspects of the Christological statements. This is apparent in the fact that the category of high priest can be applied to Jesus in this letter. The meaning and intention of Hebrews far transcend the pagan and Old Testament understanding of cult and this category therefore implies that the man characterized as a high priest was orientated both towards God and towards his fellow-men and that he also directed the latter towards God. This is borne out by the statement made in Heb 5. 1: the high priest 'is appointed to act on behalf of men in relation to God'.[27]

According to Heb 6. 20, Jesus was a 'forerunner on our behalf'. In Heb 2. 12, Jesus 'proclaims the name of God to his brethren'. According to Heb 7. 25, Jesus was able, because of the permanence of his unique offering of himself, 'to save (perfectly = for ever) those who draw near to God through him, since he always lives to make intercession for them'. Another passage that shows clearly that the author of

Hebrews had both the exalted and the crucified Jesus in mind, in other words, the permanence of Jesus' offering of himself on the cross is Heb 8. 1ff. In this passage, this function of the exalted Jesus is characterized as the most important aspect of what the author wanted to tell his readers.

Jesus' soteriological function is also expressed against the background of the superseded and insufficient priesthood of the Old Testament in one of the most important passages in this context in Hebrews (9. 11-14). In this important text, the most significant statement is made in verse 14, in which both the unique self-offering of Jesus to God in his death and the permanence and effectiveness of that self-offering in orientating believers towards God are stressed. The latter is implied in the concluding statement: so that we can 'serve the living God'.

4. The gnoseological aspect: experience of God 'through Jesus' (the significance of the transposed community with Jesus for this experience of God)

a. The concept of experience of God

i. In this section, we shall try to discover, within the theological, kerygmatic and paranetic statements made in the New Testament, an aspect of the experience of God that is Christologically determined and communicated by the risen Jesus. This means that we have to presuppose the existence of a sphere of a more or less unsystematic experience of God.

Rahner has described just such a sphere of experience in his essay on the experience of God today. In this essay, he says that 'experience of God is the ultimate and most radical and deep form of all personal spiritual experience (of love, faithfulness, hope and so on). This is a 'very concrete experience of God or of being referred to God,' Rahner has pointed out, 'that is also an experience of the inexpressible aspect of all concrete everyday experience. It is present, anonymously, in every spiritual process, but it is more clearly and systematically present in those events in which man, who is usually lost in his everyday life in individual things and tasks, is to some extent thrown back on himself'.[28] Rahner goes on to say that man experiences God clearly in 'silence, anxiety and his inexpressible longing for truth, love and community . . . in loneliness and when one is close to death'.[29]

ii. We have to amplify what Rahner says in the last part of his essay on the experience of God if the idea of an experience of God 'through

Jesus Christ' that is outlined in the New Testament is to be understood.

We are, for instance, bound to add to Rahner's affirmation that every experience of God is 'effective in faithfulness, responsibility, love and hope, beyond everything that might justify these attitudes'[30] the fact that there is an aspect of dialogue implied in this experience that is much more strongly emphasized and has therefore to be stressed particularly. In this context, social and historical experiences should also be considered as possible stimuli to an 'experience of being referred to God'.

We are also bound to mention the categories that make it possible for us to understand the universally biblical and especially the Old Testament background to the New Testament experience of God. As far as the New Testament experience of God is concerned, in which Jesus is, of course, given a position of central importance, Rahner has suggested[31] that Christianity is the literal and social objectivation of this original experience of God, an objectivization that is pure and related to Jesus Christ as the one who sets a seal on that experience.

What Rahner says here is rather too formal and insufficient to give real access to the New Testament statements. It is also possible that it is misleading to describe Jesus Christ as setting a seal on the experience of God. It is important not to claim that Christ did no more than set a seal on that experience and at the same time not say that he was above all a qualitatively new beginning or origin of experience of God. He was both the one who set a seal on and the one who originated the New Testament experience of God.[32] As far as the New Testament is concerned, Jesus Christ is the one who not only stimulated that experience of God in an exemplary way and by his words, but also made it possible for community to be created through that experience.

iii. We should also point out in this context that this experience of God is very closely connected with the New Testament theme of the relationship between the love of God and love of one's neighbour. We may, for example, take as our point of departure the Johannine *ginoskein* or loving knowledge. We can, in other words, only experience God if we love God and if we experience ourselves as loved (which cannot take place without our fellow men). We cannot be loved without our fellow-men, nor can we love God without loving our fellow-men. The love of God and love of our neighbour go together.

iv. An answer to the question about possible New Testament approaches to Rahner's view of Christianity as the pure objectivization of the original experience of God is at least implied in the material provided in the three sections that follow (b − d).[33]

v. Finally, we are bound to ask whether the experience of God presented by the New Testament points, either in spite or because of the mediation by Christ, to that directness, which has to be postulated in the light of a transcendental understanding of an unsystematic and then a systematic experience of God. Provisionally at least, we can draw attention to two passages in the gospel of John that relate to this question. The first is Jn 12. 44: 'He who believes in me believes not in me, but in him who sent me'. The second is Jn 16. 26ff, in which a statement that is apparently contradictory to the Johannine statements concerning the exalted Jesus' requests for his own is made: 'I do not say to you that I shall pray the Father for you, for the Father himself loves you . . . '

b. Paul

i. In Paul's theology, the Pneuma is the medium of openness to God or experience of God. A key statement in this teaching is made in 1 Cor 2. 10ff: 'The Spirit searches everything, even the depths of God'. An anthropological comparison is made in 2. 11 ('What person knows a man's thoughts except the spirit of the man which is in him?') with a theological statement ('So also no one comprehends the thoughts of God except the Spirit of God') so as to make the author's intention clear (verse 12): 'We have received not the spirit of the world, but the Spirit which is from God, that we might (in experience) understand the gifts bestowed on us by God'. In the context of the whole, the aim of the author is, of course, to point to the wisdom of God in the foolishness of the cross and, in this sense, Paul writes in 2. 16: 'We have the mind (Spirit) of Christ'.

In Rom 14. 17, central ideas of Paul's theology and anthopology are stated, as given by the Pneuma: 'The kingdom of God means . . . *dikaiosune* (a right relationship with God) and peace and joy in the Holy Spirit'. According to Rom 15. 13, not only 'joy and peace in faith,' but also an 'abundance of hope' are made possible by 'the power of the Holy Spirit.' In the following verse (15. 14), Paul expresses his conviction that the Christians whom he is addressing are 'filled with all knowledge (*gnosis*)'. *Gnosis* here, as in other Pauline texts, is not the knowledge that existed in the other religions of the world at Paul's time, but rather an experience of God containing a knowledge of his will and a readiness to do it.

Of particular importance to our theme of 'experience of God' are two passages in Paul's epistle to the Romans (5. 1-5 and 8. 14-27). We shall consider these now, in Sections ii and iii.

ii. Rom 5. 1-5: The apparently objectivizing concepts of peace directed towards God and 'leading towards' that are given by Christ are really related to experience of God. This is clear from the explicitly or implicitly gnoseological statements that are directed towards experience on 5. 2-5. Paul's 'boasting' (*kauchasthai*) is a speaking about the positive content of man's self-understanding. The believer does not acquire this self-understanding through his own efforts, but through community with Christ that is given in the Spirit. (This state is 'being in Christ'') In this sense it is an understanding of self 'in the Lord' expressed by 'boasting'. Since the Lord determined the present time, because he mediated the future fulfilment, the experience of 'hope of sharing the glory of God' (5. 2) also belongs to this 'boasting in Christ'. Rom 5. 3 is characteristic of a number of similar Pauline statements about experience of God, which comes about through 'sufferings'. These sufferings do not in any way hinder Christian experience of God or its expression in 'boasting'. On the contrary, they make them possible, since 'suffering produces endurance, endurance produces character and character produces hope' (verse 4). In verse 5, this idea, which is entirely orientated towards experience, is connected with the concepts of *agape* and *Pneuma*, which are here also orientated towards experience of God made possible by the event of Christ and the crucified Christ himself and expressed as given in man: '. . . because God's love has been poured into our hearts through the Holy Spirit which has been given to us'.

iii. Rom 8. 14-27: Only a few key words will be discussed in this section. These are taken from this passage because they are strictly relevant to our theme of experience of God.

According to 8. 16, the Pneuma communicates, through the 'witness' that he bears, the experience of *huiothesia* or 'adoption as sons' to our *pneuma*. This experience of *huiothesia* is linked herewith the prayer brought about by the Pneuma as an orientation to the Father of Jesus Christ (see verse 15). It is clear from this text, 8. 16, that the 'objectivizing' aspect (the expression of the Pneuma of God, the bearer of this experience from God) and the anthropological aspect of the experience itself ('our spirit') are indissolubly united. The Pneuma, as an 'objectivizing' expression, enters the structures of the believers' lives in such a way that the two cannot be separated from each other.

In verse 23, our longing for fulfilment — expressed here as a longing for *huiothesia* as the fulfilment of our hope — is described by Paul very emphatically as an 'inward groaning'. This is moreover linked with the 'groaning' or 'sighing' of creation, showing that what we have here is undoubtedly an original experience of God transformed by experience of Christ. This experience is characterized by an experience of the proximity of death (creation's 'bondage to decay', verse 21) and an overwhelming desire to break through this limitation. In verse 26, this idea is linked with that of the Pneuma and of the experience of prayer brought about by the Pneuma. The believer cannot, on his own, express his experience of longing for God and the Pneuma 'intercedes for him with sighs too deep for words'. This, then is an experience of prayer (and this is, of course, an experience of God) that comes about through the Pneuma actively working in the Christian. The parallel in 8. 34 states that Christ 'intercedes for us' and is proof that, for Paul, this is a question of the activity of the Pneuma-Kyrios himself.

The text quoted above in Section III 3 b ii: 'the Spirit of the Son of God' was sent into the hearts of believers crying 'Abba! Father!' should also be mentioned in this connection. Finally, the word used in Rom 8. 38 – *pepeismai*, 'I am sure' – expresses Paul's confidence, derived from his experience in faith of the love of God which is completely reliable. ('Nothing . . . will be able to separate us from the love of God in Christ Jesus the Lord.)

iv. It is clear from this that we have to consider the explicit experience of God that is present in the 'objectivizing' statements about the greatness of God. Such a statement is made in Rom 11. 33-26, for example. This doxology can also clearly be situated within the sphere of man's experience of the 'depths of God' (1 Cor 2. 10) that has been made possible by the Pneuma, an experience that is faith in God's universal *charis*.

v. It is also clear from several passages in Paul that this experience of God includes the *agape* of fellow-humanity. A striking example can be found in 1 Cor 13, in which Paul deals with the primacy of love quite deliberately in the middle of the long section (1 Cor 12 and 14) on the Pneuma, the charismata and those who have received the Spirit. The context shows clearly that unbelievers (1 Cor 14. 24 ff) cannot experience God simply through ecstatic or prophetic utterances. This experience is, according to Paul, unattainable without the *agape* that is manifested in such utterances.

The experience of God that is implied in Rom 11. 33-36 can only be understood when it is considered together with the experience of the powers by *dikaiosune*, freedom, life and hope and the experience of universal guilt, as expressed in Rom 1. 18 − 3. 20 (see especially Rom 7. 7 ff).

c. The Epistles and Gospel of John

For the epistles, the reader should consult what is said in 2. I. 4 above about the central theme of the first letter of John.

i. The statement made in Jn 7. 16 ff is of importance in this context in the gospel of John. Immediately following a statement about the direct nature of revelation, despite its mediation ('My teaching is not mine, but his who sent me') is the statement that 'if any man's will is to do his will, he shall know whether the teaching is from God or whether I am speaking on my own authority'. It is clear, then, from the context that this statement refers to the possibility of a Christologically based experience of God. Such experience can only take place if a man decides to do God's will in the way in which it is proclaimed by Jesus, that is, if he loves his fellow-men in the way that has been made possible by Jesus' offering of himself. This 'doing of God's will' is an authentically biblical constitutive element of the 'knowledge' (*ginoskein*) of God. 'Knowing' God here means becoming one with God in love and this implies that it is possible to have direct access to God through the Paraclete[34] and therefore to 'pray' in the widest sense.

ii. All five statements about the Paraclete in Jn 14 − 16 have something to tell us about man's experience of God, at least implicitly, in that knowledge of Jesus as the one who reveals and that of the Father are recalled by the Paraclete (Jn 14. 16-20; 14. 2-12 or 14). In this context, it is also important to consider the theme of the Paraclete who makes it possible for man to experience God in a situation of persecution and therefore also to bear witness (Jn 15. 26 ff). We should also remember the implicit theme (Jn 15. 5, 7 ff) of 'bearing fruit'.

A part is also played in this context by the Johannine statements about immanence (*menein en* ...). These are not only objectivizing statements about man's relationship with God, but also pronouncements that are indissolubly linked with the experiential aspect of knowledge, which is in turn also linked with love that is expressed in the 'keeping of the commandments' or keeping the one commandment of brotherly love (see Jn 14. 20 ff).

iii. In this context, we must also consider the extremely important statement in Jn 14. 28 that our love of Jesus, which is given by the Spirit and is impossible without love of our fellow-men, and our 'joy', which is also given by the Spirit, depend on our knowledge, which is also given by the Spirit, depend on our knowledge, which is also made

possible by our experience of faith, of God who is 'greater'. The text of
Jn 14. 28 reads: 'If you loved me, you would have rejoiced, because I
go to the Father, for the Father is greater than I'. The Father is 'greater'
because he is the origin of the Pneuma given by the glorified Jesus. He
is the original love which makes Jesus the giver of the Pneuma. The text
implies that the glorified Jesus himself was orientated towards the
Father in the sense outlined above (5. III. 3c), in other words, that he
'looked up' to the Father, who was 'greater'. This looking up to God,
who is greater, is also possible for the disciples of Jesus, but only if they
share the intention of the glorified Jesus to glorify the Father, in other
words, to reveal the Father as the one who is greater. This glorification
can only be achieved by the Spirit who was sent by the Son. According
to Jn 4. 23 ff, this experience is based on the worship of God, who is
himself the Pneuma,[35] 'in *pneuma* and *aletheia*' (this 'truth' being the
reality of God in his revelation of himself). Worshipping God means
knowing (or experiencing) him as the one who is always greater and
giving ones assent to him in faith. This can only take place, according to
the fourth evangelist, in unity with the Son who looks up to the Father
as to the one who is 'greater' and who breaks all images of God.

iv. This understanding of Jn 14. 28 is supported by the statements contained in the first epistle of John about the experience in faith of God's
greatness. (These statements are, in our present context, even more
directly instructive.) According to 1 Jn 4. 4, 'he who is in you is greater
than he who is in the world'. This is so because, as light (1 Jn 1. 5), God
transcends darkness and because, as love (see 1 Jn 4. 8, 16), he over-
comes hatred, self-seeking and lack of love in the believer. According to
1 Jn 3. 19 ff, the believer also knows by his active love of his fellow
men that absolute love is in him and precisely because of this he knows
that 'God is greater than our hearts'.

v. The ideas contained in Jn 17. 20-26 are also important for our
theme. In this passage, man's experience of God and his knowledge of
Jesus as the revealer (and as the one that is transparent to God — see
Jn 14. 6. 9 ff — and who thus, as 'truth' and 'life' forms the way to our
experience of God is connected with the unity of those who believe in
Jesus. In other words, experience of God is connected with the experience of mutual love (which leads to communication) of those who have
already responded to the gift that they have received.

d. The Epistle to the Hebrews
In this letter, the most important aspect in our context is the gnoseological question of 'seeing Jesus' (Heb 2. 8; 3. 1; 12. 2).[36] This seeing or

'looking to' Jesus does not take place for the sake of Jesus, but for the sake of God. According to Heb 6. 4, the powers of the Pneuma 'of the age to come' can be 'tasted' even now' According to 10. 19-25, the confidence to 'enter' God himself has been given by Jesus himself as the exalted high priest and this means that man already has a community wih God that he can even now experience.[37] This experience is that *pistis* is possible as a confident trust in the God of the promise, as an orientation towards the ultimate fulfilment and as perseverance in a situation of challenge here and now in looking up to the one who not only initiates our experience of faith as the believer (Heb 12. 2), that is, as the 'pioneer of our faith', but who also perfects that faith.

As in Jn 7. 17, experience of God in Hebrews is only possible by doing the will of God. This is implied in the statements about going out to the goal of the promise that is objectively the same as *pistis* in Hebrews. This is expressed in Heb 4. 11 as 'entering God's rest', as 'drawing near' in 4. 16 and 10. 22, as 'running with perseverance' in 12. 1 and as 'going forth to God outside the camp' in 13. 13. It is also clear from 13. 15 ff that, in our orientation towards God, there is an element both of praising God (13. 15) and of active fellow humanity (13. 16). Both praise of God and 'doing good and sharing what we have' are characterized by the theocentric term 'sacrifice'. By the phrase 'through him' at the beginning of verse 15, moreover, both these aspects are made dependent on the sacrificial orientation of the high priest, Jesus.

Heb 5. 11 also contains at least an embryonic reflection about man's experience of God, in the author's statement that his readers have become 'dull of hearing', in other words, that their *akoai*, their organs for hearing and obeying God, are in danger of losing their function. In this paraenesis, then, it is also a question of experiencing God and not simply a question of a blockage in intellectual ability to hear. It is in the negative sense a weakening of *metanoia* and 'running towards the goal of the promise' and, in the positive sense, a strengthening of *pistis* as the right attitude towards God's message (see Heb. 6. 11 ff; 6. 18 ff. Again, the theme of 'hearing his voice' (Heb 3. 7 — 4. 13) can be compared with this. According to Heb 10. 24 ff, Christians can protect each other from becoming 'dull of hearing'. Here too, the context is one of a Christological and soteriological drawing near to God (verse 22) and this forms a link, together with the theme of 'confession', between the terminological soteriology of the letter and its *pistis* paraenesis. The author of the letter is concerned with the question of his

Christians 'drawing near' to Jesus' sacrifice in the sacrifice of their lives and, through this, 'drawing near' to God. In other words, he is concerned with the orientation of their whole lives in the concrete towards the ultimate goal.

5. A summary of our review of the New Testament material
a. The Pauline conception as the leading model
In what follows, the Pauline idea is not exclusively, but predominantly taken as the leading model. Paul is to some extent in the centre of the New Testament. Not only chronologically, but also objectively, his theology is in the middle, between the early, pre-New Testament theology and the late theology of the New Testament itself. On the one hand, his re-interpretation of the fundamental kerygma, with its openness and breadth, provides access to the later ideas contained in the New Testament. On the other, despite all appearances and the varied forms of expression that the New Testament contains, hardly any of the theologies represented are structurally so powerfully similar to the theology of Jesus himself. The Pauline conception is not, it is true, able to present us with the fundamental question of the historical Jesus (because Paul's letters do not contain any of the synoptic material), but it can provide us with the necessary impulses.

b. A brief characterization of the three New Testament models chosen
Paul's statements fall predominantly within the category of creation. John's on the other hand, come within the category of revelation.[38] For Paul, God was the one who raised Jesus from the dead and who thus gave believers 'earnest-money' of their future resurrection from the dead, which would take place through and be connected with the resurrection of Christ. For John, on the other hand, God was the one who was revealed and glorified as love by Jesus.

In the epistle to the Hebrews, what is already present in Paul and John is expressed as a theme in specific terminology. Life in the community of the risen Jesus is expressed in Hebrews, as it is in the writings of Paul and John, as a total phenomenon, in the direction of theocentricity. The linguistic categories used are distinctively cultic, but these are transcended and indeed left far behind in the letter itself.

c. In what respects do the New Testament theological ideas agree?
Although the agreement that we are considering here applies to all New Testament ideas,[39] but we can only demonstrate this here in the three groups of New Testament writings that we have so far taken into account.

We shall try, in the context of what we said above in 5. III 3 and 4, to distinguish the agreement that exists at a fundamental level. In this attempt, we shall not overlook the great and obvious distinctions in ways of thinking, conceptual terminology and the historical situation. We shall also begin from two texts statements.

i. The first of these statements is that Jesus is the man for others, because he was also the man for God.

This point of departure is quite legitimate, because both the theocentric and the soteriological aspects of the 'late' post-paschal New Testament Christologies — in other words, of theological reflection about the risen Jesus and his function — can be demonstrated in this statement. (The theocentric aspect is contained in the 'for God' and the soeriological aspect in the 'for others'.)

As the risen Christ, Jesus is the 'man for others'. This idea is expressed in the theological models of Paul and the gospel of John (and more or less explicitly in the other New Testament writings) in the presentation of Jesus as the one who gives the Pneuma (see Jn 7. 37-39; 19. 34; 3. 34 ff). As such, Jesus is the mediator who gives not only experience of God, but also — expressed objectivizingly or pointing to a trans-subjective reality — community with God as direct contact with God. He is able to give these two elements by giving community with himself as the Pneuma-Christ by communicating *agape* as a qualitatively new gift and as a qualitatively new possibility. Jesus can only be this 'man for others' because he is also, as the risen Christ, the man for God, in other words, because he is specially united with God and, as the exalted Christ, also 'lives for God' and glorifies him. He also lives in orientation towards God by involving his own in his own theocentric orientation towards the Father, that is, by giving the brotherly love and the community with God (or experience of God) in the pneumatic community with himself that are both radicalized by the cross and the imitation of the cross. The connection between the two related poles of the 'man for others' and the 'man for God' (or the 'man in unity with God') is made clear in Jn 3. 34 ff. According to this Johannine text, because the Father 'loves' the Son (and thereby constitutes his unity with him), he has given 'all things' (that is, the fulness of the Pneuma) into his hand, so that the Son can give the Pneuma in unmeasured fulness.

ii. The second statement, 1 Cor 8. 6, can also give us a deep insight into the fundamental agreement that exists between the New Testament models. In this text, Paul tells us: 'For us there is one God, the Father, from whom are "all things" (= everything that happens in the world and all salvation) and for whom we exist (= towards whom we are orientated) and one Lord, Jesus Christ, through whom are "all things" and through whom we exist'

This text may provide the most dense statement of Christ's function as a mediator in the whole of Paul's corpus. The relationship with Christ as the 'man for God' is only apparent here. What is really visible in this statement is the sense of the 'because' ('. . . because he was also the man for God'). If the two parts of this Pauline text – the theological and the Christo-logical parts – are brought together,[40] the following statement is obtained: Everything that happens to us in history and existentially is given to us as a gift 'from God through Christ'; this gift also exists in orientation towards the absolute mystery, which is at the same time an orientation towards the radical *agape* and which only exists 'through Christ' as an orientation that is turned in this direction and that can reach its goal in Christ.

The New Testament re-interpretations of the fundamental kerygma are either explicitly or implicitly in agreement in that the *ek tou theou* and the *eis ton theon* are both expressed everywhere in the New Testament as a Christologically mediated reality. What is above all of importance in connection with our question is that the orientation towards God is given both Christologically and soteriologically. This orientation towards God is, moreover, given through the Jesus who communicates community with and experience of God and and gives 'leading towards' God (Rom 5. 2: 'access to' God), both directly and therefore including fellow-humanity and also, via this fellow-humanity, on the way towards a relationship of dialogue with God.

The fundamental soteriological structure of the New Testament Christology can be defined therefore in this way: the 'for others' follows the 'from God' and the orientation towards God.

d. A reconsideration of the concept of the absolute bringer of salvation
We have in this way given deeper content and meaning to the too formal concept of the absolute bringer of salvation; it is often found with this content and it can be relatively adequately used in this sense in the light of the New Testament situation. As we have already pointed out, then, Rahner's anthropological concept, which he uses almost exclusively in his later Christological teaching, has to be amplified by using the term that he employed more frequently in his earlier writings, namely the absolute mediator of salvation. In his essay on the one mediator and the many mediations,[41] Rahner says, for example, that the condition for the possible mediation of salvation by Christ and the

personal realization of that mediation in faith is the intercommunication of all men into the ultimate depths of their existence and its salvation and the concrete, existential realization and experience of this radical intercommunication. In the light of the New Testament, however, we are bound to add that Jesus has this function as a mediator not only as an individual (this is, of course, the primary and fundamental datum), but also as the one who unites a community of disciples, as a serving community, with himself.

It is of no importance to the New Testament datum that the concept *mesites* (mediator) only occurs as such in four places in the New Testament itself (referring to Jesus, only 1 Tim 2. 5; Heb 8. 6; 9. 15; 12. 24). For Paul and the authors who followed him, the phrase 'through Christ' was less easily misunderstood, more direct and more dynamic. 'Through Christ' points to Christ as the one who gives community with himself and establishes a relationship with God. In Paul's linguistic usage, community with Christ is the state of being in Christ that is brought about by the Pneuma. We can therefore express it in this way: 'through Christ' is being in Christ that has been included in the twofold dynamic direction of theocentricity.

'Through Christ' may, on the one hand, express – in the descending line – the fact that God has an effect on those whom he has called and therefore on the world through the pneumatic community of Christ and, on the other hand, this relationship that has been brought about by God may – in the ascending line – be in accordance with a response, since Christ includes those who are in him in his response.

6. A demarcation against a misunderstanding of the mediator and pneuma Christology within the development of dogma. Descendance and ascendance Christology

a. Mediator Christology

It is well worth while to try to define the very carefully elaborated New Testament concept of mediator of salvation in order to prevent a misunderstanding of what mediator Christology really means. In this attempt, we are concerned with Christological ideas in which the figure of a mediator is inserted as a third between the two spheres of the divine and the human.[42] We may certainly ask whether this misunderstanding, which must strike a dogmatic theologian such as Rahner as very dangerous, is not one of the causes of the rare occurrence in classical Christology and even in Rahner's Christological teaching of the concept of the mediator.

For the purpose of this demarcation, we have only to point to the arguments already indicated that Jesus Christ, as this particular mediator, does not come between God and men, but that he makes it possible for God to be experienced directly and also for men to have an eschatological community with God.

We can also say in this context that it can hardly be purely by chance that the concept 'mediator' occurs so rarely in the New Testament and that the expression 'through Christ' and other ways of expressing a community with Jesus are found instead.

In Rahner's Christological writings, the orientation towards God that forms a constitutive part of the New Testament concept of the mediator seems to be simply a question of the man Jesus in his earthly history, that is, something that is a temporal consequence of the classical theology of the incarnation, whereas it is already present in the New Testament eschatology that forms the basis of the protological statement about the incarnation.

b. Christological pneumatology

Any theological and Christological pneumatology that is developed to prepare the way for a Christological theo-logy based on the New Testament has to be safeguarded against possible misunderstandings arising from a Christology of the Spirit that may come dangerously close to a heretical form of adoptianism, of the kind that in fact has occurred in the history of dogma from the second century onwards. Paul's statement, which is basically a quotation from the Jewish-Christian tradition, in Rom 1. 3 ff ('the Son of God in power according to the Spirit of holiness ... '), is, for example, not heretically adoptianist in the second century understanding of adoptianism.[42]

On the basis of this demarcation, we can now ask whether a pneumatology should not be developed in the light of Pauline and other New Testament ideas which might act as a mediation between the traditional transcendental Christology and the New Testament Christologies in a genuine merging of these two approaches?

We are bound in this context once again to point to Rom 8. Is it perhaps not true to say that everything that can be used to safeguard the classical Christology is in fact contained in the Pauline view of the Pneuma-Christ without any possibility of distortion or narrowing down? The pneumatology postulated here should continue Paul's orientation towards the *huiothesia*.

c. Christology from above and Christology from below

In this section, we must return briefly to the two concepts of Christology from above and Christology from below in order to ask the following important questions:

Should a Christology from above (or a descendance Christology) perhaps not be traced back to the idea of mission rather than the idea of the incarnation? Should it not, in other words, be based on a Christology of mission, that is, of Christ's having been sent. This might make a Christology from below possible. Ought this not to be our aim − to look for the real meaning of a descendance Christology via the New Testament datum of a theocentricity in a descending line, to which the concept of mission belongs? This descending line of theocentricity ought then to make not only the ascending line, but also, together with that ascending line, an ascendance Christology based on anthropology, as well as a consciousness Christology possible.

7. Is the idea of the function of the risen Jesus who is now living a mythologoumenon[43] *or does it have a bearing on the matter itself referred to in a justifiable faith in Jesus?*

a. The problem and the thesis

In his book on Jesus and faith in God, R. Schäfer said that our present insight into the problem of objectizing statements about God places us at a distance from the clear two-fold image of the exalted Christ reigning alongside the Father.[44]

It is true, of course, that the problem of the juxtaposition of God and the exalted Jesus was envisaged at a very early period − even the doctrine of the Trinity assumed a demythologizing function in its formalizing aspect. It is, however, necessary to come to terms with the modern form of this problem and especially with Schäfer's expression of it, which reflects a consciousness of the problem that is based on the anthropological approach that is so frequently encountered in modern thought and is widely justified.[45]

In a context in which he is considering the transfigured humanity of Christ together with the saints as fulfilled men, Rahner has asked whether, if we look for the transfigured humanity of Christ and the saints in the experience of the hereafter in which God is to be found and where he must be if he is to be God, these may become indistinct, seem to be mere names or sounds and to disintegrate completely (only, of course, for us), in this obscurity without a name or a path through it which engulfs everything and which we call God.[46]

We must therefore ask further what the 'transformation of pre-paschal data' really is in the non-mythological sense. What really happened at the resurrection to the historical Jesus and his ability to orientate people towards God by drawing them into his community? Is what is said about the resurrection related to the 'matter itself' or is it no more than a mythological form of expression concerning the importance of the historical Jesus?

In any attempt to answer these questions, we can refer back to our previous finding that the permanence of the pre-paschal Jesus' person and claim on the one hand and the function of the risen Jesus on the other are not mutually exclusive alternatives. It is not simply a question of both – and. On the contrary, as the result of the transposition to the new level of risen being, there is a 'plus', expressed as the power of the Pneuma of the exalted Jesus in the New Testament message. This question is, however, too urgent for us to remain satisfied with a New Testament datum that may not have been subjected to sufficient reflection.

Schäfer continues, in the passage in his book quoted above, by saying that we can come to understand the 'clear two fold image of the exalted Christ reigning alongside the Father' as the correlation of the worship of God in cult which accepts Jesus' image of God as its own.[47]

This is too simple a view of the problem. The situation is really very different.[48] I would like to express it in the following statements in the form of a thesis.

The permanence of Jesus' person and claim brought about by the resurrection means this. Jesus was received into the absolute mystery that we call God, but we cannot make any statement that is more precise about his having been received in this way or form any anthropomorphic or symbolic conception of it. He comes back to us from this inexpressible mystery in a way which is not separate from ourselves and which is described in the New Testament as the effect of the Pneuma of the exalted Lord.

In the creative power of God (the concept of the Pneuma should be understood in this sense), then, the risen Jesus is the bearer of the life-giving 'function' of God himself (see 1 Cor 15. 45). He is the one who 'reveals' God in the Johannine sense: the Father,'in whom' he is and who is 'in him', does his works through him (see Jn 14. 10).

Like several other authors, Schäfer is one-sided here. We are therefore bound to point to the category 'community with Jesus' and the function both of Jesus himself and of this community with him with regard to eschatological fulfilment. We must also point to the permanent validity of the Pauline and Johannine pneumatology. Is it not possible that authors such as Schäfer are not making the whole task too easy by not going deeply and seriously into the radical ideas of Paul, the author of the fourth gospel and other New Testament authors, who were more conscious of this problem than is generally realized?

b. The importance of a pre-understanding of faith in God

It has to be affirmed − and not simply admitted − that any decision as to whether the idea of exaltation (as a conception of the present function of the risen Jesus) is mythological or not depends on a pre-understanding of faith.

What is more, it is a question of a prior gift in the light of an understanding of God. In other words, it is a question of whether we can dissociate ourselves from a basic misunderstanding of a purely transcendent God who has to be kept fundamentally and absolutely separate from the whole of creation, as the New Testament proclamation of Jesus' exaltation presupposes. Can we, then, give assent to God not only as the one who is immanent, but also as the biblical 'God for people', as Yahweh and as the God who lets people approach him closely and have community, even unity with him? Can we do this in such a radical way that this closeness, community and unity between God and man, which is expressed in the New Testament teaching about the risen Jesus and which even transcends death can be justified in the light of this particular faith in God? What is known as Jesus' resurrection from the dead and consequently the life and function of the risen Jesus 'can only be understood if we are aware of what God means'.[49] In this context, there are several statements about God 'who raises from the dead' in Paul's letters that are relevant here. (See, for example, Rom. 4. 17; 8. 11; 1 Cor 6. 14; 15. 12-20; 2 Cor 1. 9; 4. 14.)

This state of affairs is connected with what Gerhard Ebeling has expressed in the following way: the affirmation that God is 'can mean nothing other than "you have a future" . . . If we say "God" in this sense, we contradict for our part what for its part represents the clearest contradiction of all to God, that is, sin and death'.

If it is possible to believe so unimaginably strongly in God, then we are bound to have the great access to faith in the risen Jesus and his function, in other words, to the fact that a man is 'with God' in this special way by having 'not only dying, but also death finally behind him and, because of this, by being present here in this earthly life'.[50]

In this way, a future is offered to mankind and to individual man. What is meant by the absolute mystery as the God of the future is clear in that the mystery offers a future through the crucified Jesus who has been brought to life again. In the light of this understanding of the God of the future there is a possibility of believing that this one man — who was orientated towards the future of mankind — was and is 'with God'.

c. Faith in the exalted Kyrios — the ultimate concretization of the involvement of the believer in Jesus as the absolute mediator of salvation.

The sharply disruptive aspect of the question can be made clear in a new approach — to what extent does the idea of exaltation signify an ultimate concretization of the involvement of the believer in Jesus as the absolute mediator of salvation? In what way is this idea of exaltation necessary to a faith that can be justified in the light of the New Testament? The answer that we would give to this question is that it is necessary because such a relationship with a Jesus, who has not only been confirmed by God, but is also living in the power of God, cannot be made relative, but is something that concerns all Christians at all times.

If God is of such a kind that this man Jesus, who lived beyond death, can be 'with him' and if God's orientation towards the world cannot be envisaged unless the man Jesus is with God, then Jesus clearly has a very special relevance. This is his saving significance and it is clearly indicated in the New Testament and attributed to no other man. If, on the other hand, the historical Jesus, who was active here on earth, is seen simply as an eschatological event and as the bearer of a new understanding of man's existence that the believer has to accept, then it would be possible to attach this saving signfificance to another outstanding man, in which case it would have no special or absolutely soteriological relevance.[51]

It is possible to develop a functional Christology from the function of the risen Jesus, without fearing, like Wolfhart Pannenberg, that the person of the historical Jesus will evaporate in this process or that our reference back to him will be obstructed. We have in fact to work intensively in the direction of a non-mythological understanding of the concept of the transposition of the person of Jesus and his function through the resurrection.

It is most important not to see the earthly Jesus simply as an eschatological event, but also in his person or personality which reappears in an eschatological dimension in the resurrection. and whose saving significance is indissolubly linked to the resurrection of Jesus.[52]

It is also very important to keep to the single identity of the risen Jesus and the earthly and crucified Jesus. Is there, however, not a danger that this identification of the cross and the resurrection may be misunderstood in a mythological sense?[53] This is not the case. According to Rudolf Schnackenburg, this danger does not exist in Paul's case, because 'he took the cross so fully into his own existence and also took it so seriously that he inserted himself with the whole of his existence into the suffering and crucifixion of Jesus'.[54]

It depends on Paul's understanding of God whether this affirmation is correct, in other words, it depends on Paul's statements about the Pneuma that involves the believer in God's act of resurrection through suffering together with Christ and whether these statements are mythological or whether they go to the heart of the matter itself. It depends, in other words, on whether it is God himself whose creative power, as the power of the Pneuma, is effective in bringing together the believer and the man Jesus, who is hidden in the mystery of God, but who is really 'living'. The decisive question is whether God is acknowledged to be the one who is greater; this quality of being greater is fundamental and highly developed in the Old Testament, but the New Testament understanding of God as greater far transcends the Old Testament understanding in this respect.

d. The limits to what can be demythologized

In this section, 5. III 7, we have examined the whole problem from different sides. We must, however, say quite emphatically in this context that it is not simply a matter of clinging to certain word forms. It is far more important to ask a question that is entirely without any apologetic or fundamentalist intention: Is the function of the risen Jesus, as stated in the New Testament, which reaches the believer through the Pneuma, not necessary if Jesus Christ is to be at all relevant in the New Testament sense and in the teaching of the Church (which continues to be valid in reinterpretation)? The New Testament could therefore not be demythologized any more at this particular point, where the ultimate mystery, towards which all mythological means of expression eventually tend, is touched.

We must ask, then, whether the New Testament faith in Jesus can continue to be relevant in our own time, together with all the implications of the statements about God's sovereignty. These statements, after all, make a relationship of personal dialogue with Jesus and his mediation of such a relationship with God difficult and open to misunderstandings (as opposed to the Pauline view, if this is correctly understood). In fact, of course, these statements about God's sovereignty make it possible for us to grasp the radical and direct nature of this transcendental and anthropological relationship with God.

e. An attempt to outline the thesis

Although we cannot provide any logically compelling answer to the problem in this section (5. III 7), mainly because the pre-understanding necessarily belongs to our understanding of faith, we are certainly bound to make some attempt to express the essence of the New Testament and Christian proclamation of Jesus. What is more, it is important to try to do this in a way that is in accordance with the 'matter itself' and is, in this sense, a non-mythological way of thinking and speaking that is acceptable to modern man and makes faith in Jesus justifiable.

It should be pointed out in this context that an abstract theological form of statement should, by way of exception, be combined here, in this attempt, with a figurative and symbolic way of speaking.[55] It should also be borne in mind that we can, for example, experience infinity by standing on the beach and looking at its symbol, the sea — a breadth, depth and distance that we cannot encompass with our eyes.

With regard to the opposite of this absolute infinity that we call God and faith in Jesus which apparently cannot be united with infinity, we would make the following observations.

The man who believes in the New Testament sense knows that the one, special and unique man is in fact to be found in the infinite mystery which surges around him and overwhelms him despite its breadth, depth and distance and penetrates into his being with its healing and perilous strength as he breathes in. That unique man is, moreover, not present in infinity simply like one who is loved at a distance, beyond the sea. Faith in Jesus is, after all, not a being beyond. It is being closely connected with infinity through this one man. It is therefore not as though he were someone who had felt, like others, that he was involved in this mystery and that, also like others, he had disappeared into the mystery or had entered nirvana. On the contrary, faith seizes hold of him as one who belongs now to this mystery which is actively present in our world and in human life and cannot be separated from them.

In a very real sense, but one which cannot easily be imagined, he lives in this mystery without becoming merged with it and losing his human identity with the crucified Jesus or his relationship of personal dialogue with the God of infinity. The demands made by the living and crucified Jesus and his help come to the person who is open to them from and in the manner of this mystery in such a way that he experiences the surging sea of infinity with all the fear and beauty that it contains in all its obscure and nameless enigmatic quality. Nonetheless, he is able, through this man who belongs inseparably to it, to consent to it simply as love, as the meaning and goal of his life and as the meaning of human existence as a whole.

If he decides to give his consent in this way, he will receive from the dynamic power of the absolute mystery the possibility of handing on this radical love in a way that would not have been possible for him on his own. And this love which comes to him from the nameless infinity is the love of the crucified Jesus.

If, then, the man who is open to this experience 'hears the voice' from the apparently nameless and lonely making infinity and, what is more, hears it as the Logos, he is able, in dialogue, to search into this infinity with consent and trust without seeing. He is also able to search into this infinity that overwhelms him and penetrates into him for the one man Jesus who is hidden in this infinity and who searches for him from the infinity as the 'brother' and with him the 'many brethren' (Rom 8. 29).

This unseeing perception in faith or simple premonition and the subsequent search for God in the obscurity of infinity is in a very real sense the personal dialogue that is expressed symbolically and anthropomorphically in the Old and New Testaments. Through this personal dialogue, man enters into an existential relationship with the absolute mystery. His decision to keep this dialogue open or not to keep it open is a decision for or against the meaning of life.

It is also the aspect of dialogue in the process of seeking the face of Yahweh that is so often expressed in the psalms. It is also the dialogue structure of the paradoxical blending of a confession of faith and at the same time of lack of faith in the petition made to the God who is sought in obscurity to help this unbelief (see, for example, Mark 9. 24).

f. Fellow-humanity and the relationship between God and man

There is one other integral part of this 'dialogue' that has to be mentioned. It is this. There can be no search in the obscurity, which is synonymous with a destruction of the images that we have made of God, unless we cease to 'make a likeness'[56] of our fellow-man and decide instead to grant him a future in recognition of his possibilities.[57] In other words, this search into infinity is not possible without loving our fellow-men and there can be no premonition or experience of the God who speaks to us from the obscurity unless we decide not to make an image of our fellow-man. If we are, then, to experience God in this way, we have also to experience that our fellow-man is also loved and is searching for love and life. We have also to be thankful for what has been given to us in our experience of searching, however imperfect this has been, namely the love of others.

g. Summary – final question

We have certainly not proved in our examination of the subject in this section (5. III 7) that there is no mythologoumenon in the idea of Jesus as the one living now in power with God. All that we have done is to point to the conditions under which this idea does not contain a mythologoumenon and under which it is rationally justifiable to regard it as the matter itself. (Or, to express this in Christian terms, to believe as such, that is, to trust in it and to search for and love this mystery.) It is therefore relevant to summarize this section in the form of a final question.

The original question – mythology or not? – has now clearly to be asked in a different way. It can in fact be expressed in such a way that it may even point in the direction of the answer: Is this search into the obscurity of infinity really hidden by the New Testament objectivizations or is it not true to say that the door is opened to this search by these kerygmatic ideas that provide objectivization and a more or less explicit experience. Is it not, in other words, true that this opportunity is provided by the Christological mediation expressed in these ideas for a relationship with God, that is, a faith in God that enables us to have a presentiment of the radical nature of this inexpressible mystery?

8. Faith in Jesus – faith in God through Jesus?
Praying to Jesus – praying to God through Jesus?

Faith and prayer are very closely related to each other.[58] We will consider this relationship in this section.

a. Schäfer has expressed this question strikingly or has at least dealt with one important aspect of it in pointing to a mutually exclusive alternative between faith in Jesus (or praying to Jesus) and faith in God through Jesus (or praying to God through Jesus).[59] For Schäfer, only faith in God through Jesus and the corresponding praying to God through Jesus are valid. He believes that faith in Jesus and praying to Jesus are not meaningful.[60]

He bases his argument in favour of this point of view on Gerhard Ebeling's statement that faith in the religious sense can only be directed towards God.[61] (This statement is in itself important and fully justified, but it can lead to an unjustifiable narrowing down.) Schäfer, then, insists that it is only possible to believe in God 'through Jesus', not in the New Testament sense of the *dia Iesou Christou*, but rather in a too exclusive relationship with the historical Jesus, who is then only able to be a model or prototype.

Schäfer brings together an idea that is justified by Heb 12. 2 and a narrowing down of the New Testament (also Heb 12. 2) that is not justified. An example of this blending together can be found in his statements[62] that the form of Christian experience of God and the Christian understanding of God originated with Jesus and that this form appeared in his faith in God. These statements can be justified in the light of Heb 12. 2. His continuation of these statements cannot, however, be justified, when he claims that the form of the Christian experience of God is handed on by faith in God being sparked off in the historical process of the transmission of tradition. Faith in God through Jesus clearly means for Schäfer a 'faith in God by being orientated towards Jesus'.[63]

In the same way, Schäfer also thinks that the question as to whether we should pray to Jesus — despite the fact that he himself points to the different historical content of this phenomenon — should also be answered negatively. This answer is, in Schäfer's opinion, different today from what it was in an earlier period of the history of Christian faith, because of our contemporary understanding of the problem of objectivizing statements about God. To pray to God through Jesus may therefore be a loss with regard to man's power of imagination, but it does not in any way reduce the matter itself. To judge from the context in Schäfer's book,[64] this 'through Jesus' can only mean here by being orientated towards (the historical) Jesus and his prayer.

b. Attitude towards the problem

The only necessary element here is certainly faith in God through Jesus and praying to God through Jesus, at least from the point of view of the New Testament and in the light of New Testament thinking. If community with Jesus is such a necessary constitutive element in the Christian relationship with God as the New Testament in my opinion claims, however, then it must surely be possible for this community to be expressed in an address made in reply to Jesus. We have New Testament evidence of this from the earliest period of Christian history in the 'maranatha', a call to the risen Jesus to come again as the Son of Man.[65] If we look not merely at the explicit form of this address, but also at the parallels that are to be found in the New Testament, then our attention is drawn at once to the New Testament hymns to Christ. The theology of these relatively early hymns is bound to lead to an expression of what is said here in praise about Jesus in an address made in reply to

Jesus.[66]

Above all, however, it is important to point out here that the Christian faith of the New Testament cannot be separated from a real personal love for Jesus and that, because of its immanent tendency, this love had to be expressed in an address. Examples of this form of address can be found in Paul's expression of love for Jesus in 1 Cor 16. 22[67] and his statement that faith in Jesus is the answer to Jesus' love for him (Gal 2. 20). In the fourth gospel, the word *ginoskein*, expressing loving knowledge, that expresses this element.[68]

It is also important to note that the complex whole of the synoptic tradition is also preserved in the later theological ideas of the New Testament and, what is more, in such a way that the Christologically mediated theocentricity is of first importance and that there can be no alternative in the sense envisaged by Schäfer.

c. Prayer as faith made in reply

Faith in God or praying to God thus implicitly and potentially includes faith in Jesus or praying to Jesus. Praying to God through Jesus in the New Testament sense must also be open to praying to Jesus as an expression of love for Jesus.

We now have the task of amplifying these ideas and connecting them with what has already been said so far, especially about the question of mythology, in the preceding section (5. III 7). It seems to me to be especially important in any attempt to judge the whole problem of prayer not to regard it as an anthropocentric problem. It does not, in other words, begin with man and his activity or with man's address to God. On the contrary, although it is an anthropological phenomenon, it must be seen as a dialogue, in which God speaks first and man replies (in prayer).[69]

Unlike Schäfer, I believe that it is very important to decide whether what is said in the New Testament about the exalted Kyrios can be understood non-mythologically. The New Testament statements about God taking the initiative in loving and addressing man can be connected with what was said above in section 5. III 5e especially. In other words, as presence and dynamic infinity, God is, not only in an objectivizing sense, but also at the level of experience, the first and the only phenomenon that can be experienced (insofar as man, seeking faith, has not lost his ability to be quiet and listen). The way to an address made by this inexpressible mystery can, moreover, only be found via man's experience, premonition or knowledge that he is first addressed from this infinity and that his speaking is only meaningful when it is made in reply.

Prayer as a total expression of faith made in reply is therefore only possible if the Christian is open to an experience that is only present when scope is given to the address that comes as a gift from the mystery of God himself. It is, then, only possible as an expression of hearing faith and only when there is an experience of God that takes place through the radical activity of the Father's will.

Prayer as faith made in reply is also related to the *docta ignorantia* or 'negative theology' of Nicholas of Cusa, who took reason to the ultimate limit, where it was convinced of its own non-competence and became open to questioning and listening.

We must also at least point out briefly an anthropological approach which may perhaps be of decisive importance if such a faith made in reply should ever come about.

Is thankfulness to one's fellow men not a pre-condition for an under-standing, in the whole complex of prayer, of the 'word' spoken from the infinite mystery of God as the initiative and what man does as a reply?

The following three elements would seem to support this argument. Firstly, there is the structure of being given and replying in thanks. Secondly, there is the statement made in 1 Jn 4. 20 which can be applied here: if anyone does not reply in thanks to his 'brother whom he has seen', how can he reply in thanks to 'God whom he has not seen'? Thirdly, there is also the fact that thankfulness with regard to men is ultimately also thankfulness with regard to the gift that comes to us from the inexpressible mystery and through these fellow men. This is because men are not only transcendentally open to this mystery, but also open in the reverse direction, in turning to others, from this mystery.

d. In conclusion, I would once again stress that, in man's expression of faith in God 'through Jesus', the latter is in no way different from the historical Jesus who died and rose again. His permanence, which was made possible by his resurrection and is identical with his present life, as expressed in the New Testament, and his present function, must, however, be added to this.

Returning once again to the problem discussed by Schäfer (see above, 5. III 8a), we would say that there are only two possibilities for understanding Christian faith and prayer (provided that the 'special position'[70] of Jesus is not given a relative value as historically coinci-dental). The first possibility is to allow faith and prayer, as Schäfer, for example, does, to be determined by the unique impulse of the historical Jesus. (If the aim is to make a theocentric statement here in keeping with salvation history, then an attempt would be made to base Christian faith and prayer on a past action.) The second possibility is to base the unique quality accorded to Jesus in the New Testament and still valid for believers today on the present mystery of God. If the second possibility is accepted, the meaning of what has been said above (5. III 7) about the risen Jesus will be grasped.

IV. Going back to the question of Jesus himself (via the early post-paschal levels of the synoptic and kerygmatic tradition)

1. Methodological considerations

a. The possibility of asking this question

The great methodological differences that exist in modern New Testament studies has made it very difficult for this question to be asked. It seems to be possible to do so only if various methods are legitimately combined. In other words, there is a need for different methods to be used without necessarily mixing them. In this case of the question of Jesus himself, two factors are of great importance. On the one hand there is the necessary detailed work within the hermeneutical circle and on the other there is the opposite pole, that is, the understanding of lines of connection and total conceptions or the continuity of the whole. Here it is not ultimately a question of the history of traditions in individual articulations of faith, but of the history of tradition of faith itself that can be seen behind these individual articulations. It is therefore particularly relevant in the case of the question of Jesus himself to examine the objective structures and the theological concepts used.[71]

I believe that it is preferable in this context to replace the frequently used but easily misunderstood concept of the *ipsissima vox* or *ipsissima verba Jesu*, which can so quickly lead to a distortion or a narrowing down, by the concept of the *ipsissima intentio Jesu*. In this case, *intentio* should not be limited to the more superficial aspects of Jesus' consciousness. It should rather be understood in the sense of the orientation of the life and work of this unique man, which resulted from his basic situation or the deepest level of his experience. In this, the orientation of Jesus' life and effective work should be taken as a whole and from there in its individual details.

How, then, are we to understand this original intention and above all how was this intention connected with the kingdom of God? The answer to this question must be that we can only understand that intention, not by means of a process of substraction, but by studying the existing sources. The later editorial changes provide us also with certain indications without which the original meaning of the statements contained in the various logia or pericoipes and above all in the central structural complexes of the New Testament could hardly be recognized. What we have here, in other words, is not a dividing line in a process of separation, but an important question, namely, is the way in which the situation was made present by the New Testament authors and in tradition in any way important for our knowledge of the historical Jesus and his intention and also for the contemporary Christian community and the modern world.

The most obvious approach, then, to an understanding of Jesus' *ipsissima intention* or *missio* (which can be expressed gnoseologically as Jesus' consciousness of his own mission) would be through the Christological concepts used in the logia, taken in conjunction with the Christological concepts employed in other early synoptic traditions.

b. The concept of objective structures

In any attempt to go back to the question of the Jesus of history or to consider other important questions, including of the unity within the plurality of the New Testament, we have to be concerned with a special way of looking at the situation, so that we can see, beyond the differences in the modes of expression and ideas, what we have called the matter itself, which has a specific structure that can no longer be given a purely relative value.

In our particular case, the question of the historical Jesus himself, we may postulate that we have to look for an area of functions and relationships which has an unchangeable structure, in which Jesus can be clearly seen (even in the earliest post-paschal Christology) and which persists in all re-interpretations. We have finally also to be able to recognize the legitimate transposition of the original datum in the New Testament re-interpretations of the fundamental kerygma or the primordial experience of Jesus.

This approach is not possible, of course, without recourse to form criticism and other detailed work. It is, however, just as important to examine the other part of the hermeneutical circle and to gain at least an approximate grasp of the total conceptions or the total concepts. This postulation continues to be urgently necessary, even though it is important to note with care the word 'approximate' in the preceding sentence. By this I mean that this postulation is still valid even when it is recognized that it is hardly ever possible to achieve a relative method-ological precision and a similarly relative reliability in the detailed work in this other part of the hermeneutical circle (insofar as it is seen in iso-lation from the detailed work that has necessarily to precede it). Despite this difficulty, however, there is a possibility of verification in this process of elaborating the total conceptions. It provides us with the opportunity to come very much closer to the matter itself — on the basis of a solid examination of the details — than is possible in fragmen-tary work on the details.

2. *Theses about the relationship between Jesus and his disciples and God*
a. Jesus' objectivized understanding of God
There was a tendency in the approach made above, (5. II 1) to present the most fundamental structural lines — to some extent, of course, in the sense of minimal historical statements — as structural conditions based on the Jesus of history. The opposite movement of the question of the Jesus of history can be set in motion to counteract this tend-ency. It is quite justifiable to regard the absolute significance of the risen Jesus, as expressed in the New Testament and as a constitutive fact in Jesus' relationship with God, as based firmly on the Jesus of history and his understanding of and relationship with God.

The summary that follows has been elaborated on the basis of two synoptic data. The first is dialogue structure of the biblical and Jesus' image of God. The second is the anti-pharisaical character of Jesus' pro-clamation of God. The absence of any connection between these two themes is in fact only apparent. The best evidence of their interconnec-tion is to be found in the theme of the relationship between the love of God and the love of one's neighbour. The dialogue structure is clear, for example, in the commandment to love God. The anti-pharisaical char-acter of Jesus' proclamation of God, on the other hand, is clear in the radical fellow-humanity whcih is connected in Jesus' proclamation with the love of God.

i. According to Jesus' understanding of God, God is the absolute point of departure, the centre and the goal. His understanding, then, points to a radical theocentricity. This is expressed in the petition 'hallowed be thy name' in the Our Father. This petition takes precedence over the second and third petitions for the coming of the kingdom and the doing of God's will. It is only on the basis of the radical theocentricity of the first petition of the Lord's Prayer that the absolute initiative of God's mercy and, as a result of this, fellow-humanity as a response to this mercy can be known. This situation is in accordance with the Old Testament proclamation, according to which the people had to keep the covenant (and therefore the will of God) if God was to show himself as holy.

Jesus' understanding of God, then, has a certain unity of tension between God's majesty (the majesty of God as judge) and the nearness of God that had hitherto not been known as such. (God as Abba, which was the familiar way of addressing one's earthly father in Judaism at the time of Jesus; in no other case has it been proved to be a way of addressing God and, in my opinion, this is unthinkable.) This unity of tension can also be found in the earliest levels of tradition, including Q.

In our present context, the most striking characteristic of this God is that he speaks and acts first and that a response can be made to him — we reply. The unity of tension that exists here can be expressed as being Lord and being love. The word 'Abba' which Jesus used to address God is the synoptic counterpart of the loving and knowing God in 1 Jn 4. 8, 16. The power given by the Pneuma of God which enables God's mercy to continue to be effective is the result of the dialectic relationship that exists between this being Lord and being love.

ii. The eschatological objectivization of Jesus' relationship with God: the proclamation of the imminence of the kingdom of God is a constitutive element in Jesus' image of God, but it does not on its own form the 'objectivization' of Jesus' relationship with God.

iii. The continuation of the Old Testament understanding of God and the Old Testament reply to Yahweh's initiative in the synoptic tradition is to be found in the fact that the kingdom of God — in the unity of tension between the sanctification of God's name ('hallowed be thy name') and the handing on of his mercy — is effective in Jesus himself in this present era. The man who is called to this must come to a decision regarding Jesus and his activity.

This decisive function that Jesus has with regard to man's relationship with God presupposes a unique relationship on Jesus' part with God. It is clear from the sources, including the logia, that Jesus claimed this for himself. An example of this is the difference between Jesus' relationship with God as Son and that of the disciples.

iv. This relationship between Jesus and God should not be understood as a historically conditioned superstructure existing above certain social relationships (despite a number of historically conditioned expressions found in the New Testament). Much of what Jesus himself says is, of course, determined by the prevailing historical situation, but it is important here to make a distinction between this and what is still valid for later generations of believers.

The following consideration may indicate what is meant here. Jesus' understanding of God was not only anti-pharisaical, but also anti-apocalyptic. It is anti-pharisaical in that the real antithesis between Jesus and the Pharisees is to be found in their different understandings of and relationships with God. It is also anti-apocalyptic in that man's hope for the absolute future given by God is contained in Jesus himself, as is also the essage about God as judge, since God's mercy is, in the teaching of Jesus, not sentimental and effete. The apocalyptic distortion of the image of God, however, is as contradictory and fragmentary as the pharisees' view of God. This is clear from Jesus' neglect of the apocalyptic version of the first man's temptation to gain possession of God and his plan or to be able to foresee this plan. Jesus' prophetic breaking of man-made images of God is the negative evidence that Jesus' proclamation of God should and cannot be made relative by placing too much emphasis on what is historically conditioned in that proclamation.

b. Jesus' experience of God

Here we are concerned with the gnoseological aspect of what was said above (5. IV 2a) especially about the use of 'Abba' in addressing God and the proclamation of the imminent kingdom of God. Jesus' relationship with God presupposes a unique experience of God. This relationship was also conditioned, as the experience was, by a unique previously given factor (Jesus' own relationship as a gift of unity with God). This unique experience of God is discussed further below (5. V) in connection with the theme of Jesus as the believer. All that I propose to say about it here is this. It is not purely by chance that the only synoptic text in which the Aramaic form of address 'Abba' occurs is in the Gethsemane pericope at the beginning of the account of the passion. This indicates that Jesus' relationship with God was confirmed at the supreme moment of the passion. In posing the question of Jesus' experience of God, we should not overlook the fact that Jesus, according to different, but converging testimonies in the synoptic tradition, takes up a position with regard to the infinite mystery. As an example of this, we can take the tradition reflected in Mk 1. 35 (this is certainly reliable) that Jesus 'went out to a lonely place and prayed there'.[72] What we have here is obviously a consequence of Jesus' previously given unity with God. It is also clear that, in taking up this position, Jesus was able to experience God as his Father.

c. Jesus' disciples' experience of God

i. The disciples experienced God in the unity of love of neighbour that was prepared and made possible by Jesus. This love of God is connected with faith in God in the way in which Jesus taught this. It is also identical with the completely trusting and completely self-giving assent to God's will, as proclaimed by Jesus. There are clear indications in the synoptic tradition too of the type of teaching found in the first letter of John, according to which love of one's brothers is the way to knowledge of and community with God.

ii. Jesus' disciples' experience of God, in imitation of Jesus. The Christian is bound to commit himself to imitate Jesus and, therefore, to seek the face of Yahweh in the Old Testament sense. If he does not do this, he has no real justification, in the New Testament sense, for avoiding Jesus' demand that his followers should decide in favour of the kingdom of God and therefore of God himself as the Father of Jesus, by appealing to the contemporary difficulty in experiencing God. If Jesus' relationship with God presupposes a certain experience of God, then, as a result of this normative and fundamental situation, Jesus' demands made of his disciples also presuppose a certain experience of God. This can only be made for the disciples themselves in a radical form of imitation of Jesus, that is, through community with Jesus both in his relationship with God and in his fundamental fellow-humanity. (It cannot be made for the people, that is, the gentiles, who are addressed in the statement about love of one's neighbour as a norm in the judgment; see Mt 25.

Jesus' relationship with God was confirmed in his suffering and became a constitutive element in his death on the cross for the later community of disciples.[73] It is therefore not possible to wait for an experience of God before accepting Jesus' demand to make a decision in favour of God, that is, not only a fellow-humanity in the sense of a humanism that is purely concerned with this world, but also a radical fellow-humanity that is made possible by Jesus' crucifixion as the consequence of his theocentricity. It is more likely that God will be experienced in the way in which Jesus experienced him, by a decisive act of commitment, in which not only our radical fellow-humanity, but also our listening and replying to the Father (the prayer that is so clearly rooted in the New Testament) are involved. This experience of God too will only come about if we accept Jesus' deep non-conformity which led to his suffering and death on the cross.[74] This is, of course because we can only effectively serve the world if we are non-conformist in this way. This non-conformity does not bar the way to solidarity with our fellow-men. On the contrary, it is the only possible way of breaking through both the individual and the collective hardness that comes from selfishness and of handing on God's mercy in a really effective way.

3-5 Elucidations of and addenda to the theses
3. The antithesis between Jesus and the pharisees
   a. Jesus' intention
What was for Jesus the first and central aim can be seen clearly in the reasons for his opposition to the pharisees, who were the models of piety among his own people. According to Lk 15. 1 (cf. Mk 2. 15-17), the pharisees criticized Jesus for eating with 'sinners', that is, with people whom the pharisees regarded as being excluded from the people of God because they had broken the law of Israel and its interpretation by the rabbis or collaborated, as the tax collectors did, with the pagan power occupying Israel.

Although it is necessary to do so, it is not easy today to understand what it meant in the eyes of Jesus' contemporaries when Jesus 'ate' with 'tax collectors and sinners', in other words, accepted them into his community. According to the logion Lk 7. 34 (par Mt 11. 19), in which Jesus is criticized for being a 'glutton and a drunkard' precisely because he accepts into his community at table 'tax collectors and sinners', Jesus' opponents must have judged his behaviour unbelievably severely. Why did they do this?

All the claims made by Judaism of that period with regard to serious religiosity point in the opposite direction. One aspect of this was the attempt to remain apart from what was 'unclean'. The pharisees and, even more insistently, the members of the Qumran community had basically the same aim as Jesus, namely to create the true people of God, the *qahal* or *ekklesia* of Yahweh. They believed, however, that this aim could only be achieved if they remained apart from the sinners who did not know or keep the law. They therefore made the prophetic idea of a 'holy remnant' into a religious and political principle. Their aim, then, was to separate the true flock of Yahweh from Israel as a whole and to create from it the community of the holy remnant which would achieve salvation.[75]

ii. The man from Nazareth, who appeared as a prophet, aimed to destroy this whole religious structure by tearing down the wall separating the just from the sinners. This behaviour on Jesus' part must have been the most serious stumbling-block for the pharisees. It must also have been what really characterized Jesus in their eyes. The fatal antithesis between Jesus and the pharisees can be seen most sharply in this light.

In contrast to the pharisees, with the religio-political principle, Jesus had a completely different intention. His active life testified to what Vögtle has called a 'fundamental denial of the religious principle of separation'.[76] The idea of a holy remnant was very far from Jesus' mind.[77] He wanted to take God's mercy to the whole of Israel and save all men. According to Vögtle, 'from the beginning to the end of his public life, Jesus made no attempt to separate a group other the elect,[78] although he had to learn painfully that only a small part of the people really followed his call. It is not simply a question of methodology to ask whether this idea of a holy remnant was the point of departure for later Judaism, since it was only in this way, that is, by abandoning all thought of a pure community, that God's mercy could be effective in complete openness.[79]

Jesus' intention, then, was expressed in Luke's quotation from Is 61. 1 ff in his account of Jesus' first sermon in Nazareth (Lk 4. 18-21): to proclaim and to take to all men the mercy of God. If, however, no more than this were to be said about the opposition between Jesus and the pharisees, it would give rise to misunderstanding that Jesus may have done no more than simply bring a new doctrine of fellow-humanity. The antithesis between him and the Jews, however, was based on an image of God which was fundamentally different despite the common Old Testament root or on a completely different view of the relationship between man and God.

b. Jesus' criticism of his opponents' relationship with God as the negative aspect of his own experience of God

i. Although we cannot accept that Jesus had a completely undifferentiated and rejecting attitude towards the pharisees, as the situation is presented in terms of a total break between the synagogue and the Church by Matthew, who experienced this situation in his own times, it is certain that there was an extraordinarily marked opposition between Jesus and the pharisees, who were so insistent on the law, and that this opposition was fatal for Jesus.

This opposition was, of course, based on the difference between Jesus' and the pharisees' relationship with God. The clearest indication of this is to be found in the parable of the pharisee and the tax collector (Lk 18. 9-14). The perversion of this relationship is to be seen in the pharisee's making himself God's partner and expecting a return from God in response to his own achievement. He wants to tie God down to the will that he thinks he has come to possess from the Torah. In reality, of course, this attitude prevents him from understanding God's will.

ii. It is particularly relevant in this context to examine the criticism of hypocrisy which Jesus levels at the pharisees. The pharisees seem to be criticized by Jesus mainly because of the gulf between what they say and what they do (see Mt 23. 1 ff), but this does not point primarily to a discrepancy between their interpretation of the Torah and their own lives. This was undoubtedly at least partly the intention and, in the synoptic tradition, at many levels, this would seem to be very much in the foreground. In the synoptic tradition as a whole, on the other hand, and especially in the logia, it is clear that hypocrisy is only the sign pointing to a much more profound reality. Whether they are guilty or not, these men are 'hypocrites' because they claim and indeed really believe that they are carrying out the will of God in the minutest detail, whereas they are, precisely because of this, failing to carry out his real will.[80]

Jesus' opponents were simply not capable of understanding a new way of acting on God's part that went beyond their interpretation of the Torah. They were not able to be open to a divine activity that was in keeping with his activity through the prophets or even went beyond that prophetic activity. Insofar as they apply to the historical situation in which Jesus lived, his sharp words may have been spoken in a situation of rejection in the knowledge that his opponents were evading the task of passing on God's mercy on the basis of their own presuppositions and that they even wanted to prevent that mercy from being handed on (see Mt 21. 31 ff; 5. 29). The pharisees refuse — by rejecting real *metanoia* — to allow the image of God that they have fashioned on the basis of their understanding of the Torah to be broken prophetically. In this attitude of self-righteousness, they are no longer capable of remaining open to a new divine action, in other words, to the imminence of the kingdom of God in Jesus.

iii. Jesus' main concern was that God should be really recognized as God and honoured as God. He wanted God's real will to be done. Two texts providing evidence of this are Mt 21. 31 ('the tax collectors and the harlots go into the kingdom of God before you') and Lk 7. 36 ff (' . . . for she loved much'). The pharisees are contrasted with the 'children' and the 'poor'.

Other texts indicate clearly that what we have here is the negative aspect of Jesus' relationship with and experience of God in the unity of love of God and love of neighbour. The first of these is Mk 7. 8-13 (par Mt 15. 4-6). This passage points to a failure in the fellow-humanity on which God insists — in this case love of one's father and mother — for the sake of a cultic worship of God understood in a formal and legalistic sense. A failure to love one's fellow-men prevents one from really experiencing God. A similar situation is indicated in the criticism in Mt 23. 24 (cf. Lk 6. 39), levelled at the 'blind' who want to lead the blind. Another text is Mt 23. 13. Here Jesus accuses those who have the key to the kingdom, but do not enter it themselves and prevent others from entering, because they make it impossible for themselves to know the real will of God and really to experience God.

iv. As far as the other group of opponents is concerned, that is, the Sadducees, it is particularly important to note Jesus' criticism: 'You know neither the scriptures nor the power of God' (Mk 12. 24, par Mt), because their 'theological' ideas are based on formulae and apparent contradictions. The behaviour of the levite and the priest in the parable of the good Samaritan also points to the connection between a wrong relationship with God and a failure in fellow-humanity. There are also many other indications in the synoptic tradition of an experience of God brought about by carrying out the will of God. An example of this is the commandment to love one's enemies (Mt 5, 44: 'So that you may be sons of your Father who is in heaven . . . '; Mt. 5. 48: 'You must be perfect,[81] as your heavenly Father is perfect = merciful'). The demand to forgive as a condition of God's forgiveness is also an approach to experience of God, which is impossible in cult if community with one's brothers is not previously restored (Mt 5. 23 ff; cf. Mk 11. 25).

v. There is also evidence in the synoptic tradition that Jesus' disciples made it possible for others to experience God. According to Mt. 5. 16, for instance, their light was to shine before men, 'that they may see your good works and give glory to your Father, who is in heaven'. Evidence of the way in which the experience of God can be prevented is to be found in the way in which the elder son is characterized in the parable of the prodigal son (which ought rather to be called the parable of the loving Father) in Lk 15. 25 ff. Another example of this phenomenon is the implicit teaching about the possibility of experiencing God — or making this experience impossible — in the parable of the labourers in the vineyard (Mt 20. 1-15).[82]

vi. One is also tempted to ask whether it was purely a matter of historical coincidence that Jesus was not put to death by the godless, but by the most pious people among his compatriots. If this question is examined at a deeper level, the providential nature of this datum is more evident here than almost anywhere else. The composition of Mt 23 points to the great danger that threatens the community of Jesus' disciples. It is clearly their possible failure to do the real will of God or 'pharisaism as hypocricy. The evangelist places Jesus' instruction of the disciples (Mt 23. 8-12) deliberately within the framework of an indictment of the pharisees. It is only when the disciple of Jesus recognizes how dangerously easy it is for him to become a 'pharisee' that a beginning can be made in the 'new righteousness' and therefore in an experience of God in the sense in which Jesus understood it.

c. One of the consequences of the antithesis between Jesus and the pharisees was the clarification of Jesus' fundamental intention to confront men with the real God and to enable them to recognize that their own fundamental intention should be to make God's name holy ('hallowed be thy name'). Jesus was not, in other words, simply a 'man for others'. He was primarily a 'man for God'. It was only because he was first a man for God that he could be, in this radical sense, a man for others. Jesus' aim, then, was to make men open to God's work, since only God can make his name holy. He therefore tried to open them to the real will of God, so that they would hand on God's mercy (see, for example, Mt 5. 20, 48). He also aimed to make them open to the coming of God's Basileia.

It should be noted in this context that Jesus did not simply proclaim his intention in words, just as he did not merely proclaim the coming of the Basileia of God in words. In his attitude towards the poor and sinners, his proclamation and his powerful actions (see, for example, Lk 11. 20) formed a unity. We may therefore say that the kingdom of God was thrust into the present era in his person and his activity, calling for a decision on man's part and at the same time making salvation possible. It was in this way that the real will of God was expressed and Jesus' opponents were 'blind' to that will and therefore blind to the real God himself.

We may conclude by saying that it was Jesus' intention to be open himself and to make men open to God and the 'many' in a way that could only lead to the catastrophe of the failure of his work, that is, to the cross. The words of the 'imitation of the cross' therefore also belong to the expression of Jesus' anti-pharisaical intention and his understanding of God.

4. The objectivization of Jesus' relationship with God: Jesus and the Basileia of God

a. Preliminary comment and questions

Like every other man's relationship with God, Jesus' relationship was dependent on objectivizations derived from the matter itself and conditioned by historical factors. Rahner has, in this context, pointed out that Jesus objectivized and verbalized his relationship with God for himself and those who heard him by a process that has sometimes been called that of imminent expectation. In this process, the critical point of this expectation is set at a short temporal distance from the coming of the kingdom of God. Although Jesus himself rejected this, he nonetheless proclaimed, according to Rahner, an imminent expectation.

When Jesus spoke of the coming of the Basileia, he was not simply speaking of the coming of a mere 'kingdom', which could be thought of as a kind of independent reality. He was speaking of the coming of God himself and of God's taking over of sovereign rule. The statements about Jesus and the Basileia of God, then, belong, in the strict sense of the word, to the theme of Christological theo-logy.

Two questions must be asked in this context on the basis of the synoptic evidence. The first is concerned with the implications of the concept of imminent expectation. The second is concerned with what is meant by the objectivization of the experience of God through imminent expectation and its insertion into the total structure of Jesus' mission and relationship with God.

b. The implications of the concept of imminent expectation

We can explain what is meant by imminent expectation by setting out the factors that determine it, by an elucidation and demarcation of the concept itself and by examining the consequences resulting from this imminent expectation and proclamation.

In Scheme A below these three data are interrelated.

Scheme A

Open future
(anthropological)

The thrust of God
and his Basileia

}

'Imminent expectation' (historically conditioned objectivization, with reduction to the
central datum which is a consequence of the
radical theocentricity [and anthropocentricity?]

$\downarrow$

Urgency of the decision in favour of and
readiness for the Basileia of God (and task in
the evolving world in view of Jesus' proclamation of the Basileia)

i. The two factors that condition the imminent expectation Open
future: in this context, Rahner has said very pertinently that genuine
human consciousness must have an unknown future. The thrust of God
and his Basileia: The logion contained in Lk 11. 20, which provides an
interpretation of Jesus' activity within the pericope on Beelzebul, has
a direct bearing on this thrust: If it is by the finger of God that I cast
out demons, then the kingdom of God has come upon you'.

The most suitable translation of the verb *ephthasen* in this text is
'thrust forward'.[83] The verb has the following implications. The Basileia
of God continues to be a future reality. As such, however, it has come
closer and its thrust is also present in an entirely new way, in that it
thrusts forward into this era in Jesus and his activity. There are certainly apocalyptic models underlying this statement and others that
refer to the thrust of the Basileia of God, but it is true to say that the
closed apocalyptic system has been radically broken through here by
this thrust.

ii. Jesus' destruction of the apocalyptic expectation
In the fundamental sense of the word, 'expectation' is, of course, the
apocalyptic expectation of the coming of God's new world in the
imminent future. Imminent expectation of this kind and in this sense is
not present in the case of Jesus. The logion in Mk 13. 32, according to
which 'not even the angels in heaven nor the Son' know the 'day' or the
'hour' of God's ultimate action, undoubtedly forms part of the very
earliest tradition of Jesu.

There are, however, three logia — Mk 13. 30; Mk 9. 1 and Mt 10. 23
— the only three dealing with the imminent expectation in the synoptic

tradition, which do not belong, at least in their present form, to the earliest tradition. These logia are probably a transformation of central, original logia of Jesus with a re-apocalypticizing emphasis.[84]

It is possible and, in my opinion, probable, on the basis of the synoptic datum and especially the logia, that the concept of imminent expectation should be given a much more relative value in the case of Jesus. This is different from and at least partly in contrast to John the Baptist. The apocalyptic proclamation of the latter retained its valid central truth in Jesus' proclamation, but Jesus undoubtedly broke through it. There are, however, also signs of a re-apocalypticization at certain levels of the post-paschal tradition and theology.

It is not possible to restore synthetically a higher unity of the idea of 'soon' and the unknown aspect of the day, but this unity is nonetheless made possible by Jesus' destruction of the apocalyptic expectation. Jesus brought about this destruction in such a way that the coming of the Basileia was not simply stated in purely futuristic terms. The Basileia was brought into this present era in Jesus himself.

In Jesus' proclamation, there is a reduction of the apocalyptic time-scheme to a kind of mathematical point.[85] This mathematical point, as a basically abstract central datum, is a coming of the Basileia of God in the manner of a new creation which lies within the sovereign power of God. This new creation also presupposes the passing of this cosmos, in which the name of God cannot adequately be made holy.[86] This reduction — and therefore destruction — of the apocalyptic time-scheme is only possible by the prophetic destruction of the apocalytic image of God and this is the consequence of the absolute theocentricity that is reflected in Jesus' proclamation of the Basileia (and not only in the form of the first petition of the Our Father). This radical theocentricity, as the precondition of Jesus' imminent expectation, also goes together with a similarly radical anthropocentricity. This anthropocentricity is only made possible by this fundamental theocentricity. It is open to the absolute mystery and it also provides man with an open future.

It is also made possible because the original apocalyptic idea of imminent expectation was broken through by the present eschatological and present Christological aspect of Jesus' form of expectation of the Basileia. This is why it is reasonable to look for a different way of expressing what is meant by imminent expectation.[87]

iii. The consequence resulting from the imminent proclamation and the imminent expectation

This is to be found in the urgency of the decision in favour of the Basileia of God. The urgency of Jesus' task to assemble the people of God that is connected with the proclamation of the Basileia is clear from the logia. It is also conditioned by the irrevocable passing of the time during which the decision for or against the Basileia can be made.[88] A positive decision presupposes a readiness to satisfy the conditions of entry into the Basileia. These are named by Jesus as an acceptance of his own radical theocentricity, a willingness to do everything to avoid blocking this decision,[89] and to recognize the imperative that results from the proclamation of the Basileia and applies to life in this era. It is also clear from the synoptic material that it is only possible to decide in favour of the kingdom of God if a decision is also made in favour of community with Jesus. Evidence of this will be found in Lk 12. 8 parr and a series of threats and pronouncements about the judgment. The cry of woe against Chorazin (Lk 10.13 par Mt 11. 21) is an example of the latter.

As a term describing the datum in question, 'imminent expectation' ought perhaps to be replaced or at least complemented by a term such as 'constant readiness'. This would emphasize man's willingness to look forward to God's action which would result in an absolute and unique fulfilment for the whole of mankind and to satisfy the conditions of entry into the kingdom of God and therefore to decide in favour of the Basileia.

iv. The task in the evolving world in view of Jesus' proclamation of the Basileia.

This question too can only be approached meaningfully in the context of biblical theology if it is recognized that the coming of the Basileia is identical with the coming of God himself. God's forgiveness and mercy call for a reply from the man who consents to this God in the form of forgiveness and service of others.[90]

On the basis of Jesus' eschatological teaching, man's fashioning of the world for the Basileia of God can only be relevant if the works of love remain. This applies if it is recognized that Jesus' use of the apocalyptic material brings about a theological reduction to the mathematical point of a radical new creation, since even then there is a discontinuity between the world as it is now and the final kingdom of God and this leads to the question as to what is then still able to remain.

The Apocalypse of John can be used as a model for comparison with the synoptic tradition, since, even though it is late, it is a completely

Judaeo-Christian document.[91] Like Jesus, himself, the Apocalypse too does not refer explicitly to the Christian's task in the world. This question did not arise in the first century communities in the form in which it occurs nowadays. There his, however, both in the message of Jesus himself and in the Apocalypse, a place in which this fashioning of the world can be rooted and from which it can also be taken and inserted into the new creation. That place is the theme of service of one's fellow-men. The 'treasures of the peoples' that were to be brought to the 'new Jerusalem' (Rev 21. 24-27) can, in the whole context of the Apocalypse, only be interpreted in analogy with the 'righteous deeds of the saints' (Rev 19. 8; cf. 7. 14; 22. 14) that 'follow them' (Rev 14. 13) into the new creation. The condition for this entry of man's works from this era into the new creation as a continuity from below is that there is also a continuity from above. In other words, the God of Jesus is not only the one who is to come and who 'was there' in the old covenant, but also the one who is already here for his people with his power and his faithfulness to his promise. What, then, is important for Jesus' disciples is whether they give their consent to this incalculable God whose behaviour is so different from that which men would expect and who overthrows all man's concepts and wishes. The scandal caused by Jesus' proclamation of the Basileia reduced to the mathematical point has to be sustained, for the sake of faith in God and the prophetic faith which destroys again and again the ideas that men have of God.

The carrying out of this task includes not only individual love of one's fellow men, but also the humanization of the secondary structures of society as a whole and cannot be conceived without this aspect. The relationship with and experience of God that takes place within the carrying out of this task presupposes God's central revelation of the cross in the New Testament. What is already present in the synoptic tradition in statements such as the one made in Mk 8. 35 and in such demands as 'let him deny himself, take up his cross and follow me' (Mk 8. 34 parr) is made explicit in the later New Testament writings. Taken in isolation and interpreted individualistically, the logion: 'Whoever loses his life . . . will save it' (Mk 8. 35) is easily misunderstood. It cannot, however, be misunderstood if it is related to the salvation of the whole world by means of the law of salvation as formulated in Jn 12. 24: 'If it (the grain of wheat) dies, it bears much fruit'.[92]

In the light of the New Testament teaching, then, evolution and increased fellow-humanity within the framework of this evolution can be understood as an integral aspect within the process of fulfilment through death, which is related to the whole of mankind. In the reduction to passing away (the radical judgment) and new creation, Jesus' message of the Basileia means that the law of salvation defined in Jn 12. 24 also applies to the world as a whole.

Life and work within the evolving world are in this way orientated towards the fulfilled community with absolute love. This takes place in such a way that aspects of Christian life that have hitherto hardly been sensed are disclosed. These include new and more promising opportunities to learn how the way towards the ultimate fulfilment can be followed by 'dying' and how to stand, because of this, not outside, but really inside this evolving world and serve it, 'bearing much fruit'.

The statements found in the New Testament should not, then, be incorporated into an evolving view of the world. On the contrary, this evolving view of the world clearly forms part of Jesus' message of the Basileia interpreted in this way,[93] so that the real God can 'rule' in the sense of Jesus' proclamation and in the sense of 1 Cor 15. 28.

c. The total structure provided in the synoptic tradition for the objectivization of Jesus' experience of God

We can now verify what was said above (5. IV 3 b ii) about the objectivization of Jesus' relationship with God in the imminent expectation, but only if it is inserted into the total structure of Jesus' relationship wih God as presented in the synoptic tradition. The objectivization of Jesus' relationship with God into the future is conditioned by an objectivization in the present (see Scheme B I). The line pointing towards the future, as presented in 5. IV 3 b ii, has to be complemented by the aspect of promise and the 'abundance' of promises (see Scheme B II).

As a third stage (see Scheme B III), the three points of objectivization distinguished so far are related to each other. In other words, it is not simply a question of combing the two partial schemes, B I and B II, but rather a question of indicating the relationship between Jesus' mission (together with his response to having been sent) and the thrust of the kingdom of God on the one hand and the form of objectivization that is orientated towards the future on the other.

One further comment has to be made on these schemes. It should be borne in mind when studying the three diagrams (B I, II and III) particularly that the objectivizing terms referring to the New Testament ('mission' and so on) can also be understood in the gnoseological sense (in the case of 'mission', thus seen from the point of view of Jesus' consciousness of mission). In the case of such concepts as 'response', 'faithfulness to the mission' and so on, it should be remembered that these are also seen from the standpoint of Jesus' own consciousness. The structure of relationships to which these concepts point cannot be understood unless both the objectivizing and the explicitly or implicitly anthropological and gnoseological forms of expression are also taken into consideration.

i. The present aspect — mission and response

Scheme B I

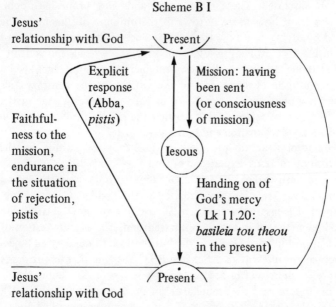

Jesus'
relationship with God

Present

Explicit
response
(Abba,
pistis)

Mission: having
been sent
(or consciousness
of mission)

Faithful-
ness to the
mission,
endurance in
the situation
of rejection,
pistis

Iesous

Handing on of
God's mercy
(Lk 11.20:
basileia tou theou
in the present)

Jesus'
relationship with God

Present

It will be noticed that this first scheme does not take as its point of departure Jesus' expectation of the Basileia in the future. Jesus' expectation was different from all the apocalyptic imminent expectations in that, because of his person and his work, it had a present aspect. The scheme therefore takes as its point of departure Jesus' expectation in this present.

The curve forming the framework of the scheme indicates the sphere of consciousness within which the various forms of objectivization of Jesus' relationship with God should be understood.

The two points of reference indicated at the top and the bottom of the scheme should not be seen as signs for God and the world. Both point to points of objectivization in Jesus' relationship with God. Even the point of reference at the bottom should be understood in this sense.

Each is also orientated towards the other, although it should be borne in mind that the point at the top — Jesus' mission as 'having been sent' or as 'consciousness of mission' — has priority.

The line from the point at the top ('mission') passes from Jesus' 'having been sent', through his consciousness of his own mission to the 'handing on of God's mercy'. This concept is — to some extent in accordance with Lk 4. 17 ff — connected with the thrust of the *basileia tou theou* into this era (Lk 11. 20).

The response, as the realization of Jesus' relationship with God, is indicated by two separate, but converging lines. Although they are drawn separately on the diagram, they cannot be in fact separated. This response takes place within the framework of the idea of mission, insofar as this — in the fulfilment of the 'handing on of God's mercy' and the experience of God which takes place within this process of handing on — is endured (faithfulness to this mission, endurance in the situation of rejection, the 'temptations' of Jesus). This is shown in the diagram by making the line from Jesus' mission through the handing on of God's mercy to the point of objectivization at the bottom turn back again to the point of objectivization at the top. This endurance in mission is, however, borne up (see the arrow from *Iesous* to the point of objectivization at the top) by the closeness and love of the Father, which was experienced by Jesus when he was sent, and Jesus' explicit response to it. Jesus was, in other words, only able to be the 'man for others' because he was primarily the 'man for God'.

ii. The line coming from the Old Testament and pointing to the future
Scheme B II

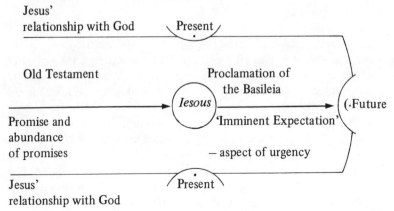

The new aspect in this scheme (B II) is that the line from Jesus to the point of objectivization described as imminent expectation (relationship with God as the one who is coming and experience of the thrust of his power) is based firmly on the Old Testament and is inconceivable without the Old Testament. In this context I would refer back to what was said above (see 2. II 1) about the concepts 'promise' and 'abundance of promises'.[94]

iii. The openness of Jesus' consciousness of mission and his response to God's future

Scheme B III

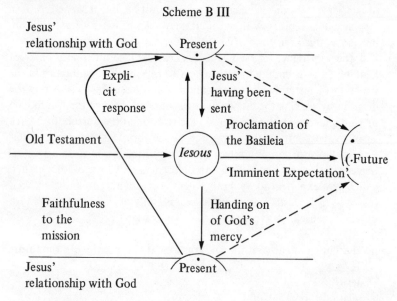

There are two dotted lines in this scheme (B III) which are not in the previous two diagrams (B I and II). These point from the points of reference in the present at the top and the bottom of the diagram to the point of reference in the future. They have been added for the following reasons.

Both Jesus' consciousness of his own mission and his response were open to God's future, because he knew and experienced his Father as Yahweh or as the God who had a future as a condition of his being.[95] (This is indicated by the upper dotted line.) Paul's concept *arrabon* (earnest-money or pledge) provides an excellent model for the dynamism of the Basileia already thrusting into the present era. The

Pneuma, in whose power the ultimate fulfilment will take place, is already active in the present, in the direction of the future fulfilment.[96] The dynamic power of the Pneuma, which is able to bear up Christian life here and now and to fulfil it, should be understood in this sense. According to the synoptic tradition, Jesus' present activity is similarly important only in its orientation towards fulfilment in the future. (This is indicated by the lower dotted line.) This is so because the God of Jesus is of such a kind that he transcends the possibilities open to the present era in the direction of a future that is open to the infinity of love.

iv. Jesus as the central point of the structure of relationships pointing in the direction of the Basileia of God

Iesous is the central point of all the lines in the structure of relationships shown in all three stages of Scheme B. This is justified by the situation represented in the diagrams. Because of his function in the present, Jesus had an indissoluble connection with the Basileia (see once again Lk 11.20) and therefore a central function in making a relationship with God possible. (This function was made explicit in the New Testament after the Easter event.)

The same applies to the line pointing to the future. According to Lk 12. 8 ff, the fate of the human race at the last judgement will depend on whether men have — in the present — consented to or rejected community with Jesus. We can refer here to the earliest post-paschal Christology to support this thesis. It is especially here that Jesus is seen in the light of the future, that is, as the Son of Man or Judge who is to come.

The position of the word *Iesous* at the point of intersection of the lines also shows that the connection between eschatology and theology is only present in the sonship of Jesus.[97] If the future sphere of salvation of the kingdom of God is at the same time to be a reality in the present, there must be a foundation for this pre-realization. That foundation is Jesus' activity, made possible by God and carried out on his instruction (see again Lk 11. 20). Jesus' activity is the way in which the Basileia is encountered. Jesus, in the function of messenger that is inseparable from his person, is the sign in which the Basileia is encountered.[98]

v. Summary

The objectivization of Jesus' relationship with God, which comes from the future as an imminent expectation and is directed towards the future as such, thus retains the emphasis given to it by Rahner in my exposition, but I have, I think, made the structure of relationships within which it is situated a good deal clearer. This is a distinct gain, because it enables Rahner's objectivization theory to be seen as it really is, and not simply as a one-sided statement. If, then, this objectivization of Jesus' relationship with God in imminent expectation is no longer seen in isolation (and therefore as not in accordance with the New Testament datum), but is inserted into the whole sphere of relationships, we can perhaps summarize the theme 'Jesus and the *Basileia tou theou*' usefully as 'Jesus and God'.

5. Description of the concepts 'Father' and Son'

The concepts 'Father' and 'Son' are characteristic of Jesus' specific relationship with God as outlined in the early synoptic tradition of the New Testament. 'Father' is used by Jesus in a special sense as a way of addressing God. 'Son' is derived from this way of naming God 'Father', the title 'Father' being therefore primary, 'Son' secondary. The logia in which Jesus appears as the 'Son' can, however, be traced back to Jesus himself.[99]

Both these terms are even more difficult to interpret nowadays. A description, based on a stimulus provided by J.B. Metz,[100] can help us to understand how the New Testament concepts of God's fatherhood and Jesus' sonship (including the sonship of the exalted Christ) can be interpreted in a non-mythological way.

On the basis of the New Testament datum, Metz has suggested that the name of God cannot be interpreted simply by means of the primary psychological categories of fatherhood. He is convinced that the term 'Father', which is so closely linked to the message of the coming of the kingdom of God, refers in Jesus' statements to the 'arrival of the power of unconditional love which destroys all human comparisons'. Jesus, Metz claims, 'made experience of God primarily an experience of freedom'.

Various texts in the epistle to the Galatians can be used to justify this description of these concepts. In Gal 4. 7 and 5. 1, for example, sonship and freedom are correlative. This correlation does not simply apply to Jesus' existence on this earth. It is also eschatological and points to the future, in which the risen Jesus is present. Because of this, it also applies to Jesus' disciples' relationship with God in the present, post-paschal period.

According to R. Schäfer,[101] the relationship 'Father-Son' goes back to the 'subordination' of man which cannot be 'abolished' and is open not only to love, but also to freedom. The relationship of the Son with the Father, then, is a 'subordination' in freedom and trust to the one whose rule is love. 'In using the name "Father", Jesus declares that God's rule is not tyrannical or arbitrary', Schäfer maintains. For Jesus, God's rule was 'not an oppressive burden, but a precious discovery which made all other possessions lose their value'.

It is possible, then, to regard the concept 'Father' as a symbol for 'creative love of the kind that makes freedom possible'. This is not an empty formula or an unknown mathematical quantity. It is rather a consciously indadequate expression of something that is on the one hand a mystery that escapes our grasp and on the other a reality that is experienced and to which we give our consent.

V. Jesus as the believer
1. The New Testament datum and questions
The two most important New Testament documents dealing with the faith of Jesus himself are the gospel of Mark and the Epistle of the Hebrews. I believe that this theme can also be found in Paul's Letters.

Individual authors in the New Testament have different concepts of faith, but all these understandings of faith are similar in that none of them depart fundamentally from the Old Testament idea of *'emunah.* In other words, the New Testament concept of faith is never a one-sided *pistis* in the sense that was rejected by Martin Buber. In the New Testament, the personal relationship that is constituted by trusting self-giving and is only raised to a qualitatively new level by the confession of God's saving action in Jesus — at least insofar as community with Jesus makes radical faith possible — is preserved.

If *pistis* in the New Testament were primarily and always a 'believing that' or a regarding of certain saving facts as true, it would be difficult to think of Jesus as a believer. In the two New Testament documents mentioned above, however, there is, as the basis of a Christological use of the concept of pistis, a trusting faith in prayer in Mark and a standing firm in trusting the God of the promise in Hebrews. These concepts, in my opinion, provide access to the important Christological statement that is expressed most unambiguously and in a very comprehensive way in Heb 12. 2. In view of the fact that there are no strictly verbal parallels for the faith of Jesus himself in the other New Testament documents, we are bound to ask whether other objective parallels do not make up for this absence in the rest of the New Testament. There is also the related question as to whether the explicit statement of Jesus as the believer is so rare in the New Testament.

2. Jesus as the 'pioneer and perfecter of our faith' (Heb 12. 2)

According to Heb 12. 2, Jesus is the *archegos* and *teleiotes* of *pistis*.
Since the concept of faith in Hebrews points to the confirmation of
hupo-stasis (Heb 11. 1: faith as holding firm with regard to 'things
hoped for') in contestation and ignominy,[102] it would be unacceptable
to translate *archegos* simply as 'originator'.[103] Jesus should rather be
seen as the 'pioneer' or 'leader' of faith, the one who begins or initiates.
Jesus should be understood not simply in the manner of an example,
but rather as the one who lived this faith in a unique way and whose
faith has now attained permanence, with the result that he now gives
his own the power to believe in this way. In other words, Jesus' disciples can — according to the context (Heb 12. 1) — 'run with perseverance' to the goal of the promise.

What we have here, then, is not an exemplary, but a causal faith.
This is clear not only from the concepts used in Heb. 12. 2a (*archegos*
and *teleiotes* are correlative here), but also from the soteriological dimension that appears in Heb 12. 2 b. In Hebrews, the cross and 'seated
at the right hand of the throne of the Majesty in heaven' (Heb 8. 1) undoubtedly have this soteriological aspect. There is also the statement in
Heb 5. 9, according to which Jesus is the 'cause (*aitios*) of eternal salvation'. Finally, the concept of 'high-priest', which plays such an important part in the letter, is also related to this. Heb 3. 1, which also contains a twofold statement about Jesus, should also be seen in conjunction with Heb 12. 1. According to this text, Jesus was the *apostolos* and
high priest of our confession'. Jesus, then, was the *archegos*, the
'pioneer' or 'leader', precisely as the *apostolos*, the one who was sent by
the Father, just as he was the perfecter of our faith as the high priest. If
Christ was, in his function as *archegos* and *teleiotes*, unmistakably
separated from all *metochoi*, that is, those who share in his way, he was
nonetheless commensurable at one point. That point was faith. He also
believed, in the manner of the 'men of old' mentioned in Heb 11.

The statements made in Heb 3. 2 (Jesus as *pistos* or 'faithful') and
2. 13 ('I will put my trust in him; a quotation from the Old Testament,
Is 8. 17; 2 Sam 22. 3, LXX) should also be taken in conjunction with
the basic datum of Heb 12. 2 (Jesus as the 'pioneer' or 'leader' in faith).
Finally, there are two more texts which should be considered in this
context: Heb 2. 17 and 5. 8. 'Learning obedience' in the latter is inter-
changeable in the letter to the Hebrews with *pistis*.[104]

3. Jesus' faith in prayer according to Mk 9. 23

According to this text, Jesus repeats the half doubting, half trusting words spoken by the father of the epileptic boy, whom his disciples has not been able to cure, in a rhetorical question. He asks: What does that mean 'If you can'? and goes on 'All things are possible to him who believes.'

In this combination of ideas, the one who believes can only be Jesus himself. Because of his 'faith', he is the one for whom healing is possible. This supposition is confirmed by the conclusion of the passage. In verse 29, Jesus says that 'prayer' is the condition on which the possibility or impossibility of healing depends.[105] It is clear from this that faith and prayer are parallel concepts. This datum leads us inevitably to the statement in Mk 11. 22 ff about the faith in prayer that moves mountains. This statement can, in my opinion, only be meaningful as a primarily Christological pronouncement. Understood in any other sense, it is absurd.[106]

Possibly the best way of explaining Mk 9. 29 is to ask another question. How can 'prayer' be understood here as a means of healing or, to put this question in a more general form, as the means par excellence of helping one's fellow-men? In answering this question, we must above all take into consideration what we have said above in this context. Prayer here, then, does not refer to an isolated cultic practice, but to a total expression of life.[107] As such, it can be compared with faith which expresses itself in word (and response) and action.

In Mk 9. 24, the faith of the father who asks for his son to be healed is also related to the healing and the word of the power of faith. This is a point of view that is always prevalent in Matthew. One is bound to ask here whether several different traditions have been assembled in this passage in Mark, resulting in the ambivalent state of affairs in verses 22-22-24. In my opinion, this is improbable. The ambivalence is not authentic, because a powerful faith in prayer is attributed in Mk 9 only to Jesus, the father of the epileptic boy paradoxically expressing only his search for faith in unbelief. In connection with Jesus' faith, this can only be related to the healing of the boy.[108]

4. Parallels in the rest of the New Testament

a. There is a direct line from Jesus' faith in pray (Mk 9. 23), that is, his unconditional trust in God's power and readiness to help, to his prayer in Gethsemane and his offering of himself on the cross. Prayer, in the sense in which it is used in Mk 9. 23 and 11. 22 ff. includes faithfulness to his mission to the point of death. If this faith in prayer is only possible for Jesus' disciples in community with Jesus, then prayer on the part of a disciple that does not at the same time also imply an imitation of the cross (Mk 8. 34) or 'suffering together with Christ' (Rom 8. 17) cannot participate in the dynamism of Jesus' faith.

b. In the Epistle to the Hebrews, the theme of Jesus as the one who initiated faith is linked with that of his 'trials' or 'temptations' (*peirasmoi*). The statement made in K. 22. 28: 'You are those who have continued with me in my 'trials' is probably one of the very earliest texts in the synoptic tradition. In any case, it is certain that the theme as such goes back to the earliest tradition[109] The statement about Jesus' *peirasmoi* in Lk 22 is certainly evidence that the Jesus of history was 'threatened by crises of identity', even when he was abandoned on the cross, which is interpreted in Mark (or in the pre-Marcan tradition) in Ps 22. 2. Jesus' temptations are identical with the situation of rejection and the aporia that led to the catastrophe of the death on the cross, just as the latter can be linked with Jesus' mission and his function with regard to the Basileia that was contained in his mission.

Jesus' followers, then, associated, during Jesus' historical existence, with a man who, as a real person, had his own personal characteristics and whose life was marked by uncertainty in the form of these temptations.[110] They also knew him as a man who had a very special mission and a unique commitment and who lived in the dynamism of one who bore the Pneuma. His life was also, despite all its controversial elements, a single whole.[111] It lacked the fragmentary nature that would have been the consequence of guilt. When, then, his disciples came to believe in his resurrection, this resulted in the inevitable theological consequence, based on the conviction that the Pneuma had been associated with this man Jesus, that he had been 'in every respect tempted as we are, yet without sinning' (Heb 4. 15; cf. 2. 18; 7. 27; see also 2 Cor 5. 21; cf. Rom 6. 10; 8. 3). This statement should be compared with the pronouncements made about faith in Hebrews.

c. The problem that produces the apparent discrepancy between the statements referring to Jesus' sinlessness and his temptations has only been satisfactorily solved by Karl Rahner. He has made a distinction between Jesus' reflective consciousness on the one hand and his 'most original and central situation which sustained everything else that he knew or did' on the other and traced this back to his relationship with God.[112]

d. Our understanding of Jesus as the one who 'prayed' and trusted

(Mk 9. 23, taken in conjunction with Mk 11) can, despite the uniqueness of the Marcan statement about Jesus' faith as well as that in Hebrews, be supported by unambiguous parallels in the New Testament. As the one who trusted and gave himself completely or the one who 'prayed' in this sense, Jesus is also present in the gospel of Luke. The Lucan statement about Jesus on the cross ('Father, into thy hands I commend my spirit', Lk 23. 46) can be justified in the light of the statements made in the synoptic tradition about the earthly Jesus' radical commitment to his mission and his equally radical theocentricity.[113] In spite of the absence in Matthew of any parallel to Mk 9. 23, the former gospel is clearly parallel, since Matthew has taken over the Marcan tradition of Gethsemane and the crucifixion. Matthew is also noticeably marked by an unambiguous theocentricity.[114]

In the case of Paul, the closest parallel is the author's concept of 'obedience' and 'subordination' on Jesus' part. This is also connected with Paul's *pistis Christou*.

In the gospel of John, Jesus' obedience and his absolutely trusting prayer is made much more radical by the theme of Jesus' unity with God.[115]

e. We must now ask why most of the New Testament authors avoid making a direct statement about Jesus' faith. We can certainly say, on the basis of the parallels, that this has nothing to do with the argument of the later theological tradition,[116] namely that faith was excluded in the case of Jesus because of his direct vision of God while still on earth. This fact is, in most of the New Testament writings, the result of an attempt to accommodate the communities of believers, for whom believing was an attitude on their part towards God through Jesus. It may also have been the result of an attempt to give greater emphasis to the aspects, that were also stressed in Heb 12. 2, of Jesus as the 'pioneer' or 'leader' and 'perfecter' of faith. Indeed, the only New Testament author who really succeeded in making a theologically balanced and completely justified statement about the faith of Jesus himself was the writer of the letter to the Hebrews. He did this, in Heb 12. 2, on the basis of his specific Christological and soteriological insight.[117]

5. Christ's faith in Paul?

a. I must first give my reasons for dealing with this question at this particular point. I am of the opinion that the argument that Jesus can also be seen as the subject of *pistis* (in other words as a believer) in Paul can be verified in the context of Paul's theology of *dikaiosune* and *pistis*.

Since it is impossible to go in detail into that context here, however, we must limit ourselves to a few basic indications, which should not be regarded as of decisive importance within the framework of this chapter. What is more, the close connection between the Pauline idea of the *pistis Christou*, with which we shall be dealing in this section, and the theme that will be discussed in the following section (5. V. 6) has also played a part in our decision to place the section on Christ's faith in Paul here.

b. The two most important Pauline texts for our understanding of the Pauline theology in this respect are Rom 3. 21 ff and 3. 26.

According to Rom 3. 21 ff, 'now the *dikaiosune* of God has been manifested apart from the law, although the law and the prophets bear witness to it, the *dikaiosune* of God (which has been manifested) *dia pisteos Iesou Christou* for all who believe'. This statement, together with the parallel text in Rom 1. 17, forms a framework including the passage 1. 18-3. 20. What is indicated in 3. 21 (as in 1. 17) is the powerful manifestation of the 'righteousness' (*dikaoisune*) of God himself. In other words, God reveals his *dikaiosune* in a new way to 'all who believe'.

The expression 'the law and the prophets bear witness to it' points, as do other similar expressions in the New Testament, to the fact that verse 21 is concerned with the event of Jesus.

The subject of verse 21 ('the righteousness of God') is repeated in verse 22. The expression in this second verse, *dia pisteos Iesou Christou*, is a more precise definition for the expression 'manifestation of God's righteousness' in verse 21. *Dia pisteos Iesou Christou* does not mean 'through faith *in* Jesus Christ', but 'through the *pistis* of Jesus Christ himself'. The powerful manifestation of the *dikaoisune* of God is not, after, achieved through what comes from man or even through Christians' faith in Christ. It comes about through something that is from God and to God in his unique 'Son'.[118]

Pistis Christou in this context is the means by which God reveals his *dikaiosune*. This faith of Christ is essentially Christ's obedience to death as an orientation towards his 'life for God' (Rom 6. 10).

c. The fundamental presupposition for this argument is that Paul was able to use *pistis* in the same context with different, but mutually related meanings. He used it to mean a right relationship on God's part towards his people, a right relationship on Christ's part towards God (Christ being understood here as the unique man, the second Adam) and a right relationship on man's part towards God 'through Christ'.

The fundamental thesis, then, is that *pistis* was used by Paul to indicate a total reality. Various aspects of this emerge at different times in Paul's writing.

We may therefore assume that there was, according to Paul, a *pistis* of God as faithfulness (to his promise). This *pistis* is parallel to *dikaiosune* and is used in the sense of a right relationship on God's part towards men. A clear example is to be found in Rom 3. 3.[119]

This thesis can be summarized as follows: God's *pistis* — and with it, his *dikaiosune*, which is a parallel concept — is revealed in Christ's pistis and this is expressed, as a human attitude and mode of behaviour, in Christ's 'obedience'.

What we have here, then, is a way of expressing God's communication of himself. What is in God is revealed by Jesus, who makes this revelation real by the way in which he believes, in other words, by his radically trusting obedience.

d. The handing on of this reality of *pistis* is implicit in Rom 3. 26, in which the words *ton ek pisteos Iesou* should, in my opinion, be seen as a parallel to *to ek pisteos Abraam* in Rom 4. 16. In both cases, the genitive points to the subject of the *pistis* and in both cases too, although the theological level is different, there is a corporative idea present. The phrase 'the one out of the *pistis* of Christ' in Rom 3. 26 means, then, 'the one out of the *pistis* communicated through the Pneuma in being in Christ'.

e. This is in accordance with another argument, namely that Rom ff can be interpreted in the light of Christological understanding of *dikaiosune* that is apparent in 1 Cor 1. 30: Christ as our *dikaiosune* from God'.

God's righteousness was not simply revealed somehow in the event of Christ. It was revealed by Christ's having been revealed as the 'Son of God'.[120] This means that the right relationship on God's part towards those whom he has chosen was revealed by his revealing the response (that is, the right relationship of those whom he had chosen towards him) to them 'in Christ' and in this way made this response possible (see Rom 8. 29; Gal 4. 6; 3. 26).

We have in this case to make a distinction between the descending and the ascending lines (God's activity towards men and their response to him). With regard to the descending line, we may say that God's mercy and faithfulness are revealed in Christ, who carried out God's saving will in his obedience to death and in so doing completed and revealed the passage into 'life for God' Rom 6. 10) and in this way opened the way to universal salvation. As for the ascending line, 'in Christ,' in other words, in the community with Christ brought about by the Pneuma, the believer can himself become 'righteousness of God (2 Cor 5. 21) or he can 'live for God in Christ Jesus (Rom 6. 11).

f. Finally, this view is also made possible by Paul's Christ-Pneuma theology (see 2 Cor 3. 17; 1 Cor 15. 45; Rom 8. 10b; 8. 2). 'Out of faith' (or 'out of the *pistis* of Christ', Rom 3. 26) or 'righteousness' objectively mean the same as 'living for God in Christ' and 'being led by the Spirit' (Gal 5. 18; Rom 8. 14).

This Christological and pneumatological interpretation of the concept of *dikaiosune* makes it possible for us to understand this very difficult term, by detaching it from the whole of Paul's thought and fitting it back into that thought. In this context, the alternative definitions, *dikaiosune* as power and *dikaiosune* as a gift', can perhaps be elaborated into a useful synthesis. This interpretation is also capable of preserving Paul's anthropological intention and even revealing the deepest level of this intention. This could not be done so radically in any other way.

6. The connection between the faith in prayer of the earthly Jesus and the function of the exalted Jesus

If the earthly Jesus' *pistis* was in fact a faith in prayer, then the 'intercession' of the exalted Jesus (Rom 8. 34; Heb 7. 35; 1 Jn 2. 1 ff) is the transformation of that faith after the Easter event. What we have here are statements about the prayer of the exalted Jesus taking place within his fulfilled orientation as a Son towards the Father. Believers can only address the Father as such because the Pneuma of the Son calls 'Abba' in them (Gal 4. 6). This is a case of the permanence of Jesus' offering of himself that was his trusting offering of himself 'in prayer' on earth that culminated in his death on the cross.

The clearest statement about Jesus' faith can be found, then, in the letter to the Hebrews. It is clearer than Paul's statements, for example, because Jesus is included among those who have borne witness to faith in Heb 11. This is not the case in Paul's writing, in which Jesus' faith is only implied in such instrumental expressions as those found in Rom 3. 22 (*dia* . . .). The expression 'Jesus' faith' can easily be misunderstood – in the sense of being confined to the attitude of Jesus while here on earth – and for this reason it should not be forgotten that the epistle to the Hebrews also stresses the permanence of Jesus' faith. This permanence can be found especially in the exalted Jesus' 'intercession' for men

(Heb 7. 25), in the statements about the 'blood' of Jesus in heaven as an expression of the soteriologically effective permanence of his offering of himself on the cross[121] and, as a consequence of this, Jesus' function as the high priest as the 'perfecter of our faith' (Heb 12. 2).

Jesus' original openness to the absolute mystery of God (which he possessed, according to Paul) made it possible − through the Pneuma − for his own to be open to God. In Paul's writings too, despite many statements which appear to contradict it, Jesus' faith is not a 'believing that' in the sense in which Buber used this phrase, but rather a faith in dialogue in the God who is able to raise the dead to life through the Pneuma. This is the highest way of expressing what appears in the synoptic concept of faith as an unconditional trust in God's power and readiness to help men.

Gerhard Ebeling has expressed the relationship between Jesus' faith and the faith of his disciples after the Easter event in a way that throws light on our problem[122] He said that the 'witness of faith' became the 'ground of faith' through his resurrection.

7. The significance of the idea of Jesus as the believer for the total theological context of Christology

The idea of Jesus as the believer can be regarded as a meaningful way of representing a central Christological datum, namely that the risen Jesus' orientation towards God, which was of such soteriological importance (this is, of course, the ascending line of theocentricity), was originally based in Jesus' earthly life. The relationship between Christology and, on the one hand, soteriology (the idea of the cross and therefore of the radicalized *agape*) and, on the other, ecclesiology, eschatology and the Old Testament history of the promise should be seen in the light of this central statement of Christological theo-logy. We will now deal with each of these relationships briefly in turn.

The relationship between Christology and soteriology can be distinguished in the fact that Jesus' giving of himself on the cross was the culmination of his trusting offering of himself while he was on earth and carrying out his mission, in which God was revealed in a unique way as *agape*. This throws a new light on our fundamental statement that Jesus could only be a man for others because he was at the same time the 'man for God'.

With regard to the relationship between Christology and ecclesiology, it is faith through community with Jesus, this one believer, that constitutes the community of believing disciples in their service of the world, so that the *agape* of the cross can be effective in the world.

In this attempt to discover the total theological and Christological context within which the idea of Jesus as the believer is placed, the theology of the first letter of John and the gospel of John is of great importance. We may summarize this theology by saying that faith and love belong together because faith is knowing the absolute love which men are called to hand on to others. Faith can be a knowledge of love for Jesus' disciples because Jesus himself revealed absolute love. What is more, Jesus revealed love through his knowledge of the Father (see Jn 10. 15; 17. 25) and his conformity with the will of the Father (see, for example, Jn 5. 19 ff). The Marcan counterpart to this is, of course, Jesus' faith. The disciples, in community with Jesus, hand on the love that they have received from Jesus, just as Jesus received it from the Father.[123]

Finally, we will briefly consider the relationship between Christology and eschatology. The objectivization of Jesus' relationship with God from the future and into the future (see the three Schemes, A, B II and B III) can be justified in the light of the presentation of the Christological significance in the Epistle to the Hebrews of Jesus function as the 'pioneer and perfecter of our faith'. Jesus was, in other words, the one who, within the framework of the author's understanding of the concept of *pistis*, was at the origin of the ascending line, the *eis ton theon*. He was, in other words, at the beginning of *pistis* as a standing firm in trusting the God of the promise.

8. The notion of Jesus' faith as an approach to a legitimate Christology of consciousness. The significance of the Christological theocentricity based on Jesus' faith

a. What has so far been said about Jesus' faith should provide a New Testament approach to what Rahner has rightly called a Christology of consciousness.

How can this possibly be the case in the New Testament documents that have not been safeguarded by dogmatic formulations, when the 'heretical' abbreviations and distortions that have occurred throughout the history of the development of dogma are borne in mind? Even if the Nestorian Christology can only be regarded as really heretical if it is compared with the theology of the Alexandrian school, what Rahner has said in this context does not apply exclusively to the beginning of the twentieth century. In every case where, on the basis of a human reality, there are secondary and derived contents of the human consciousness, sometimes occurring in combination with each other, and these contents of consciousness or conscious attitudes are presented as correct Christological interpretations, then, Rahner has claimed, the result has always been a rationalistic and therefore heretical Christology.

In the light of the New Testament, our answer must be that Jesus' faith, as expressed in the New Testament, cannot be levelled down, despite its structural similarity with the faith of the Old Testament 'witnesses', as revealed in Heb 11. The concept, the 'faith of Jesus', can only be understood in the New Testament sense within the framework of a unique mission and as faithfulness to that mission. It is related to a special community with God and a special possession of the Pneuma. Because of this, it has nothing to do with any attempt to raise a man up though a 'combination of secondary contents of his consciousness' or with the fairly recent attempts to raise Jesus up as a model. Faith here does not point to an evaluation of this kind of combination as exemplary. It points rather to the offering of the whole man as a gift of himself. The faith of Jesus is therefore orientated towards the inclusion of those who imitate Jesus in his *pistis*. The idea of Jesus' faith, then, may also help to safeguard Jesus' humanity, without neglecting the reality of Jesus insofar as that is not purely human.

b. Those who support a dogmatic theology in which the Christology of Chalcedon is preserved are bound to ask, with good reason, for a clarification of certain aspects of this specification of Jesus as the believer. How, for example, could Jesus, as the one who initiated faith, also have been the originator of the faith of others? How can Jesus' uniqueness be safeguarded in spite of or in the context of statements about his faith? We would offer the following initial attempts at clarification.

It should not be forgotten that there is a close connection between the *eis ton theon* ('towards God') and the *ek tou theou* ('from God'), the latter taking precedence, of course. There is also the futuristic eschatological theme that is present in Jesus' faith (Heb 12. 2: Jesus as the 'perfecter of our faith'). Both this eschatological aspect and the possible conclusion drawn from the future for the present point most clearly to the uniqueness of Jesus as the one who believed, not only as a model for faith, but also as the originator of faith. Finally, the diversity of concepts of faith in the New Testament, as opposed to the classical definition of faith ('regarding as true'), should also be borne in mind.

c. We have demonstrated, then, that Jesus as the believer is possibly the most striking place on which to base the Christological and soteriological *eis ton theon* in the earthly life of Jesus.

In this connection, however, we are bound to show briefly why this *eis ton theon* is so fundamental for the image and experience of God within the Christological theo-logy. This image and experience of God only occur when there is a response to God's communication of himself in the man who comes to this image or has this experience of God, in other words, when the ascending line (the *eis ton theon*) is present in that man. As far as the Christological theology is concerned, what is of decisive importance is whether there is Christocentricity — in itself and in the soteriological sense — in that ascending line. A very important part is also played in this Christological theo-logy by the attitude of the risen Jesus. Can this be seen theocentrically as the permanence of the earthly Jesus' attitude of faith and obedience?

It is only when the *eis ton theon* is present in this way that Christology is open to a theology of the Trinity. This is because there cannot be a theology (or reality) of the Trinity without the permanence of the relationship in dialogue which is only present as the living permanence of the *eis ton theon* (the response) of the earthly Jesus.[124]

VI. Summary and conclusion: the relationship between the Christological theo-logy of the New Testament and the Old Testament theology of Yahweh

1. The structural similarity between the relationship with God in the post-paschal New Testament and the pre-paschal relationship with God on the part of Jesus and his disciples

The structural similarity between the themes outlined in the two sections, 5. III and 5. IV, can be characterized in the following way. On the one hand, it is clear from the relationship with God of the post-paschal Christian, who, like Paul, thinks that it is only possible to turn to God 'through Christ' and his Pneuma (in the sense in which God wants this orientation towards him). On the other hand, there are those aspects of the relationship with God on the part of Jesus himself and the disciples who followed him in Galilee and to Jerusalem. The outline of Jesus' own faith provided in the preceding section (5. V) should be an aid to understanding here, but the structural similarity between the contents of the two sections, 5 III and 5. IV, can only be fully understood if the transformation of the pre-paschal data and the permanence of Jesus' person and function in that transformation are recognized. It is only when this structural similarity is accepted that the question of the continuity between the Old and New Testaments (and the question of what is new in the New Testament) can be meaningfully answered.

2. Newness and continuity in the relationship between the Christological theo-logy of the New Testament and the Old Testament theology of Yahweh

a. What is new in the New Testament as opposed to the Old?

This question can be answered in a simple sentence — the new element is Jesus Christ.[125] Jesus did not simply do away with the old covenant or invalidate it. On the contrary, he enabled it to achieve its ultimate goal.

Faith in Christ does not reduce the monotheism of the Old Testament and its justifiably intense and emphatic confession: 'Hear, O Israel: the Lord (Yahweh) our God is one (Lord)' (Deut 6. 4-9). On the contrary, it renews it and makes it more radical. Christianity in the New Testament is in no sense a mystical religion that is isolated from the creative fulness and depth of the Old Testament life of faith. On the contrary, it is this same life of faith in its ultimate depth and experienced in a new way.

The misunderstanding that man's relationship with God 'through Christ' is a complication of the simple Old Testament relationship with God is probably based on a too individualistic concept of the relationship with God. Anyone who believes that the only uncomplicated relationship with God is the one between the individual soul and God is bound to think of any communal turning towards God as a disruption of this simplicity and to deny the theological and sociological structure — which is present by virtue of creation or transcendentally and anthropologically — at the basis of the communal (although, of course, unique) orientation of the Son and his disciples towards God. In this way, he also denies the constitutive element of the present life for God in Christ Jesus, through which Christians are prepared for eschatological fulfilment (which, moreover, has the same structure).[126]

The Christocentricity of the New Testament, then, does not imply any reduction of the dynamic dialogue structure of the Old Testament faith in God's promise. On the contrary, it is a confirmation or validation of the promise (Rom 15. 8). In it, the Pneuma bestows a share in the radical self-offering of the crucified Jesus and therefore community with Jesus, which raises man's relationship with God in dialogue to a qualitatively new level. The truth, made manifest in the cross, that 'God is love' (1 Jn 4. 8, 16) throws light on the way in which the Old Testament life of faith was not simply preserved, but made new and more intense in the New Testament.

b. In this way, Jesus was the *yehoshu'a* (Yahweh is salvation). This name can be accepted in its full New Testament significance, even if its occurance in Lk 1.31 and Mt 1.21 is not taken into account. The salvation that comes to man from Jesus, then, is that of community with this *yehoshu'a,* in other words, with the one who was not his salvation, but the salvation of Yahweh. The original revelation of God which contains everything in embryonic form in itself, was the revelation of the name of Yahweh in the Old Testament.[127] This does not God's communication of himself through a unique man, but is on the contrary open to the thrust of Yahweh's presence, even in the unsuspected manner of the event of Jesus.

Faith in Christ is not a Christocentricity in the sense of a subcutaneous monophytism, according to which the origin and the goal are only to be found in Christ. It is rather, in the sense in which it occurs in Heb 12.2, both the faith of Jesus (Jesus himself being seen in continuity with the Old Testament tradition of faith as theocentric) and the faith of Jesus' disciples in the Yahweh who became their Father through their community with Jesus.

c. What is new in the New Testament and the connection between the New and the Old Testaments can be understood in the light of the idea of the Pneuma. In the New Testament, because of the link with the unique Son of God, the Pneuma is the medium of direct contact with God, not only for individual bearers of the Spirit, but also for all believers in community with Jesus and, either potentially or intentionally, for all men.[128]

d. In the New Testament, the question of God is not a question as to whether God exists, but, as in the Old Testament, it is a question about the true God. In the New Testament too, there is the question about the destruction of the established image of God, that is, the idol, and the orientation of men's attention, which is no longer inhibited because of the destruction of the idol. This question is the same as the other question as to how it is possible for man to be or become open to the real will of this God and Father of Jesus.

3. Our position with regard to Buber's criticism of the New Testament concept of pistis

At the beginning of this chapter, we referred to Martin Buber's thesis, which was, within the problem discussed in this chapter, the most decisive and most clearly defined question presented in connection with the justification of faith in Christ. It is worth while recalling it here. Why was the faith of Judaism not sufficient for the one who called for the revelation in Jesus? Why does that faith not suffice, although it is — certainly in the form in which Buber has understood it and handed it on — something very great from which man can undoubtedly live? We have reached the point now where we can attempt to answer Buber's question.

a. Buber's thesis does not give adequate recognition to the abundance of promises contained in the Old Testament. It is not as though the Old Testament promises are seen as less important in New Testament Christianity than they are in Judaism. On the contrary, the promises made to the patriarchs are not simply fulfilled or done away with — they are irreversibly made valid and effective. The revelation of Jesus means that the promises of the old covenant point to something much greater than can be seen from the Old Testament alone. In this sense, Buber lacks the radical vision of the God of the old covenant as the one who is always greater that is the true view that emerges from the biblical message.

It is perhaps possible to say, rather boldly, that God took a risk by introducing this complication of the event of Christ into his history of salvation. What he risked was a reduction or even a distortion of the significance of the Old Testament and the possible continuation of the Old Testament in Judaism. He took the risk that there might be believers in Jesus in whom the relationship with and experience of God was less than, for example, in the Judaism of the Chasidim or Buber himself (although this form of Judaism could hardly have come about without the influence of Christianity).

Why, then, did God take this risk? He did so because he wanted to give the *perisson* or 'abundance', the measureless fulness of the Spirit (see Jn 3. 34 ff; see also, in Paul, Rom 5. 17, 20; 8. 31; 5. 5), since he wanted to make his communication of himself irreversible by making the man Jesus identical with his word of revelation.

b. The event of Jesus made faith in and community with God fundamentally so open to a constantly new transcendental experience that it is no longer possible to think of partnership with this God as a strictly legal relationship. 'Partnership' is, even in the New Testament, proclamation, as a participation in the sonship of the one Son, a genuine dialogue. Indeed, this participation brings about the state of partnership and the latter cannot be perverted so long as community with Jesus is preserved, since it is in Jesus that its non-pervertible character has become definitive and irreversible.[129]

The synthesis between *'emunah* and *pistis* (or rather, *pistis* as contact and *pistis* as acceptance[130]), that can be regarded as justified from the Christian point of view and also as factually present in the New Testament, can be found in the fact that the believer in the New Testament is included in the *'emunah* of Jesus and this acceptance takes place through the confession that God raised Jesus from the dead. This confession is a verbal consent given to community with Jesus.

c. In reply to the question as to why the faith of Judaism had to be transcended, we would point to the task of the people of God with regard to the world. God called the new man (the 'new Adam' of Rom 5. 12-21) and the new community united with him in service to fulfil his promises, that is, to carry out what he planned to do in preparation for the fulfilment of his Basileia. The service of the world, which is performed by the Church and which transcends the function of the Old Testament people of God, can only be given a Christological motivation.[131]

d. The ultimately decisive factor, which cannot be present without the revelation of Jesus, is community with Jesus or the crucified Jesus himself who was confirmed by God, as the one who made *paschein* or suffering possible as *sumpaschein* or suffering together with and orientated this *sumpaschein* towards *sumdoxasthenai* or being glorified together with (Rom 8. 17). This crucified Jesus can only in this context be the revelation of 'God is love' and can only in this context really overcome the world (1 Jn 4. 8, 16; 5. 4 ff).[132]

Buber provides an interpretion of Mk 9. 23 (Jesus as the believer)[133] which has many points of contact with the interpretation given above (5. V 3). His aim is to use this interpretation to support his thesis that Jesus' 'faith' was more closely related to the Old Testament *'emunah* than to the *pistis* of the New Testament. We are therefore bound to ask whether there is any difference between Buber's understanding and that of the second evangelist.

Mark stresses not only the idea of Jesus' uniqueness, but also, at least implicitly, a central idea which Buber has not seen or recognized. The prayer in faith, which the evangelist mentions in Mk 9. 23 and 11. 22 ff, must, if we are to grasp his understanding of Jesus' faith, be taken together with his central idea that Jesus gave his life for others (see, for example, Mk 10. 45) and that he called on others to imitate him and be associated closely with him. This is also illustrated in Jn 15. 5: 'Apart from me you can do nothing'. God has, as it were, ordained that there can be no relationship with God, as salvation, without the on who, through his dying, 'bears much fruit'

Finally, what is radically new and higher is the God who communicates himself to man in Jesus Christ and whose self-communication in this way can only be experienced in man's response, in other words, in community with Jesus himself, who gives himself to God in response and who responds to God's saving will. (This is, of course, theocentricity in an ascending line.) It is only in this way that we can approach an 'image of God' (which again and again has to be broken through by the power of the Pneuma) as presented by the New Testament, a relationship with God, a *koinonia* (1 Jn 1. 3) and community with this God.

6. Theses for new approaches to a contemporary Christology based on the New Testament

I. Introductory theses

1. Jesus' hunanity as a point of departure

It is no longer possible, as it was in the past, to take Jesus' divine nature as a point of departure in Christological thinking. It is more in accordance with contemporary anthropological thought to take Jesus' humanity as a point of departure. The New Testament can be of great help here, not only in the light it throws on the historical Jesus, but also in its statements about the risen Jesus.

This proposition is to some extent a prelude to all the theses that follow. Taking carefully into consideration the fundamental content of this proposition, then, it should be clear from the very beginning that the theses that follow ought, in the light of the New Testament way of thinking, to satisfy the demand that the point of departure in each case will be Jesus as man. The second proposition contained in this first thesis is also directly related to the other theses outlined in this chapter in taking Jesus' humanity as the point of departure, as is, for example, the thesis discussed in 6. III. 3 below.

2. The Church's doctrines and the New Testament — the problem of safeguarding the unique aspect of Jesus

At each period in the history of the Church, the unique aspect of Jesus as the absolute bringer of salvation and his unique relationship with God has to be safeguarded in formulae that are in accordance with the way of thinking that is current at the time.

For a long time, the formulae of the classical Christology fulfilled this function by means of a descendance theology, taking the divine nature of the Logos as its point of departure. Taken as a whole, the formulae used in this classical Christology formed a closed system, safeguarding — quite adequately for the period — the unique aspect of

Jesus. In view of the situation outlined above (6.I 1), however, we have to find a new way of safeguarding faith in Jesus as the absolute bringer of salvation and his special unity with God. New approaches to this type of Christology cannot be made, however, on the basis of the New Testament, by following the unhistorical method of ignoring the definitions made by the Church throughout history. They can only be made by maintaining a close and positive link with the Church's traditional teaching, while at the same time critically examining it. A matter of primary importance in these theses, then, is to point constantly to the relationship between the classical Christology and the new approaches to Christology that can be made on the basis of the New Testament.

This, then, in outline, is the problem of the relationship between the Church's official doctrines and the kerygma of the early Church, as recorded in the New Testament.

Our elucidation begins with the concluding statement in this first thesis, that is, the assumptions made in 6. I 1-2 confront us with a problem. This problem is concerned with the relationship between the Church's doctrines and the kerygma.

The official doctrines of the Church[2] are indisputably interwoven with the tradition of interpretation derived from the New Testament and the Church's consciousness of faith. This statement should not, however, make us lose sight of the priority and the mediation of what is primary on the one hand and the aim of the 'primordial datum', the earthly and exalted Jesus in his identiy, on the other. The Church's official teaching cannot have the same function as the New Testament. The relationship between them cannot be understood as part of a closely interconnected structure of elements of equal function and priority. On the contrary, what we have in the New Testament is the record of a dynamic procedure with its point of departure in the primordial datum that 'speeds on' (see 2 Thess 3. 1) and aims to seize hold of the world (see Rom 1. 16 ff).

a. The point of departure: a merging together of the New Testament and the modern ways of thinking

In the first chapter of this book, we discussed the relationship between the primordial datum, the New Testament, our modern consciousness of faith and our modern way of thinking under its aspect of a merging together of different spheres of thought, but did not consider the Church's official teaching in this context. This point of departure can be represented in the following way (Scheme C I):

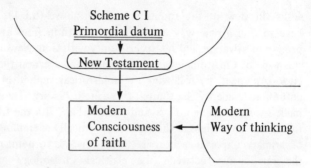

b. The function of the Church's doctrine within the fundamental structure of relationships in the merging together of different spheres of thought

In this context, it is clear that an important part is bound to be played by the question of the function of the official teaching of the Church and therefore the function of the Church itself, within the situation outlined in Scheme C I. Before we do this, however we can illustrate the function that the Church's doctrines have for our modern understanding of faith with the fundamental structure of relationships in a second scheme (C II).

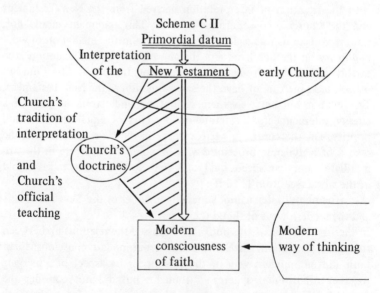

By not including the Church's doctrines' within the main line running from the primordial datum through the 'interpretation of the early Church (New Testament)' to the 'modern consciousness of faith', it is possible to show that the latter is directly related to the primordial datum and also to the kerygma of the early Church (New Testament), without which the primordial datum cannot be reached. On the other hand, it is also important to show that the Church's teaching has a corrective function which is primary, but which does not exclude functions. The arrows pointing from the primordial datum (and including the 'New Testament') and passing through 'Church's doctrines' to the 'modern consciousness of faith' also show that the latter bears the stamp of the 'Church's doctrines'.

The shading in the triangle formed by 'New Testament', 'Church's doctrines' and 'modern consciousness of faith' shows that the main line from the primordial datum to the 'modern consciousness of faith' cannot exist without the tradition of interpretation in the early Church. The 'Church's doctrines' have become the safeguard and to some extent also the written record of this tradition.

c. The significance of the Church's official doctrines and the primordial datum expressed in the New Testament for the unity of the Church. The significance of the Church's doctrines for the Church is only partly and by no means sufficiently indicated by the shaded area in Scheme C II. The 'Church's doctrines' do not simply have a corrective function, in other words, the task of warning the Church of a possible omission of nineteen thousand years of interpretation (or part of this tradition) in the Church and a consequent loss of continuity with the Church of the past. They also have a basic function in ensuring the unity of the Church today. This unity has also to be safeguarded in the outward form of expression of faith, even if we believe today that this safeguard only applies to the substance necessary for the unity of faith in Jesus. In any case, we have to take care to prevent legitimate theological pluralism (unity in plurality) from degenerating into a series of juxtaposed and unconnected theologies.

An attempt is made in the following Scheme (C III) to throw light on the significance of the 'Church's doctrines' and the primordial datum (that is, the earthly and exalted Jesus in his identity) for the unity of the Church.

Scheme C III

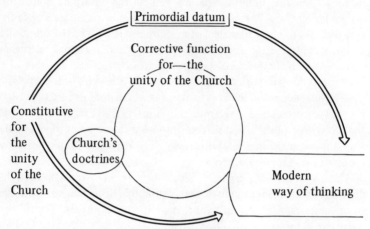

The corrective function for the unity of the whole Church's consciousness of faith is indicated in the Scheme by the lines from the 'Church's doctrines'. The whole Church does not, however, form a completely closed circle, but is open to the 'modern way of thinking' (not only the modern way of thinking exclusively within the Church) and to the great number of people who determine this way of thinking and are determined by it and at whose service the Church is.

The lines from the 'Church's doctrines', with their corrective function, do not, however, show what constitutes the unity of the Church. In the diagram, the tendency, as indicated by these single lines, of the 'Church's doctrines' to unity in faith is therefore enclosed within the stronger, double lines from the primordial datum. In this way, the dynamic movement from this datum is shown as constitutive for the Church's unity and as open to service of the world.

The factor that we have called the 'Church's doctrines' has the function of guaranteeing the possibility of communication between Christians within the unity of Jesus' community (as created by him), as a presupposition of the unity of the Church.

It is on the basis of the corrective function of such arrangements of words (which points to dangers to the unity of the Church) as necessary factors that the open reality of the 'whole Church' is at the same time constituted. This means that it is necessary to reach agreement about arrangements of words in questions of central importance to Christianity at all periods of history. (These will, of course, always include early formulae, as far as at least part of the Church is concerned.)

These arrangements of words can only have a corrective function if they are adapted to the language of the period. This certainly cannot be said of every individual arrangement of words used in every period of the Church's history. Despite the relative validity of these arrangements, because of the continuity of the Church (or its identity with itself with regard to faith throughout the centuries), they can be reformed precisely as arrangements of words.

d. The total structure of relationships within which the New Testament and the Church's doctrines are situated.

The arrangements of words and the interpretations reserved in earlier arrangements of words, however valuable they may be, do not form the dynamic centre of the Church's unity. This centre of unity is found in the 'primordial datum' that thrusts forward into the presence of the Church. That datum is the Pneuma-Kyrios.

This can be made clear in a combination of the previous Schemes. This combination, Scheme C IV, shows the lines from the 'primordial datum' both in the direction of a 'merging together of different ways of thinking' (C I and C II) and in the direction of the 'unity of the Church' (C III).

Total Scheme C IV

The sequence of theses 6. II. 1 to 6. IV

In the first place, we have to consider to what extent the individual statements of the classical Christology can be verified in the light of the New Testament (theses 6. II 1 to 7).

In the second place, we have to ask how the New Testament can guarantee the unique aspect of Jesus within this complex, in case the classical form of guarantee cannot be applied here (theses 6. II 3 to 5).

In the third place, the best guarantee here is to trace the Christological problem back to its central problem, as this is apparent in the light of the New Testament, and its bracketing together with eschatology, soteriology and ecclesiology (theses 6. III 1 to 6; eschatology, see 6. II 5).

Finally, we have to consider the possibility of a communication between a transcendental Christology and a biblical way of thinking in dialogue (thesis 6. IV).

II. The classical Christology and the critical function of the New Testament

1. The origin of the statements made in the New Testament about the pre-existence of Jesus

The New Testament statements about the pre-existence of Jesus and the corresponding statements made about his incarnation came about, in accordance with the intention of demonstrating the unique aspect of Jesus, on the basis of historically conditioned factors in the Hellenistic, that is, the Jewish and gentile Christian, world. In Judaeo-Christian Palestine, these statements about Jesus' pre-existence were not needed to safeguard the unique aspect of Jesus, nor could they be verified. They can be replaced by the concept of mission.

On the one hand, the protological statements made in the New Testament (that is, statements about Jesus' pre-existence, incarnation and mediation of creation) can be understood on the basis of Judaeo-Hellenistic speculation about personified and pre-existent wisdom. On the other hand, they can be seen as answers to the questions posed by those in the religious environment surrounding the gentile, Hellenistic Christian communities (that is, in an atmosphere of early gnostic thought and possibly also in the light of other philosophical systems containing a protology).

The New Testament statements about the pre-existence of Jesus made within this spiritual environment should not, however, be understood simply as (negative) safeguards. They were not made simply to safeguard the unique, saving significance of Jesus. They came about rather as the result of a positive intention on the part of the Christian community to preserve what it already possessed. They therefore form part of a theological complex in which Jesus' victorious power over the cosmos is positively demonstrated.

It is true that the ontic formulations of the classical descendance Christology were evolved from these New Testament statements. The safeguards, which are implied in these New Testament statements, were developed in the course of the history of dogma, but even in the latter they do not function simply as safeguards.

Nowadays, this kind of positive demonstration of Christ's power over the world, as recorded in the New Testament statements about his pre-existence, can only be understood as an attempt to safeguard the unique, saving significance of Jesus. This would at least seem to be its primary function in modern Christology.

In the statements made in the synoptic tradition, which belong to the Palestinian Jewish Christian world and which go back, in their essential form, to Jesus himself, the concept of Jesus' mission is implicit. This concept provides an adequate safeguard for the special saving significance of Jesus.

To take a Christology of the Son as a point of departure for a contemporary Christology of pre-existence would be a misunderstanding of the New Testament.[6]

As for Christ's mediation of creation, the fundamental text here is 1 Cor 8. 6, which has so often in the past been given a one-sided interpretation. This text is not simply concerned with the mediation of creation. What is expressed in it is Christ's mediation of universal salvation. This is in accordance with the fundamental principle that the end also determines — precisely as the end — the beginning.

Paul combines both the original concept of mission and the initial approach to an understanding of pre-existence. The concept of the Son's mission cannot, however, be unambiguously based, in Gal 4. 4 and Rom 8. 3, on a mission derived from pre-existence, if Paul did not explicitly refuse to allow his Hellenistic communities to believe in pre-existence.[7]

2. Logos and incarnation in John

In the fourth gospel, as the New Testament point of departure for these terms, Logos and incarnation do not have the same meaning as they do in the classical Christology. The gnostic scheme of the descending and ascending revealer is broken through by the inner orientation of the incarnation. This is orientated towards the death on the cross. As in the New Testament as a whole, there is no incarnation in the gospel of John that is isolated from soteriology and regarded as purely Christological.

a. The fourth evangelist used the concepts of Logos and incarnation — the first of which (Logos) occurs in the hymn that is found in a changed form in Jn 1 — in his reinterpretation of the fundamental post-paschal kerygma of the death and resurrection of Jesus. Like the other New Testament authors, he is not primarily interested in an incarnation that is isolated from the cross and resurrection as central to soteriology and regarded as purely Christological. This is true even though this way of regarding the incarnation that came about at a later period in the history of dogma also tends in the direction of a soteriological aspect in the sense of the union between divinity and humanity.

b. Scheme D below indicates the difference between the gnostic scheme of the descending and ascending revealer and the Johannine incarnation of the Logos as the revealed Word.

Scheme D

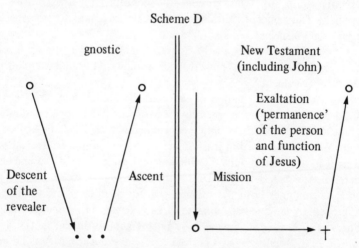

According to the gnostic or early gnostic way of thinking, the function of the revealer was, generally speaking, to redeem the sparks of light (the souls) that had been banished into matter by giving them knowledge (*gnosis*) of their membership of the world of light. This revealer had no real earthly human history. This can be seen in the tendency in the gnostic texts to ascribe the real death of Jesus on the cross not to the revealer himself, but to a subordinate figure representing him or to explain this death as unreal and only apparent. The three dots at the bottom of the Scheme on the gnostic side show that nothing concrete or earthly took place in the revealer's existence. According to the mythology of gnosticism, the revealer, who was above in the world of light, returned unchanged to this place above, because he had never really been below.

According to the New Testament (including the gospel of John), the mission came from the open space at the 'level' of God or from the dynamic power of the Pneuma. The man Jesus, who was given this mission, was, of course, not regarded as pre-existent in the temporal sense. The line of this mission points to the culmination of this mission in Jesus' experience of his death on the cross and also in God's confirmation of this way in the resurrection of exaltation which constitutes the permanence of Jesus' person and function. This brings the ultimate goal of Jesus' way above with God. The starting point of the line of his mission was above in this sense. The man Jesus is thus seen, in the New Testament (and John) as the absolute revealer who passed through a human fate and death as a real man.

c. Even apparently gnostic sounding statements such as 'I came from the Father and have come into the world; again, I am leaving the world and going to the Father' (Jn 16. 28) should be understood in this way. They provide a re-interpretation of what the synoptic tradition presents as a unique, saving mission, but do it in early gnostic language.

The statement in Jn 10. 17 ff (the aim of the Father's 'commandment' to the Son whom he sent out of his 'pre-existence' was that the Son should 'lay down his life' in order to 'take it up again') is in accordance with the early kerygma of the fulfilment of the Father's will as far as the death on the cross and the resurrection from that death, if it goes beyond the early tradition to the point where the 'taking up again of life' is finally (as the goal or end) linked with the 'laying down of life'.[8]

d. In the fourth gospel, then, the unique, saving significance of Jesus is constituted by the death on the cross, as confirmed by God. This is the case in John not only in the factual order of salvation, but also — in analogy with the idea of transcendence — because the world is as it is. It is, in other words, according to John, darkness and the light of absolute love could only be revealed by the self-offering of a man whom God had made his own.

3. Safeguarding the unique aspect of Jesus in the New Testament

The New Testament contains Christological statements that, quite apart from the protological statements, adequately safeguard the unique aspect of Jesus (non-titular Christology of the synoptic tradition; Paul: power of the Pneuma, *eikon*; John: Christology of the revealer)

a. As far as the non-titular Christology of the synoptic tradition is concerned, the unique significance of Jesus is safeguarded in an open but extremely dynamic way. For example, Lk 12. 8 ff can be compared with Lk 10. 21 ff., in which Jesus 'rejoices' in the Spirit. The vitality and dynamism of Jesus' faith is expressed in such statements about what Jesus does at least as strongly as or even more strongly than (or perhaps in a more original way than) in the later titular formulae.[9]

b. Paul's epistles contain a number of statements about the unique aspect of Jesus unity with God and his saving significance. These include, for example, his preaching about Jesus as Kyrios, his use of the word *eikon* and the title 'Son of God' for Christ and his statement that the risen Jesus possesses the Pneuma of God. Paul's safeguarding of the unique character of Jesus is also clear from his statements about Jesus' pre-existence (even though these are very open and cannot be interpreted temporally) and his use of the particular passage in the hymn in which Christ is addressed 'in the form of God' (Phil 2. 6). These statements about the unique significance of Jesus are still important safeguards, even though there is no preaching about God in Rom 9. 5, as opposed to a current view in Paul's time.

c. In John, the incarnation is much more closely linked with the idea of revelation and only loosely associated with that of creation, with the result that we have to look for it, not in Paul, but in Jn 1. 1 ff, within the framework of the hymn about the Logos taken over by the fourth evangelist. In contrast to the statements about Jesus' pre-existence, the Christology of the revealer is of primary importance in John. The statements about the pre-existence have, as opposed to the idea of revelation, a serving function. In Paul, the term *eikon*, which is used in the theology of creation, also has a similar part to play.

d. One aspect of our problem should not be forgotten. The man Jesus of Nazareth, with his individual qualities and fate, was the absolute bringer of salvation. Within the framework of a Christology based on the Old Testament monotheism of faith in Yahweh (which is preserved fundamentally in the New Testament), this fact can only be seen as an establishment. In the context of the Christological concept of mission, this establishment as a free act on God's part, is very similar to the 'establishment' of the mission of any Old Testament prophet. This establishment is related to the permanence of Jesus' person and function, insofar as only he received the fulness of the Pneuma.

4. The meaning of the concept 'pre-existence'

Pre-existence means that God is able to want to communicate himself in this very intensive way, that is, through the revelation of Jesus. He is Yahweh in the sense in which this name can be understood in the light of God's communication of himself in Jesus.

If we reason on the basis of Paul's theology, the pre-existence of Jesus is really that of the Pneuma (as the power of God requiring self-communication), since it is his possession of the Pneuma that constitutes the unique aspect of Jesus. A parallel can be found here in the Christology of the Logos (or revealer) in the fourth gospel.

a. The concept of pre-existence and the biblical idea of God

The meaning of the concept of pre-existence can be understood in the light of the biblical idea of God. In the Bible, God is not Aristotle's 'unmoved mover', but Yahweh. He is the God who is there and who comes, the God who is orientated towards self-communication and the God who has his *ru'ah* (his Spirit) as the power of his revelation of himself.

The doctrine of pre-existence cannot be understood in the light of an isolated Christology. It can only be fully understood on the basis of a Christological theo-logy. The Son's mission does not mean that the one who was to be sent existed as such before he was sent. In other words, we do not have to assume that he was pre-existent in the temporal sense. In my view, the Son's mission may imply, in the Pauline sense and in the sense in which it is used in the rest of the New Testament, the creation of the man Jesus. Here, we have, however, to bear in mind that Jesus' mission (or commission) was initiated by God in different ways according to the different levels of tradition. At a very early level of tradition, it was apparently connected, according to the fourth gospel, with Jesus' baptism and then, quite consistently, made earlier.

Pre-existence is, for modern theologians, a cipher without any real content for the fact that the possibility of an absolute bringer of salvation or a self-communication on the part of God (in this particular sense which qualitatively transcends everything else) must be based in the divine plan and indeed in God himself. As a logical consequence, pre-existence is inevitable. This is also the consequence that led to the doctrine of the Trinity, since — if the unique significance of Jesus has to be recognized and safeguarded — it is necessary to have a theology of the Trinity that can be united with faith in Yahweh.

Should the idea of pre-existence perhaps be differently represented? This might be expedient and even possible from the point of view of pastoral theology, but as long as the relationship between God and the world is expressed in temporal categories — and it will always be necessary to do this because every relationship is historical — it will not be possible to avoid thinking about the traditional concept of pre-existence and considering its function as a safeguard.[11]

In this question of pre-existence, the soteriology of the New Testament (that is, Paul, especially the letters to the Colossians and the Ephesians, and the gospel of John) must also be taken into account. The pre-existence of Jesus is related to the pre-existence of those whom God wishes to save through Jesus, that is, those whom he chose in Christ before the beginning of the world and who were predestined according to his will (see Eph 1. 4 ff; Rom 8. 28).[12] The unique character of the mission of the absolute mediator of salvation, which is founded in God himself, is in no way reduced by this pre-existence of those who have been predestined and chosen for salvation. Jesus' uniqueness (and at the same time the relationship between his pre-existence and the predestination of his own) is present in the concept of God's communication of himself, which is a consequence of the sending of the absolute mediator of salvation.

b. Jesus' pre-existence in Paul and John

i. The second proposition in this thesis (6. II 4) says that it is the Pneuma, as the dynamic power of God acting in the direction of his communication of himself that makes the absolute bringer of salvation, and therefore the idea of pre-existence, possible in Paul's theology.

Despite appearances, the Christology (of the revealer) found in John's teaching about the Logos is closely parallel. The Logos of Jn 1. 1-1-14 is not in accordance with the history of traditions, but is, as far as its content is concerned, identical with the Paraclete in the farewell discourses, which is, in turn, identical with the Pneuma in the whole teaching of the gospel. The Johannine equation, Jesus is the Logos (that is, the revealed Word of God made concrete in a historical man), and the other statement made in the prologue, namely that this Logos is *theos* (that is, the revealer is divine and is united in a unique way with God) are parallel with the Pauline equation, the Lord is the Pneuma (2 Cor 3. 17; see also 1 Cor 15. 45).

In the hymn that forms the prologue to the fourth gospel, then, the Logos is called *theos*. This means that he is loved by the Father, has a special unity with him and can receive and give 'without measure' (see Jn 3. 34 ff) the Pneuma, through the Father's love.

According to John, the Son is pre-existent in the Father's love and 'glory' (see Jn 17. 5, 24). It is clear from the context of Jn 17 that this idea is very close to that of the Pneuma. The love with which the Father loved Jesus (see Jn 17. 26) is probably identical in the evangelist's understanding of the situation with the Pneuma. Even more important is the text in Jn 7. 39, ' . . . for as yet the Pneuma had not been given, because Jesus was not yet glorified'. According to this statement, the Pneuma was not communicated until Jesus had been glorified and exalted. This is not an isolated statement. It expresses a constant theological principle of the fourth gospel.[13] This, then, is further evidence of the fact that the author of the gospel did not take over the gnostic myth of the descending and ascending revealer, but broke through that myth and the related false concept of pre-existence applied to the concrete revealer. In gnostic mythology, the revealer would not have to wait until the coming of the 'hour' (his death on the cross, his resurrection and his ascension to the Father) before giving the Pneuma.

ii. It is, of course, possible to object that the consequence of this New Testament datum would be, not a Trinity, but a 'Binity'. We shall discuss this problem more fully below (6. II 7), but in the meantime it has to be pointed out that there is no polarity between a theology of the Pneuma and a theology of the Logos or the Son of God which might necessarily result in a doctrine of only two modes of subsistence. It is in any case clear from the Pauline Christology of the Pneuma and, in a different way, from the Johannine Christology that, according to both authors, God committed himself. God's raising Jesus by his Pneuma and making him a 'life-giving Pneuma' (1 Cor 15. 45) means that God to some extent invested his Pneuma in this man Jesus as the power of his divinity and as his own vitality. The statement 'God is love' (1 Jn 4. 8, 16) is of central importance and could only be made as a result of the kerygma of Jesus' offering of himself. It can be interpreted, in the sense of a Christological theo-logy, as God's being self-offering of a pouring out of himself as an infinity that always remains constant. The text that we have already mentioned in this context in the gospel of John (jn 3. 34 ff) can be similarly interpreted.

iii. The idea of the incarnation — insofar as this is connected with the concept of the Logos (or revealer) — is only one of the two possible ways of expressing God's communication of himself that we have to consider here. The other is the 'new creation' mentioned, for example, in 2 Cor 5. 17. Although the text refers to Christians who are 'in Christ', what is implied is that Christ himself was originally the 'new creation', that he is, in other words, the unique *ktisis* in whom what was created in the first creation (Gen 2) in a mediated way is now radically created in an absolute way.[14]

5. Christology in the unity of eschatology and protology

The protological statements in the New Testament Christology (pre-existence, the mediation of creation and so on) can be understood as safeguarding projections of eschatology. According to Paul, the mission of the Son is the sending of the one who is able to draw others into his own relationship with God as a Son (that is, into the fulfilled *huiothesia* or sonship; see Rom 8. 29).

What has to be emphasized even more strongly than the idea of the unity existing between God and man is man's being made in the image of God and God's plan to bring what is made in his image, through the latter's community with Jesus, to fulfilment in the eschaton.

As opposed to the classical Christology, which does not overlook the question of time, a new Christological approach is bound to take into account the unity of present and future eschatology.

a. The problem

From the historical point of view, the eschatological Christological statements are primary and the protological statements have been derived from them. The Hellenistic Christian communities had the intention, when the protological kerygma was developed, of proclaiming the lordship of Jesus as Kyrios over the world and the beginning of his rule with the Church's mission.

These ideas cannot, however, be taken over unquestioningly and applied to modern theological thinking. We are bound to ask what significance the protological statements in the New Testament can have for us today. The answer that suggests itself is that they should be understood as safeguarding projections of eschatology. The word 'projection' is not used here in the psychological sense. By projection we mean that the content of the eschatological kerygma is projected back, in a special kind of theological process, into the *proton* or beginning. The underlying theological principle has been defined as 'what applies at the end must also determine the beginning'.[15]

The concept 'safeguarding projections' may, however, give rise to a theological misunderstanding, namely that there is no basis in the reality of God in what is expressed in this protology or that there is no pre-existence in the real sense. The answer to this problem is that the protological statements made in the New Testament have a basis of reality so long as the pre-existent God — his pre-existent Pneuma and his thrust to communicate himself that was already present in embryo in the old covenant[16] — is a reality. In other words, the New Testament protology is real if this God is not a God of the philosophers, but Yahweh.

b. Paul's eschatology as a model

The most appropriate text is Rom 8. 29, which contains a statement about the eschatological aim of God's work of salvation and God's protological knowledge in advance. The Son's mission is directed towards his bringing the 'many brethren' whom he was to gain into the relationship with God which he himself has as the 'image' (*eikon*) and the Son of God.

Eikon is a concept which is related to the theology of creation (see 1 Cor 11. 7; 15. 49; cf. Gen 1. 27) and which is of great importance in Paul's Christology.[17] Christ as the *eikon* of God is the risen Christ who is fully determined by the Pneuma and, as such, the fulfilment of what was established in the first creation, qualitatively transcending all expectations. This Christological concept of the *eikon* is also seen, in Paul's theology, in the light of the future eschatology. In other words, the end is seen as the aim of the beginning.

A similar teaching is contained in the parallel between Adam and Christ. It is clear from the 'last Adam' (1 Cor 15. 45) as the 'life-giving Pneuma' what the aim of the 'first Adam' at the original act of creation was. Paul is thinking ahead here to the eschaton and from the eschaton back to the beginning again. He is, in other words, thinking forward from the plan of the God who wants this fulfilment and back from the eschatological fulfilment in the future. It is not difficult to trace Paul's reasoning here. The Pneuma, which determines the present for Christians, is, in Paul's teaching, in the vitality of the Christian existence that makes it possible, the *arrabon* or earnest-money for the fulfilment at the end and at the same time the power that prepares those who are in community with Christ for this ultimate fulfilment and finally brings it about in the general resurrection.

Paul also relates this idea, in which the beginning is seen from the fulfilment at the end, to Christ himself, for example, in 1 Cor 8. 6. The realization 'through Christ' of the entire saving event that comes from God is the protological counterpart in Paul's teaching to his eschatological statement in 1 Cor 15. 28. Despite Paul's different terminology and way of thinking, this is certainly the place in the New Testament where the structure of the eschatology of Jesus, according to which the kingdom of God, which is to be fulfilled in the future, is thrusting forward into this present era, is best preserved.

If we compare Paul's Christology of the Pneuma with the classical Christology of the Church, it is clear that the first provides us with the possibility of going beyond the concepts of the classical teaching and of giving content and meaning to the protological statements on the basis of Paul's statements about eschatological fulfilment. As a descendance Christology, the classical teaching is determined by a clearly protological approach and, together with its formally correct, but nonetheless problematical central concept of the incarnation or the divine Logos, is transcended by the biblical idea of a *huiothesia* orientated towards the future and needing a *huios* or Son who is both *eikon* and Pneuma.

The connection between God and humanity, that is, God's communication of himself to man, can, in the light of the concept of *huiothesia*, be seen in terms of personal dialogue. This way of regarding the self-communication of God avoids other possibly erroneous ways that may result from a Christology based on an abstract understanding of divinity and humanity. The statements about pre-existence, then, act as a safeguard in modern Christology that this man Jesus is a Son in such a way that he can include all other men in his original relationship as a Son.

Objectivizing statements made *a posteriori* about the eschatological fulfilment (such as that made, for example, in Rom 8 29) are bound to lead to an extension of the transcendental approach. This means that anthropology must be more open to the eschatological future.[18]

c. Present and future Christology

The present aspect of Christology should not be overemphasized to the extent that the future element is thrust into the background. This would be a narrowing down and a distortion of the content of the classical Christology, which is derived from the protological statements of the New Testament and of those statements themselves. This is what emerges at least from a brief glance at New Testament eschatology and Christology as reflected in the Pauline letters, where the present and the future aspects form a dynamic unity. The same conclusion can be drawn from what is presumably the earliest post-paschal Christology.[19]

This tension between the already present and the future that has not yet come was therefore present at the very beginning of the history of Christianity, although the 'not yet' was so thrusting at the beginning and the eyes of the early Christians were so firmly fixed on the Jesus whom they expected to come as the Son of Man and Judge that the 'already present' was for the most part only implicit. This tension should be preserved even now in Christology. It should be discernible in all contemporary approaches to the subject.

The aspect of time is in no sense overlooked in the classical Christology of descendance, but despite this there is a tendency to stress the present both in this classical Christology and in the classical ecclesiology of the 'Church triumphant'.

Rahner's transcendental Christology may appear at first sight to be too firmly fixed to the present, but it is in fact open to the future. As far as I can see, the evolving approach is included within this transcendental Christology in a way that is quite justifiable in the light of the New Testament. It is not in any way limited to an immanently progressive humanization and it does not result in a diminution of the dynamic power of God thrusting towards absolute fulfilment.[20] The future aspect of the tension between present and future in the New Testament must, however, be more strongly stressed and its importance for Christology today must also be emphasized. This must be done if only for the sake of the connection between Christology and the biblical proclamation of the God who works for the fulfilment of his kingdom.[21]

The 'present' Christology of the gospel of John and the epistles to the Ephesians and the Colossians should not be played off against the unity of the present and the future in the Christology found in the synoptic gospels and the other letters of Paul. This is because there is no real discontinuity, but a legitimate re-interpretation of a dynamic unity that has been proclaimed from the very beginning, perhaps with the help of other means of expression. In the case of Paul's letters to the Ephesians and the Colossians, the idea of 'growing towards Christ' is equivalent to the future statements in the other Pauline letters.[22]

6. Formalized statements in the classical Christology and the New Testament proclamation of the exaltation Jesus

The classical Christology expresses in formalized statements what can 'only' be found in the New Testament in the proclamation of the risen Jesus, his relationship with God and his present and future eschatological function.

According to theses 6. II 1 and 5 above, the protological statements cannot be used as counter-evidence. These and other statements about Jesus' sovereignty of divinity have a different theological structure from the doctrine of the communication of idioms, which is an extreme and easily misunderstood mode of expression for the doctrine of the hypostatic union. There is no point of contact in the New Testament for the *communicatio idiomatum*.

The correlation that is closest in any new approach to the classical Christology, but at the same time based on the Pauline model, is a Christology of the Pneuma.

a. Formalized statements and the proclamation of the exaltation
This Thesis (6. II 6) is the real corner-stone of the first group of theses (6. II 1-7). The word 'only' in the first sentence does not imply a diminution. On the contrary, it indicates that the primordial datum — the exalted Kyrios who is, in his person and function, the permanence of the person and function of the Jesus of history — can be verified and is of supreme importance. It is, then, 'only' if this is the case that the preceding theses will be in agreement with the traditional teaching of the Church and at the same time perhaps helpful in leading us forward.

The objection may be raised that to stress the exaltation in this way may lead to a reduction of interest in the historical person of Jesus. (This has already happened to some extent in Protestant theology.[23]) In reply to this objection, we may say that the personal identity of the exalted and the earthly Jesus is envisaged and certainly not left out of account in this approach. If this is done, a statement made about Jesus living now will not be wrongly interpreted as a making present of the kerygma of the Jesus of history, but regarded primarily as a statement about a 'person' who makes a relationship with God in dialogue (in the biblical sense) possible.

Looking at the Jesus who is living now in the present and is personally identical with the earthly and crucified Jesus should be called an *articulus stantis et cadentis Christologiae*, since it is only when Jesus is viewed with this presupposition in mind that he can have a unique, saving significance. The inevitable result of limiting ourselves to look simply at the historical Jesus is that Jesus is levelled down to the category of an important prophet or rabbi.

On the other hand, it is not possible to speak in Christology of a God-man existing from eternity, because such a God-man did not exist before the incarnation or the mission.[24] What can, however, be stated in Christology is the saving significance which the man Jesus, who was confirmed by God when he was raised by him from the dead and was established in his transformed function by the Pneuma, has now and in the future eschatological fulfilment. What we have, then, to safeguard is the Christology of the exalted Jesus.

b. The *communicatio idiomatum*

This way of expressing Christological properties is, in the light of the New Testament, very open to misunderstanding and would seem, moreover, to be a mere repetition of earlier formulae or at the most a reinterpretation of these formulae. We are also bound to ask in this context whether it is possible, on the basis of the New Testament, to verify a positive presentation of this Christological teaching and an affirmation that the experience in faith of God's unique presence in Jesus cannot take place without a *communicatio idiomatum*.

Although we cannot undertake a detailed investigation here, we may assume that there are not any statements in the New Testament containing a communication of properties or at least no statements that have the structure of such a communication. This is because there is nothing in the New Testament that ignores the concrete person of Jesus. There is no abstract divine being in the New Testament, whereas the point of departure for the communication of properties in the classical Christology is the (Trinitarian) *essentia*, that is, an 'essence' abstracted from the person of Jesus. This essence is, moreover, also conceived as different from the person (or mode of subsistence) of Jesus.

It can be verified that the Christological statements made in the New Testament that are quoted in support of this theory do not have the structure of a communication of properties. There are several New Testament statements about Jesus' sovereignty which safeguard his unique aspect and his divinity, but which are not structured as communications of properties. This is particularly noticeable in the case of those texts which the Catholic dogmatic theologican Diekamp[25] quoted as providing the basis. These are Rom 8. 32; 1 Cor 2. 8; Acts 20. 28; 1 Jn 3. 16; Jn 3. 13; 8. 58. The concepts 'Son of God' (Rom 8. 32) and 'Kyrios of glory' (1 Cor 2. 8) are not statements indicating the mode of subsistence of the Trinity. The 'Son of Man' (Jn 3. 13) is not a way of indicating Christ's human nature in the sense in which this term is used in the classical Christology. Acts 20. 28 means that God obtained the community with the blood 'of his own', that is his own Son.[26] In Jn 3. 16, not God, but Jesus is the subject of the sentence.

Even the New Testament statements which Diekamp did not cite and according to which the Logos ᴜ. Jesus could perhaps be called 'God' (these were more suitable for Diekamp's purpose) do not provide any basis for the *communicatio idiomatum*. According to Jn 1. 1, 'and the Word was God'. 'Logos' here is not the second mode of subsistence of the Trinity, but God's revealed word. Thomas' words in Jn 20. 20, 'My Lord and my God' attribute to Jesus a unity with God in the sense of Jn 14. 9 ff, that is, that the one who sees him sees the Father, in other words, that Jesus is transparent to the Father as his revealer.

The only text in which Jesus may perhaps be called God is 1 Jn 5. 20: 'This is the true God and eternal life'. This sentence, however, cannot simply be applied only to Jesus. It can also be applied to the one previously named as 'true' and therefore it is the Father who is meant in 1 Jn 5. 20b. The statement refers to the Father 'in whom' we are by being in his Son, Jesus Christ. It also refers to the Father and Son in the usual Johannine orientation.[27]

Finally, there is no statement in Rom 9. 5 that Jesus is God. All that this text contains is a doxology to the Father which forms a conclusion to the preceding argument. Together with the doxology to the Father in Rom 11. 33-36, this text forms an inclusion or framework for the argument in Rom 9. 6-11. 32.[28]

The *communicatio idiomatum* can have the function of safeguarding faith in the unique aspect of Jesus as the absolute bringer of salvation and precisely for this reason it may not be suitable for all generations of Christians, because this way of expressing Jesus' 'divinity' has no structural basis in the New Testament.

The doctrine of the *communicatio idiomatum* was developed in a particular spiritual climate or context, in which the classical Christology with its ontic categories was current. Before looking for a basis for the communication of properties in the New Testament, then, the protological statements that are a pre-condition for this doctrine should be examined, their New Testament meaning should be checked and it should be established whether they are historically conditioned.

It is, then, only in this particular spiritual context that the doctrine of the communication of properties could have been a legitimate and possibly necessary safeguard for faith in Jesus. Outside this spiritual climate, the only one in which this doctrine is intelligible, it can only lead to a monophysitic misunderstanding. It is also undoubtedly misleading for anyone who is not able to follow this way of thinking easily.

It is therefore hardly possible to claim, as Rahner has done, that the whole doctrine of the hypostatic union is contained in this teaching or that experience in faith of God's unique presence in Jesus cannot be achieved without a *communicatio idiomatum*. This claim cannot be made as a necessary condition or to protect the privileged position of the statements made in the New Testament about Jesus' sovereignty.

In fact, the doctrine of the *communicatio idiomatum* is nowadays only understood by a relatively small circle of specialists in dogmatic theology (and especially the history of that theology). It is no longer used in catechetics or in homilies and in these and related spheres other ways have to be found for safeguarding the unique significance of Jesus. We have already tried to provide stimuli for this and further suggestions are made in the theses that follow (6 III 1-6).

c. The function of Paul's Christology of the Pneuma
In the Pauline Christology based on the Pneuma, which is dominated by this thinking about the risen and exalted Jesus, there is a complete safeguard of everything that the classical Christology aimed to safeguard. Paul, however, provides these safeguards in a different way. There are no formalized, ontic statements, but rather a dynamic form of expression concerned with the power of God active through the Pneuma-Kyrios and orientated towards the community of believers and the world.[29]

7. Christology and the doctrine of the Trinity
Since the doctrine of the Trinity only came about as a result of the revelation of Jesus, a pre-incarnatory doctrine of the Trinity can, in accordance with the constant character of the New Testament Christologies, only be interpreted in a post-incarnatory sense. New approaches to the doctrine of the Trinity are also conditioned by new approaches in Christology.

a. The problem: 2 Cor 3. 17 ('The Kyrios is the Pneuma') as a point of departure
It should be clear from the preceding sections and especially from Scheme D and the accompanying elucidation (6. II 2b above) that a pre-incarnatory doctrine of the Trinity (in other words, an attempt to formulate a doctrine of God as a Trinitarian doctrine orientated towards God's communication of himself in the man Jesus, but without that man and therefore without the 'God-man') can be interpreted in the light of a post-incarnational doctrine (that is, a teaching in which the dialogue between God and the man Jesus or the 'God-man' plays a part).[30]

A number of new approaches to a theology of the Trinity closely linked to Christology will be found in several of the theses outlined above (6. II 1-6) and below (6. III 1-3). The problem that is raised in thesis 6. III 1 provided the stimulus for the central chapter 5 on the New Testament. The New Testament basis for a theology of the Trinity is discussed more fully in that thesis.

We are, however, bound to ask here how any doctrine of the Trinity can be maintained and safeguarded, when the New Testament appears to point less to a Trinity and more to a 'Binity'.

The theologian (including the New Testament scholar) has to ask a methodological question here — will his study be orientated more in the direction of the Church's doctrines or more towards the New Testament (in the sense indicated in Scheme C, towards the New Testament including the Church's tradition of interpretation and the Church's doctrines as a corrective)?

If the theologian decides in favour of the New Testament approach, we can then ask him whether he will not perhaps run the risk of prematurely cutting himself off from the Church's doctrine of the Trinity. I. Hermann, for example, claimed that Paul's teaching contained no real doctrine of the Trinity.[31] Rahner's reply to this was that it was only possible to make this claim if one's point of departure was a very primitive doctrine of the Trinity.[32] Hermann's one-sided, distorted view was clearly the result of a defective knowledge of dogmatic theology and a serious failure to understand the findings of exegesis. It is worth looking a little more closely at this example.

Hermann uses the image of the sun and its rays in his elucidation of the central Pauline text 'the Kyrios is the Pneuma' (2 Cor. 3. 17). 'I experience the Kyrios as the Pneuma in the way in which I experience the sun and its rays', Hermann says. 'The Pneuma is the unceasing radiation of the exalted Lord. This radiation affects man. He observes the power of radiation — the Pneuma — and knows that it is the Lord, just as he observes the warmths of the sun's rays and knows that it is the sun'.[33] The structure of relationships that Hermann finds in Paul is illustrated in the following Scheme E I.

Scheme E I

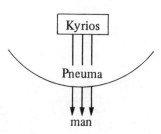

b. God, Kyrios and Pneuma

This scheme (which is only provisional) and Hermann's thesis only partly embrace the Pauline datum. According to the words of 2 Cor 3. 17, this picture of the Kyrios and the Pneuma is justified. In it only the Kyrios and the Pneuma are seen as active. Hermann therefore limited himself to these two factors and, of course, the third factor, man as affected by the power of radiation from the Kyrios. He did this mainly because of an error in exegesis. Although he dealt in great detail with the passage preceding 2 Cor 3. 17, he neglected to examine the following passage, in which the relationship between Jesus and the Father is of paramount importance, especially because of the concept used (*eikon*). In fact, Hermann's image of the sun and its rays can only be applied correctly if the Father is included in it. Hermann compared the Kyrios only to the sun. This comparison would hardly have been possible for Paul, who would have seen the Father as the (original) sun, the Son as the ray or rays coming from the Father (in the sense of the *eikon* or 'image') and the Pneuma as the brightness[34] or warmth[35] which the sun produces by its rays.[36]

This image of the sun, its rays and its warmth (or brilliance) illustrating the theology of the Trinity is not quite sufficient. The Pneuma is not simply the medium in which God affects the believer through Christ. It is above all the creative power of God himself.[37]

The following Scheme E II is therefore more appropriate, since it shows not only the Father as *theos* (as the origin of the structure of relationships), but also the Pneuma as the creative power of God. What is more, the Pneuma also appears not only between the Kyrios and man, but also — and primarily — with the origin, that is, *theos*.

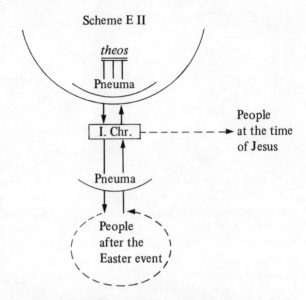

Scheme E II

In accordance with the theology of Paul, who stressed not only the *ek tou theou*, but also the *eis ton theon*, a double line is shown. On the one hand, the line leading from the God who is powerful in the Pneuma through I. Chr.[38] points to people in the period following the Easter event and this is made possible by the Pneuma given abundantly to the Kyrios by the Father. The line then points from the people living after the Easter event through their experience of the Pneuma, in which they enter into a relationship with the Kyrios Christ as the mediator, back to the Father as the origin of the Pneuma. The dotted line in the diagram encircling 'people after the Easter event' indicates the need for the line coming from *theos* as 'absolute love' to include men as well so that it can then return through Christ to the Father.

It should be noted that the two lines from *theos* to I. Chr. and from I. Chr. back to *theos* are not simply the beginning of the one leading to 'people after the Easter event' or the continuation of the one coming from those people. They also have an importance of their own, showing the unique relationship in dialogue between the Kyrios and the Father. The relationship between the Father and the Son, who wants to include the 'many brethren' in his huiothesia through the Pneuma, which he 'is', is in itself a theology of the Trinity, both in the ecumenical and in the immanent sense.

It is therefore obvious that there are only two 'persons' here in the

New Testament sense of 'centres of action' — the *theos pater* and the 'man' Jesus. This relationship in dialogue is trinitarian insofar as God is, through the Pneuma as his own personal potentiality, is of such a kind that this relationship and its soteriological effect are possible. The relationship between the two, God and the man Jesus (as any man) could not, of course, constitute a Trinity, which could only come about (as a formalized safeguard) by this relationship being placed, through the gift of the fullness of the Pneuma, at a completely new level that could not be attained by man and that is contrasted with the relationship between God and any other man.

c. A possible approach to the real difference between the second and third modes of subsistence of the Trinity in the light of Pauline and Johannine theology

It is obviously that the real difference that exists between the God who affirms himself in Christ and the God who communicates the central depths of his own existence in the Pneuma must be made clearer.[39] If this is not done, the foundation is removed from the doctrine of the Trinity in the traditional sense and even in a formalized and safe-guarding sense.

Even if the problem is accentuated in this way, it is still possible to link together the New Testament datum and the formalized doctrine of the Trinity. The real difference postulated by the doctrine of the Trinity can be traced back in the teaching of Paul (and at least materially in the rest of the New Testament) to the real difference between the mode of existence of the earthly Jesus and that of the exalted Jesus who has at his disposal the fulness of the Pneuma.

The structure of relationships resulting from this thesis can be made clear in the following Scheme E III.

Scheme E III

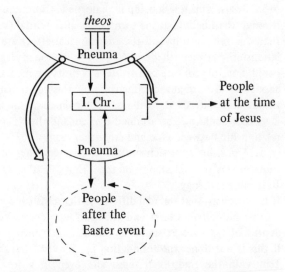

The third mode of subsistence (or 'person') in the formalized doctrine of the Trinity can be affirmed theologically provided that the
exalted Christ's possession of the Pneuma and therefore the gift of the
Pneuma experienced by the early Christian community was in fact
made possible by God's power of the Pneuma. From the point of view
of the New Testament, then, there are two modes of subsistence connected with the Pneuma indicated in the upper part of the Scheme. (Or,
to express this idea differently, two modes of subsistence are constituted by this Pneuma.) On the one hand, there is Yahweh's openness to
self-communication in the man Jesus. By this we mean self-communication in this man in his concrete historical person together with his permanence achieved by the act of resurrection. On the other hand, there
is God's communication of himself (this is merged together with the
permanence of Jesus) into the hearts of those who believe in him in the
outpouring of love through the Holy Spirit (see Rom 5. 5).

Two lines, then, go from the Pneuma as power of the origin, the
theos pater, to the two modes of subsistence constituted by the origin.
One of these lines goes to I. Chr., the earthly and exalted man Jesus in
his personal identity. His concrete historicity is additionally indicated
by the arrow which goes from I. Chr. to 'people at the time of Jesus'.
The second line goes from the Pneuma in the upper part of the diagram
(that is, the Pneuma as the power of creation of God himself) to the

Pneuma shown below in connection with 1 Chr. In Paul's theology, this should be seen as being in the most intimate way connected with the exalted Kyrios and, in the formalized sense, as being the point of departure for the third mode of subsistence of the classical theology of the Trinity. There is a merging together of the second and third modes of subsistence through the personal identity of the earthly Jesus and the exalted Pneuma-Kyrios, just as there is also a merging together of these two modes of existence with the first origin, the *theos pater*, as indicated by the two pairs of lines, that is, the pair of lines in Scheme E II and the additional pair of lines in Scheme E III.[40]

d. The safeguarding function of the doctrine of the second and third modes of subsistence in the Trinity

If the Kyrios Christ is seen in his relationship with the Father, the *eikon* relationship as determined by the Pneuma, the point of departure of the doctrine of the Trinity can be quite easily seen. If we look simply at the Kyrios and the Pneuma, that point of departure is in danger of being obscured. The Pneuma comes from God and makes the Kyrios God's *eikon*. For this reason, it is more than a personal potentiality or power belonging to the Kyrios. The Pneuma is, of course, also functional, but it would be a form of anthropomorphism to regard it as no more than functional, because the personal power of God himself is more than and different from that of man.[41]

The doctrine of the third mode of subsistence, then, safeguards what the New Testament has to say about the exalted Jesus of the Pneuma-Christ and is, in the New Testament, the central kerygma. (We have described this above as an *articulus stantis et cadentis Christologiae*.)

The doctrine of the second mode of subsistence safeguards the radical and historical communication of himself by God in a man, without which the communication of the Pneuma through an exalted Jesus would be no more than a myth, making the kerygma a form of gnosticism or at the most a philosophical essay. The merging together of the second and the third modes of subsistence is of inestimable importance for the whole doctrine and it is achieved by the personal identity of the historical and the risen Jesus, as we have already seen. The doctrine of the second and the third modes of subsistence prevents us from believing, erroneously, that what is important is that Jesus continued to be proclaimed by committed Christians and that it was of no importance in this commitment whether Christians were or were not interested in the present life and function of that Jesus.

e. An approach to a doctrine of the Trinity from a theology of the cross

Jürgen Moltmann has attempted to formulate a doctrine of the Trinity on the basis of a theology of the death of Jesus.[42] We can also approach a doctrine of the Trinity on the basis of what we have said so far. The kerygma of the exalted Jesus is safeguarded, as we have seen, by this doctrine and, since the exalted and the crucified Jesus are identical, a theology of the Trinity can be based on the permanence of Jesus' offering of himself on the cross.

This can be more adequately demonstrated by the theology of Paul than, for example, by Jesus' cry from the cross in Mark. The eschatological dimension of Paul's soteriology is of particular importance in this connection.

The permanence of Jesus' offering of himself on the cross should be taken together with the *hupotassesthai* or subjection of the exalted Jesus to the Father in the fulfilment (1 Cor 15. 28, because it would be wrong to separate the theology of the resurrection (1 Cor 15) from the theology of the cross (1 Cor 1-3).[43] On the basis of the idea of the cross it is possible to develop a theology of the Trinity, as long as this idea of Jesus' death is extended into the eschatological dimension or is at least seen in the light of God's plan of eschatological fulfilment. What is more, a doctrine of the Trinity can only be evolved on the basis of the eschatological aim of the *huiothesia* or sonship if the cross and the radical working out of God's love (see Rom 8. 31-39; 5. 8-11) are also taken into consideration.[44]

A theology of the Trinity of this kind (and faith in Jesus as the absolute bringer of salvation), is however, only possible if the theology of Paul, the first letter of John and other similar or related Scriptures are seen to be in continuity with Jesus himself. Finally, this theology of the Trinity would act as a safeguard for the theology of Yahweh as the God who is there for man.

f. The significance of the theology of Paul and John for the theses outlined in this section (6. II 1-7)

In these theses, the ideas of the classical Christology and the doctrine of the Trinity have been confronted with those of the New Testament. In the latter, the writings of Paul and John have played a very important part, while the synoptic tradition has receded into the background. There are three main reasons for this.

Firstly, despite their very different modes of expression and patterns of thought, these late New Testament theologies are in continuity with Jesus and the synoptic tradition. Secondly, looking at the exalted Jesus who is now living with the Father (this pattern emerges most clearly from the theologies of Paul and John) is an *articulus stantis et cadentis Christologiae*. Thirdly, the development of the Church's dogma in the centuries that followed was in the first place based on these late New Testament writings. This means that any interchange between dogma and scriptural exegesis cannot take place simply on the basis of the synoptic tradition. This interchange is not possible without the mediation of these late writings.[45]

III. The central problem and the structure of relationships of the New Testament Christology in its relevance for new approaches

1. Monotheism of Yahweh and Faith in Christ

The entire problem of Christology and the doctrine of the Trinity can, in the light of the New Testament, be traced back to the central problem of monotheism and Christocentricity. This central problem is identical with the question as to whether the Christocentricity of the New Testament should be understood as life lived in accordance with the example and teaching of the earthly Jesus or as community with Jesus living now.

This thesis expresses on the one hand the central problem of Christology and the doctrine of the Trinity as posed by the New Testament and, on the other, the most important question of all for Christian faith today. Before discussing this problem in detail, it is necessary to make a preliminary comment on monotheism.

The Old Testament pronouncement: 'Hear, O Israel: Yahweh our God is one' (Deut 6. 4-9) does not apply less to Christians than to those living under the old covenant. On the contrary, it applies to them in a more radical and intensive way. In this sense, it can and indeed must be said that Christians are monotheists. The concept of monotheism (like the concept 'theism') is, however, employed in many different ways and can therefore easily be misunderstood. A better term in this context is 'monotheism of Yahweh' or Yahweh monotheism', since the Christian is not simply a monotheist in the sense in which the term is used in Greek philosophy. He is also a monotheist in the sense in which it occurs in the Old Testament, that is, by the Second Isaiah or the late prophets who stressed the unique aspect of Yahweh as the God who is there and who is to come. Although the monotheism of the Greek philosophers should in no sense be underestimated, that of the Old Testament prophets qualitatively far transcends it.

This radicalization of the concept of God (in the sense of making

God more personal and stressing the eschatological aspect and the dialogue between God and man) has made it possible for us to understand his communication of himself as the God who is and is to come through the one man Jesus as the absolute mediator of salvation. It has also thrown light on the problem that arises in connection with the Christocentricity of the New Testament as an apparent complication of this Yahweh monotheism.

The theological basis of the theses 6. III 2-6

These theses place emphasis on the dialogue structure of the relationship with God in the Bible. The foundation for this dialogue structure is laid in the Old Testament and the structure is laid in the Old Testament and the structure is made more radical and expressed in a qualitatively new way in the New Testament.

The key-word 'Jesus as the believer' in the thesis 6. III 3 below points to the connection between this thesis and those that follow (6. III. 4-6). The meaning of Jesus' faith as such is made clear in the culmination of this reality. As the believer, that is, as the one who gives himself in trust and love, Jesus became the one who died on the cross and thus revealed absolute *agape*.

The revelation of this *agape* had to continue and this extension of *agape* forms the content of the theses that follows 6. III 3 (6. III 4-6). It had to be handed on by the community of Jesus' disciples (the Church) as the community serving the world (thesis 6. III 6), which includes that serving the modern world (thesis 6. III. 5). This handing on of absolute *agape* is, however, only possible if the community is at the same time a saving community with the real Jesus who is living now and with his temptations and suffering, which are orientated towards glory (see thesis 6. III 4).

2. The significance of the Old Testament for new approaches to Christology today

In any new approaches to Christology today, it is necessary to strengthen the link with the Old Testament and emphasize the aspect of personal dialogue that characterizes the biblical relationship with God. Jesus is the one who validated the Old Testament promises and made the relationship with God in personal dialogue radical, at the same time fulfilling it.

Here, we will only add one comment to what we have already said in chapters 2 and 5 above. The fulfilment of what was initiated in the revelation of the name of Yahweh as the original revelation of God in which everything was contained in embryo is most easily discernible in 1 Cor 15. 28 (' ... so that God may be everything to everyone'). The present activity of the Pneuma of the Kyrios is directed towards Jesus' handing over of the Basileia to the Father and mediating the fulfilment of this God being 'everything to everyone'.

3. The theocentricity of Jesus himself as constituting a Christology of dialogue

The New Testament solution of the central problem stated in thesis 6. III 1 above is to be found in a Christology based on a personal dialogue. It is of great importance from the Christological and soteriological points of view that the significance both of the *ek tou theou* and above all of the *eis ton theon* for the New Testament expression of the principle of personal dialogue should be recognized.

One way in which the *eis ton theon* is expressed with regard to the Jesus of history is the description of Jesus as the believer. This is a clear approach in the New Testament to a Christology of consciousness.

This ascending line of theocentricity can also be applied to the risen Jesus. It is also of decisive importance in indicating the function of the risen Jesus for Christians' relationships with God after the Easter event. It is this datum above all that establishes the permanence of Jesus' person and cause, as based on the New Testament.

In this thesis, Jesus is described as the believer. This term, as applied to Jesus, can be easily misunderstood. To prevent misunderstanding, then, I would suggest the following precautions. It should not be made absolute. In view of the literal use of the term that is relatively rare and at times not generally recognized, the main emphasis should be placed on the objective parallels. The idea of Jesus as the believer should not be regarded as the point of departure par excellence for a Christology of consciousness, but rather as a characteristic and important, though rare, expression of the whole New Testament approach. The meaning of faith in the synoptic tradition and the epistle to the Hebrews should also be clearly understood. One final important safeguard for the application of 'believer' to Jesus is an understanding of the theology underlying Heb 12. 2. This contains not only the idea that Jesus initiated faith, but also the notion that he brought it to eschatological fulfilment.

4. The basis of New Testament soteriology

It is not only Jesus' death on the cross, seen in isolation, that saves. Salvation is also brought about by community with the crucified and risen Jesus, who has made it possible for death to be overcome (*sumdoxasthenai*) through community with him (*sumpaschein*).

As this thesis has already been extensively discussed in the preceding chapters, no further comment is needed here.

5. Christology and soteriology within the framework of radical agape
Christology and soteriology have to be interpreted within the framework of the New Testament idea of *agape* as made radical by Jesus' offering of himself. (This also applies to the primary and secondary sociological structures.) The meaning of Christology within an evolving view of the world has also to be taken into account in this context, especially in view of the need to humanize social relationships. The Christological law of salvation of 'bearing fruit by dying' should also be included in any consideration of the preparation for the coming of the kingdom of God.

This *sumpaschein* or suffering together with Jesus as community with him cannot be understood separately from radical *agape*. This means that, like the New Testament *sumpaschein*, this *agape* is only possible as *sunagapan Christo* or loving together with Christ. The discussion in Chapter 5 of the statement that Jesus is the man for others because he is the man for God is relevant here. What Moltmann has shown to be the hard kernel of a responsible political theology is also implied in this thesis.[46]

Jesus brought into this world a power in which he was able to proclaim and communicate God's mercy to men. This power can make us open to our fellow-men. It cannot, however, be made freely available when the message of the cross and community with the crucified Jesus is regarded as inhibiting and is therefore eliminated (as it is, for example, in the Marxist criticism of Christianity). It becomes available only when it is accepted as the dynamism that is present in this state of openness and as an opportunity to break through man's selfish turning in on himself and make him open to the *agape* that is so needed by the world. The Johannine statement about bearing fruit through dying (Jn 12. 24) can also be applied here.[47]

Finally, it should be pointed out that the connection between the cross – or the imitation of the cross – and *agape* is a necessary precondition for this thesis.

6. The connection between Christology and ecclesiology

Another New Testament approach to Christology can be based on the connection between Christology and ecclesiology. Jesus is not only the model, but also the origin for salvation through community with him, that is, in the post-paschal sense, being in Christ or immanence. Christology in the New Testament sense cannot be fully understood if we think in terms of the model of a great number of people to be saved confronted by Jesus seen in isolation. On the contrary, Jesus should be seen as being in a relationship with his community of disciples (the Church), as a community serving the world. The mission that Jesus gave to his disciples is, in the chronological sense, the interpretative correlation to the mission of Jesus himself.

a. The theme of this thesis

It is not possible to evolve a New Testament Christology without considering the ecclesiastical implications, because it is, in the New Testament, always primarily functional or relational (that is, within the relationship with the Father, the disciples and men).[48]

There is an example in Jn 17. 10 (' . . . I am glorified in them') of what is meant by this connection between Christology and ecclesiology. The community of disciples is not only soteriologically, but also Christologically relevant for the world. The community of disciples is the glorification of Jesus and Christology cannot be conceived without this glorification of Jesus, which came about soteriologically.[39]

What is said about Jesus from the Christological point of view is not dependent on this glorification of Jesus in his own and is not constituted by this glorification. This process takes place through the love of the Father, which was directed towards the one man, Jesus, 'before the foundation of the world' (see Jn 17. 24).

New Testament Christology is above all based on this pre-existent possession and regaining of glory which is in turn based on the love of the Father. It also exists in that love, that is, in unity with the Father as the supreme concept that also includes earthly activity. Although it is not constituted by it, then, Christology cannot be dissociated from ecclesiology. This connection between Christology and ecclesiology and the relevance of ecclesiology for Christology are only possible if the relationship between Jesus and his disciples is not regarded simply as a model.

b. The exemplary character and community-forming function of Jesus as models of Christology

Jesus is frequently described nowadays as exemplary, in the sense of providing a model, but this is quite inadequate from the Christological point of view. The aspect of imitation is not in the foreground in most of the texts in the New Testament that are relevant to Christology and ecclesiology. The disciples or followers of Jesus are not, for example, saved because they resemble him. The category of an isolated model should perhaps be replaced by two other categories. The first of these can be described as making a community possible and the second by the simple word 'for', which is connected with Jesus' mission. These two categories may act as a norm for the interrelationship between Christology and ecclesiology.

The first of these two categories, that of making a community possible, is made visible in the Jesus of history in the power which was given to him by the Spirit of God to enable him to hand on God's mercy by establishing a community above all for the outcasts (that is, the tax-collectors and sinners). This community with Jesus was established after the Easter event by the Pneuma and it is now communicated to believers so that they will be in community with each other and for the world and their brothers. This, then, is the second category — the community with Jesus is a missionary task for others. (See also below, 6. III 6c.)

This is illustrated in Rom 8. 29. According to the literal translation of this text (the only one that can be accepted in the context of Paul's theology), those whom God predestined and chose were 'formed together' (*summorphous* with 'the image of the Son of God' (*tes eikonos tou huiou autou*).[50] Jesus' disciples are not in the same relationship with him as statues are with the model, the shape of which they are given, yet on which they are in no way dependent despite the similarity of shape. On the contrary, Jesus is original for his disciples and for the community of the disciples with Jesus and with each other that is constituted by Jesus. It is only in this solidarity with Jesus, brought about by the Pneuma, that the disciples were able to remain in the relationship that accompanied community with God and Jesus' mission, was salvation for them and made it possible for them to serve their fellowmen. In the following Scheme F, an attempt is made to illustrate this. This is done in the diagram by showing the members of the community of disciples linked to Jesus and through Jesus to each other and by combining this structure of relationships with that indicated in Scheme B III above.

Scheme F

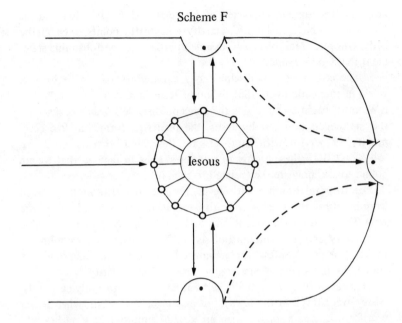

The disciples, then, were constituted as a community with Jesus by their solidarity with him. Because of this, what applies to him also applies to them. Like him, they too were sent, handed on the mercy of God, responded to the Father by turning towards him and persisting in a situation of contestation in a faith that was rooted in the Old Testamen and finally were open to the God of the future.

It is only if we regard Jesus' function as that of the one who makes it possible for us to have access to God and our fellow-men by giving us community with himself that we can dispense with the need to raise him up to the level of a model that is valid in every conceivable respect.

It is very important to stress this in view of the common tendency nowadays to by-pass the central New Testament kerygma by regarding Jesus simply as the earthly Jesus, by not being satisfied with the statement that his cause simply continued and finding a substitute for the authentic New Testament that has been abandoned in this way and above all by attempting to make Jesus an ideal man with an ideal exemplary character in a way that cannot be substantiated in the New Testament itself.

This criticism of an ideal abstract image of Jesus is, I think, a valid one, despite the New Testament statements about Jesus' sinlessness and the unique character of his relationship with God and his fellow-men which, in his life, activity and death, points, even in the early synoptic tradition, to a possible approach to the Johannine statement that God is *agape*.

c. The community of disciples as a community of service for the world in connection with the mission of Jesus himself

i. We must begin by clarifying the concept 'disciple'. Are these disciples the messengers sent out by Jesus, the men who formed a close community of service with him? Or are they all Christians, all Jesus' followers? Both these groups of 'disciples' exist in fact, so that we are bound to ask, how are they related to each other?

For their relationship with Jesus, the category that we have called 'community with Jesus' is constitutive even in the earliest levels of the New Testament. It is constitutive as a confessing community, a table community and a community of service.[51] For example, according to Lk 12, 8 ff par, 'confess' (or 'acknowledge') means affirming solidarity with Jesus and 'denying' means saying no to this solidarity.

This category of community with Jesus is valid not only before the Easter event (even in the logia), but also after that event, when it was transformed, not primarily into an idea of imitation, but rather into faith in a relationship, to which the word 'community' can really be applied. This relationship is expressed by Paul as being 'in Christ'.

The most important of the three aspects of community with Jesus for our purpose is that of the community of service. In the context of the activity of the historical Jesus, this concept can only be applied to the small circle of disciples. This particular concept, however, throws light on the inner meaning of this community with Jesus. It is clear that the concept of a serving community is the only positive New Testament alternative to the category of the isolated model that should, in our opinion, be rejected.

ii. The other two aspects of community with Jesus that we mentioned above, the confessing and the table community, also play a part in the post-paschal transformation of the community with Jesus that constitutes the Church. Whereas the confessing and the table community would, however, constitute the Church as an isolated factor, the community of service plays a decisive part with regard to the community of disciples as such. This is because, after the Easter event, not only the small circle of those holding office or exercising a function in this serving community, but also the whole Church community as such is a community with Jesus of service for the world. This, of course, also applies to every individual Christian.

iii. Ecclesiology is relevant to Christology for four main reasons. Firstly, the aim of Jesus before the Easter event was to gather the people of the covenant for Yahweh. He was mainly active, in other words, in a gathering movement.[52]

After the Easter event, this aim was changed. This is clear, for example, from Rom 11, in which the author reflects about the universal mission and the promises made to Israel. Jesus' aim was then the salvation not only of the Jews, but also the gentiles. (The latter in fact came first in time.)

Secondly, the basic structure underlying this aim is the analogy between the mission given to Jesus by God and the mission given to the disciples as messengers of the Basileia by Jesus.[53]

Thirdly, even before the Easter event, there was a hard and radical imitation of Jesus within this community of service.[54] This was an early form of the later *sumpaschein* or imitation of the cross.

Fourthly, we may conclude from the basic structure that existed before the Easter event (Jesus' sending of the disciples as messengers to gather the people of Israel in analogy with his own mission) that the idea of Jesus' disciples in the gospel of Matthew is legitimate. According to Matthew every Christian is regarded as a disciple ('make disciples of all nations', Mt. 28 19).[55]

The idea of the Church in 1 Pet 2. 5, 9 is also clearly legitimate. Here the Church is described as a 'holy priesthood'. It has, in other words, a relationship of 'for' with regard to the world, not in the purely cultic sense, but in the sense of a total commitment. After the Easter event, not only those holding office in the Church, but also all followers of Christ are involved in the community of service for the world. This datum exists above all because of the presence of the Kyrios in the whole community of disciples (see Mt 18. 20; 28. 20). This enlargement of the mission is of particular importance. After the Easter event, the community of Jesus' disciples were not sent only to the people specially chosen by God, the 'kingdom of priests' (Exod 19. 6). As the new people of God and a 'holy priesthood', it was sent out to all people.

iv. If we are to understand the Church after the Easter event (and today), it is in my opinion extremely important to grasp the fact that the whole phenomenon has the character of having been previously formed (historical Jesus — disciples in the narrower sense — disciples in the wider sense or followers).

From this vantage point too, Jesus can be seen as the one whose function, as the absolute bringer of salvation, is not that of being a model, but that of making community possible and indeed bringing it about. This means that the idea of mission and service is of central importance from the ecclesiological point of view, because it can act as a point of departure for Christology as a theology of Jesus' mission or as a doctrine of Jesus as the one sent by God.

v. The image of the Church and its task that emerges from this outline is extremely dynamic. It is, like the description that we have given of Jesus' mission, quite opposed to the earlier, static concept of the Church. There is, however, also a danger inherent in this image. On the one hand, there is a danger in the misunderstanding that may arise in connection with a Church that simply preserves what it possesses and retains its believers, so that it comes to lose its special dynamism, that is, the dynamism of Jesus himself, with regard to the world and can only share in the dynamism that really belongs to the world and social evolution. The Church as seen in the light of the New Testament, on the other hand, has an irreplaceable task with regard to the world. The Church has above all to serve Jesus' task and intention, insofar as Jesus is present in the Church together with his intention, that is, the essential aim of his life.[56]

The community of Jesus' disciples (and each individual member of it) is, because of the nature of the mission, always in a state of tension. On the one hand, there is task of serving the world and, on the other, it has to be tied to Jesus and to be in accordance with the kind of community in which Jesus aims to live. This is so not for the sake of the community itself, nor for the sake of those who already belong to it, but above all because of the mission.

The inner existence of the Church and brotherly love in it is, from the Christological point of view, rooted in Jesus' community with his Father (see, for example, Jn 17. 21: 'that they may all be one, even as thou, Father, art in me and I in thee') and, on that basis, it is also Christologically relevant. Correlative with this inner existence is the function of the community of disciples that is directed outwards towards the formation of a community with those outside (the tax-collectors and sinners, for instance). This is in analogy with Jesus' mission to the world (see Jn 17. 18).[57]

It is only when the reality of the missionary community with Jesus is taken quite seriously that there can be a theological basis for this mission. It is not a question of the Church spreading as the organization of all the baptized. It is rather a question of a growth in the number of those who are committed to the proclamation and realization of Jesus' intention, the saving will of God.

vi. The specific function of the smaller circle of disciples (which nowadays consists of those to whom the proclamation of the Christian message, teaching and the office of president of the liturgical assembly are entrusted) is to integrate the function of the whole community of disciples as a Christologically based missionary community. This means that the smaller circle of those holding office has to be at the service of the whole community by helping the members of that Church to function in service of the world, by enabling their capacity to function in this way to grow and, rather in the sense of Eph 4. 11 ff, by equipping them for the 'work of ministry'. In other words, those holding office have the task of helping all the members of the body of Christ to become incorporated in the mission of the head of the community.

vii. The concept 'community with Jesus' also leads to a relativization and a safeguarding of Jesus' unique character. The safeguarding is in fact contained in the process of relativization. In it, the real humanity of Jesus is safeguarded insofar as he has 'many brethren' who are in unity with him. The safeguard of Jesus' uniqueness is also contained within this category of community with Jesus insofar as he himself constitutes that community and in this way gives *koinonia* – or salvation – with God.

  d. Rahner's idea of the Church

i. If it is true to say that, in the light of the New Testament, community with Jesus and above all missionary community for the world are central ecclesiological concepts, then the question that has to be asked of every ecclesiology is whether full justice is done to these concepts in it.

The best point of departure for Rahner's ecclesiology is his article on mission and implicit Christianity in *Sacramentum Mundi*.[58] There are also several other detailed discussions of the Church in the manual of pastoral theology containing contributions by Rahner.[59] The emphases that characterize Rahner's view of the Church, however, emerge with particular clarity in the article in *Sacramentum Mundi*.

We may mention here some of the fundamental ideas contained in this article on ecclesiology. He insists, for example, that everyone must somehow or other be able to be a member of the Church. This, he goes on, implies that there must be degrees of Church membership. These degrees will range from explicit, baptized membership down to a non-official implicit Christianity, which can or ought to be called a valid Christianity, even though it cannot and will not call itself that.[60]

Even though there is little in the New Testament to indicate a recognition of anonymous or implicit believers, we can still agree with Rahner's thesis as being in accordance with the intention of the New Testament, since it is clear that this must always be confronted with modern ways of thinking and approaching reality. As a New Testament scholar, I would certainly accept this intention on condition that the basic constitutive elements of New Testament ecclesiology are not overlooked.

It is undoubtedly true that Rahner's idea of implicit Christianity makes it possible for us Christians to avoid indifferentism and dogmatic narrowness and still not question the Church or the Christian mission. We can also be open in the human and the Christian sense towards those who think differently and at the same time also approach them with orthodox faith. Indeed, the idea of implicit Christianity makes us free to proclaim our faith and to missionize.

The concept also has a corrective function and can enable us to understand what is meant by the idea of a missionary community with Jesus for the world in the New Testament. This is an extremely valuable idea, so long as no attempt is made to fashion it into an ecclesiological system.

ii. Nonetheless, it is important to note that Rahner stresses ecclesiology in his Christology far less than it would seem to be in the New Testament. In this section, we shall try to find some of the reasons for this.

In the first place, we must consider the gnoseological aspects. Taking this as his point of departure may have determined the inner emphasis that Rahner placed on his ecclesiological considerations. The gnoseological significance of the Church in the sense of the explicit aspect of what is present outside the Church at least in an unthematic form[61] has certainly to be supplemented, in the light of the New Testament findings, by the idea of a community of service with Jesus for the World.

Implicit Christianity as a formal gnoseological concept should be completely open to this. An illustration of this principle is Rahner's affirmation that the proclamation of the explicit Word confronts man with a radical decision., despite the appeal in Scripture (Acts 17. 23) to his unthematic way of worshipping.[62] If Rahner's approach is combined with the various New Testament approaches, the result will inevitably be a conditioning of our criticism of the lack of differentiation in Rahner's idea of degrees of Church membership.[63]

Rahner's ecclesiological emphases originate in his open but abstract transcendental Christology. It is easy to misinterpret this Christology because it is so abstract. As a result of the transcendental and anthropological connection between Jesus and the whole of mankind, Jesus is not seen sufficiently explicitly as the one who was sent and as the origin and central point of the community of those who were also sent.

This abstract transcendental approach, which is often wrongly misunderstood, can, if an attempt is made to universalize it, lead to an unjustified by-passing of the most important element, in my opinion, that can be derived from the New Testament. The concrete mediation between Christology and ecclesiology by the idea of a community of service for the world that is present in the New Testament may perhaps be insufficiently expressed. This may in turn result in a change of emphasis. Both from the Christological and from the ecclesiological points of view, the aspects of mission and the 'for' may be underestimated. We may therefore legitimately ask whether, in Rahner's article in *Sacramentum Mundi* and in his Christology, the Church, in the sense in which it appears in Scripture (especially 1 Pet 2. 5, 9 and Eph 4. 12), does not really emerge at all clearly because, although Rahner's approach is certainly open to the New Testament 'for', this 'for' is not sufficiently concrete and does not, for this reason, sufficiently determine the idea as a whole.

iii. We are now in a position to criticize and correct Rahner's idea of degrees of Church membership. A distinction must be made between the concept of the Church that is present in this idea, a concept in which Christianity and Church membership would seem to be merged together with the result that even implicit Christians would appear to belong to the Church as well, and the New Testament concept of the Church as the community of Jesus' disciples (or the body of Christ, the 'holy priesthood', 'living stones built into a spiritual house' and so on). The Church membership of those who belonged to the community of Jesus' disciples in the New Testament sense (or who belong today to that community) cannot be distinguished in degree from the Church membership of those whom Rahner has called implicit Christians. The distinction is qualitative. A distinction in degree cannot be reconciled with the New Testament point of departure for ecclesiology, because the constitutive element in the case of the latter is the specific election to the confessing and missionary community with Jesus and this community is certainly not different in degree from implicit Christianity.

We are therefore bound to emphasize that there is a membership of the community of Jesus' disciples which is different not only in degree, but also and above all qualitatively from membership of the Church. This affirmation is not contrary to Rahner's intention. The very reverse is true — it supports it. In the light of the New Testament, it is quite legitimate to ask whether the concept of Church should be understood in such a wide sense as it is in Rahner's article, in which it apparently includes the whole of mankind, so long as men do not exclude themselves by explicitly rejecting what they always are because of God's grace.

I would therefore suggest that the term 'Church membership' might better be replaced by the idea of the transcendental possibility of belonging to the explicit community with the absolute bringer of salvatin. This would help to overcome the difficulty discussed here by retaining the transcendental Christological approach in our approach to ecclesiology.

iv. To conclude this section 6. IV, we will consider briefly the parable of the judgement in Mt 25. 31-46. There can be no doubt that, as Rahner has said, a love that is so radical and so without reservations in its acceptance of man must implicitly affirm Christ in faith and love. This affirmation of Christ, then, is in a very real sense, the basis of implicit Christianity.

This conclusion cannot, however, be applied unquestioningly to a distinction in degree between different modes of Church membership. The passage in Mt 25. 31-46 cannot be quoted in an undifferentiated manner as support for the concept 'Christian'. In the most relevant text (Mt 25. 32), it is clear that the *ethne* or gentiles will appear, at the last judgement, before the throne of the Son of Man.

The same text, however, also applies as a criterion of judgment to the man who is a disciple of Jesus because of his community with Jesus. It applies to him, however, in a very specific way. It is clear not only from this passage in the gospel of Matthew, but also from other demands made of the disciples by Jesus in the New Testament that judgment will be passed on him both in accordance with the criterion of his service of Jesus in serving his 'brethren' and on the basis of whether he has carried out the mission given to him by Jesus in his explicitly accepted community with Jesus. This mission is to help others to become Jesus' disciples as well and therefore also explicitly to enter Jesus' community of service.

This community is directed towards the handing on of God's mercy and therefore towards active love of the kind expressed in Matthew 25. It is also orientated towards sharing Jesus' soteriological 'for' in community with him. The man who is an explicit disciple of Jesus because of election and grace is judged, then, not only on the basis of his service of and activity for his fellow-men, but also in accordance with his community with Jesus as a community for the world.

IV. Communication between a transcendental Christology and a biblical way of thinking in personal dialogue

The transcendental approach is open to a Christology based on the New Testament. It is therefore possible to achieve communication between the classical descendance Christology, the transcendental anthropological ascendance Christology and the way of thinking that characterizes the New Testament Christologies of personal dialogue. This can be done with the help of the concept of theocentricity in a descending line and that of theocentricity in an ascending line.

The abstract concept of the absolute bringer of salvation can be given content and meaning by the Christological ideas contained in the New Testament.

1. The intention

The aim in the elucidation of this final thesis that constitutes the penultimate section of this chapter is to show the extent to which a battery of concepts of the kind necessary in any dialogue between a dogmatic theologian and a New Testment exegete can be employed and extended. Another, related aim is to examine how far it is possible to succeed in establishing communication between Rahner's transcendental approach and the New Testament way of thinking in personal dialogue.

Three (or four) possible approaches to this problem will be followed in the Schemes below. In the first two, Schemes G I and II, the two systematic points of departure for this encounter with the New Testament way of thinking in personal dialogue are outlined. Rahner's transcendental approach to Christology (G II) is undoubtedly determined, as far as its concrete form is concerned, by the Christology of descendance, but is distinguished from it by its fundamental openness to the possibility of being amplified by New Testament lines (especially those from God and towards God). In the descendance theology pure and simple, on the other hand, as illustrated in Scheme G I, the descending line from God is overemphasized.

Scheme G III shows G II (the transcendental approach) amplified by New Testament lines Christologically and in Scheme G IV, G II is amplified soteriologically and ecclesiologically. An attempt is made here to represent the objectivizing New Testament lines as anthropologically open.

2. Descendance theology – openness in the transcendental approach

Schemes G I and G II

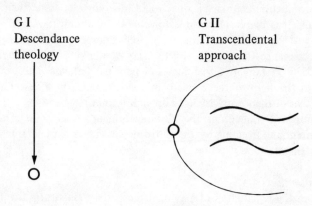

G I
Descendance
theology

G II
Transcendental
approach

It is possible to provide this extremely simple diagram for descendance theology (G I) because the descent and the union of divinity and humanity at the goal are all that have to be indicated.

Scheme G II shows Rahner's transcendental approach and can be interpreted transcendentally both anthropologically and – in the ultimate culmination of transcendental thinking – Christologically. It points to man's openness or that of the absolute bringer of salvation to the absolute mystery and does this, moreover, at the level of what is transcendentally already present. The wavy lines inside the space that is open to eternity are signs representing the capacity of all openness to receive into itself various forms of free obedience, trust and worship.

3. Transcendental Christology and Christological theocentricity in the New Testament

Scheme G III

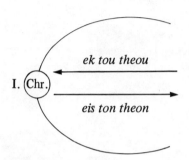

In this Scheme, an explicit link is made between transcendental Christology and the two lines representing the biblical datum of 'from God' and 'towards God', in other words, Christological theocentricity in the descending and the ascending lines. What is transcendentally already present is in the foreground in Scheme G II, but in this Scheme attention is drawn principally to the aspect of dialogue in the expression of the mutual relationship between the absolute mediator of salvation and the mystery that is known as God.

4. New Testament soteriology and ecclesiology combined with transcendental Christology

If we are to go another step forward and include those people who belong to Jesus in this relationship of personal dialogue, in other words, if we attempt to represent schematically the realization of the soteriological function of the absolute bringer of salvation, this can only be done in two separate diagrams. The first Scheme (G IV) has been deliberately left incomplete and represents the category of the model that is defective from the Christological and soteriological points of view. The second (Scheme G V) shows the full New Testament datum. In it, what is illustrated in Scheme F above is transposed to the structure of relationship under consideration here. The *ek tou theo* and the *eis ton theon* of Scheme G III have been replaced in this Scheme by anthropologically open expressions.

Scheme G IV

(not only:)

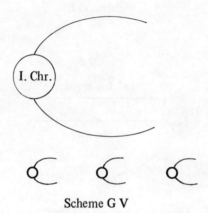

Scheme G V

(but rather:)

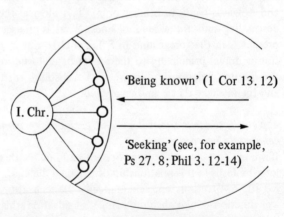

'Being known' (1 Cor 13. 12)

'Seeking' (see, for example, Ps 27. 8; Phil 3. 12-14)

The aspect of dialogue shown in the transcendental Scheme is primarily objectivizing within the New Testament. Within the framework of this Scheme, it is assumed that the absolute mystery can be attained by man so long as he is open to it. A further assumption is that there is another line running in the opposite direction, in other words, from the absolute mystery. If man is open to this mystery, it can be attained through this openness. This mystery can, moreover, be discussed in a relatively more adequate way from the biblical point of view, that is, anthropomorphically and in terms of personal dialogue (in other words, to some extent as an objectivization) than from the abstract gnoseo-logical point of view.

The point of departure for the Christology of ascendance is man in his abstract and transcendental openness. It is, however, possible that his fate depends on the absolute mystery to which he is open and on the affirmation of that openness.

The theocentricity in an ascending line, however, is a statement of a relationship with God as the aim. In it, the aspect of dialogue is thematic. Within the Christological and soteriological pattern indicated in Scheme G V, man's fate depends on whether he responds to the *eis ton theon* of Jesus as the absolute bringer of salvation.

The real difference between transcendental Christological thinking and New Testament Christological thinking is that the aspect of dialogue that is implied in the transcendental approach is made explicit and thematic in the New Testament approach.

This explicitation of the aspect of dialogue within the transcendental approach is necessary if we are to understand the New Testament. We are, after, all, living in an era of post-Cartesian, anthropological thinking. This explicitation is moreover necessary in any dialogue between dogmatic theologians and biblical exegetes.

The inclusion of the two lines of dialogue in the Scheme does not mean that the exegete cannot accept the transcendental approach. It is much more a question of finding a battery of concepts which will make communication between the exegete's way of thinking and that of the dogmatic theologian possible.

It is necessary to try to combine the two approaches, because the transcendental approach, as a reflection about the possibility of the biblical approach in dialogue, cannot be sufficiently amplified as it is and because any dialogue between the dogmatic theologian and the New Testament exegete may be blocked in the absence of a battery of concepts capable of dealing with the New Testament datum.

5. *Summary*

One objection that may be raised is that transcendental openness may perhaps be brought to an end by the aspect of dialogue that is at least partly determined by the objectivizing thinking of the New Testament. To this I would reply that there is no danger of this happening because the aspect of dialogue is already implicitly present in the transcendental approach, at least as a possibility. The objection is also invalid because anthropomorphisms of the kind that are encountered in the biblical way of thinking in dialogue are theologically transparent and are relatively better able to go to the heart of the matter than abstract thought. Finally, the danger of an end to transcendental openness is minimal because the aspect of dialogue can be expressed in such a way that their objective conformity with the openness of the transcendental approach is easily recognizable. Our aim, in this section especially, has been to point to this openness and this aim has largely determined the choice of terms used in Scheme G V. The two lines of dialogue in this Scheme have been called 'being known' and 'seeking'. Both of these terms indicate transcendental openness.

V. Conclusion: the significance of the Church's doctrines and New Testament statements for modern theology and proclamation

We would like to conclude this book by going back to the theme of the relationship between the Church's traditional doctrines and the New Testament, in view of the fact that it is of fundamental importance to the interchange of ideas between exegesis and dogmatic theology.

We have described the Church's doctrines as acting as a corrective in the positive sense. As we have seen in our discussion of I. Hermann's thesis (see above, 6. II 7), this corrective can help us to look more actively for a datum that can be verified exegetically and perhaps even to find one.

The dialogue between the Church's official formulations and the New Testament also throws a much sharper light on the classical doctrines of Christology and the Trinity precisely as formulations. The transcendental approach is also seen in the same perspective. The exegete is able to see what is expressed by these formalized doctrines of Christology and the Trinity and this understanding is an important precondition for fruitful dialogue with the systematic theologian.

The question is frequently raised: is it valuable to consider these dogmatic formulations as such and not simply or exclusively as safeguards? In reply to this question, I would say that it is valuable insofar as something can be known from many of the Church's doctrines that would perhaps not have been known otherwise, although in theory it should be possible to gain such knowledge from the New Testament.

It is also possible to say that, although many of the formulations of the Church's magisterium are not in themselves dynamic, they are able to set the dynamism that comes from the primordial datum itself free. This primordial datum, after all, normally reaches us via the New Testament and the tradition of the Church's interpretation.

A situation of controversy and a successful merging together of biblical thinking with the thought of each successive generation can often lead to the liberation of the primordial datum in a specific way, with the result that later generations of Christians can make use not only of the continuity with the underlying intention of the Church's doctrines, but also the original dynamism itself.

I am bound to admit that it is quite possible to establish communication between the classical doctrines of the Church (especially as interpreted by Rahner) and the New Testament datum. Nonetheless, despite the positive effect of the setting free of dynamism by these doctrines, to which we have just referred, the critical question still arises: should the Church's doctrines as a whole not be understood primarily as a corrective? Another, related question is: does the theological position of the Church's doctrines, as indicated above in Scheme C II, not go to the heart of the matter? The Church's doctrines are not placed in the diagram at the centre of the main stream from the primordial datum to modern consciousness of faith, but rather in a side stream which is connected with the main stream and also has an important functional significance.

It should be clear from a consideration of the matter itself and also on the basis of pastoral theology that the way towards modern theology and proclamation is not directly via the Church's doctrines. We must therefore ask whether the kerygma that comes from the primordial datum and its significance for modern man would not be more easily understood if we were to look for new interpretations (intelligibly formulated) on the basis of the New Testament. One condition is valid here: continuity with the history of dogma will not be broken if the matter that the Church is seeking to express in its tradition of interpretation (often in a way that is conditioned by the prevailing historical situation) is kept in sight and contact is not lost with other believers in the whole Church.

Because of the central importance of Christology, the path that must be followed is that outlined in theses 6. II 6 and III 1-6 above and, of course, in the whole of Chapter 5. We cannot nowadays safeguard faith in Jesus from the periphery consisting of later, historically conditioned dogmatic definitions. This safeguarding process has to begin at the centre, to which all Christological and Trinitarian problems can be traced back. That centre is, of course, to be found in the New Testament.

The New Testament way to a re-interpretation of the content of the Church's faith in Christ in the form in which it is needed by pastoral theology in particular should be more suitable than that of the classical Christology. A pre-condition for following this way, however, is that it is not primarily the literal text of the New Testament that would be followed, but rather the matter underlying the formulations of the New Testament. Another pre-condition for the success of this venture is the merging together of biblical and modern ways of thinking.

It is true, of course, that many of those holding office or exercising functions in the Church today are deeply influenced by the traditional dogmatic formulations. This also applies to a large number of lay Christians. It would be wrong simply to deprive these Christians of these official definitions. Such a step might damage the Church's *agape*. For such people, the first step ought to be a re-interpretation of the formulations themselves.

If we see the matter as a whole, we are bound to come to the conclusion that it is impossible to avoid a communication between both ways, that is, the way of re-interpretation going back to the origins and the way of a theologically justified translation of the Church's dogmatic formulations.

The most urgent aspect of this process is to make the mystery that is present in the statements about God and our approach to God through Jesus known as such[64] and to encourage this necessary reductio in mysterium. This applies on the one hand to any attempt to go beyond the limits imposed by the central datum of Christian faith in new formulations. On the other hand, serious difficulties are experienced by pastors and lay people who were brought up in an earlier theological tradition. The dogmatic formulations with which these people are so familar are often found to be an inadequate expressions and safeguards of a mystery that should be accepted in the strict sense.

As soon as the mystery of the New Testament and Church pronouncements about faith is grasped, it becomes clear that there is ultimately no adequate way in which the datum can possibly be expressed in historically conditioned formulations. It is only by means of an authentic, responsible and pastorally sound *reductio in mysterium* that heretical misunderstandings, for example of the Trinity as tritheistic or Christology as monophysitic, can be avoided.

In any attempt to find new interpretations that can be of use in pastoral theology, the question of abbreviated formulae in which these reinterpretations can be expressed in their entirety, but in a very concise form is bound to arise. Rahner recognized the value of such short formulae and has made a number of suggestions on the basis of his own theological approach.[65] In my opinion, however, there are many New Testament texts which can provide better material for such short formulae than the classical Christological or Trinitarian doctrines, which are, of their very nature, too abstract. These New Testament formulae at least enable the emphases to be placed in a more adequate way. They have, however, to be translated into a language that can be understood today if they are to perform this function properly.

Points of departure for such abbreviated New Testament formulae are, for example, 1 Jn 4. 16a and 1 Cor 16. 22,[66] the non-titular Christology of the early tradition, such Christological statements as those in Rom 8. 29 and a great number of possibly quite fruitful ideas and formulae in the epistle to the Hebrews. Even the titular Christology of the New Testament can be utilized for such short formulae. The term 'Son of God' could, for example, be re-interpreted in the sense of freedom and *huiothesia* and even such overworked concepts as *soter* and Kyrios ought to be open to a fresh interpretation.

Notes

N.B.: *Works cited by the authors are given − for the most part − in the original editions, since the particular emphases and names referred to are often altered, or even omitted, in the standard English translations.*

1. The relevance of the Bible for modern theology and the problem of co-operation between dogmatic theology and exegesis

[1] K. Rahner, *Schriften zur Theologie* V (Einsiedeln, 1962), pp. 33-53, especially p. 41. (Cf. *Theological Investigations,* vol. V).

[2] This raises the whole problem of revelation. See Rahner's article in *Sacramentum Mundi* III, pp. 819-843 and the article on Scripture and Holy Scripture, *Sacramentum Mundi* IV, pp. 428-441. The Old and New Testament Scriptures cannot be isolated from revelation of the kind that exists outside Israel and Christianity.

[3] K. Rahner, *Über die Schriftinspiration* (Freiburg, 1958), see especially pp. 52 and 56 ff.

[4] This also applies even if Jerome's words about an ignorance of Scripture being equivalent to an ignorance of Christ himself *(ignoratio scripturarum . . . ignoratio Christi est*; *Comm. in Is., Prol., PL* 24, 17) are taken with a grain of salt, in other words, not in the narrow sense in which they are possibly used by Jerome himself and for which he might have been criticized, for example, by Augustine.

[5] For the connection between the doctrine of the inspiration of Scripture, as a doctrine constituting the Church, and ecclesiology, see Karl Rahner, *op. cit.*

[6] See K.-H. Ohlig's continuation of Rahner's teaching and application of it to Christology in *Woher nimmt die Bibel ihre Autorität ? Zum Verhältnis von Schriftkanon, Kirche und Jesus* (Düsseldorf, 1970), pp. 97-100, 191-194.

[7] A basic question here is: how can it be shown that it is worth while studying the New Testament with this aim in mind? The aim should in this case be a merging together of biblical and modern ways of thinking, as outlined in 1. III. 5 below.

[8] In this context, I would stress explicitly that the exegetical contribution has to be made also for pastoral theology, which cannot, in the last resort, be separated from dogmatic theology.

[9] See W. Thüsing, 'Die Botschaft des Neuen Testaments − Hemmnis

oder Triebkraft der gesellschaftlichen Entwicklung? ' *Gul* 43 (1970), pp. 136-148.

[10] See F.J. Schierse, 'Was hat die Kirche mit Jesus zu tun? Zur gegenwärtigen Problemlage biblischer Exegese und kirchlicher Verkündigung', *Das theologische Interview* 2 (Düsseldorf, 1969), p. 36; *ibid.*, in his review of my book *Per Christum in Deum, ThRv* 63 (1968), p. 384. See also my reply in the foreword to the second edition of *Per Christum in Deum* (Münster, 1969), p. xi ff.

[11] I have only mentioned exegesis and dogmatic theology in this context, because they are for us the fundamental disciplines.

[12] K. Rahner, *Zur Reform des Theologiestudiums*, Quaestiones Disputatae 41 (Freiburg, 1969).

[13] See K. Rahner's article on Scripture and Holy Scripture in *Sacramentum Mundi* IV, p. 441.

[14] M. Buber, 'Der Mensch von heute und die jüdische Bibel', Werke II, *Schriften zur Bibel* (Munich and Heidelberg, 1964), p. 869.

2. Questions and notes on transcendental Christology

[1] The prologue to the gospel of John (Jn 1.1 ff) was originally a hymn to Christ which the author used and supplemented. It does not contain any speculation about the Logos in the Hellenistic sense or in the sense of later patristic theology. The author of the gospel regarded it as the earliest expression of the Christological theme of revelation.

[2] See E. Schweizer, 'Pneuma ktl.', *ThWNT* VI, pp. 428-431.

[3] See E. Schweizer, *op. cit.*; W. Thüsing, *Per Christum in Deum. Studien zum Verhältnis von Christozentrik und Theozentrik in den paulinischen Hauptbriefen* (Münster, [2]1969), pp. 155-159. (This work is cited in all footnotes below as *Per Christum in Deum*.)

[4] I. Hermann, *Kyrios und Pneuma* (Munich, 1961), p. 113; *Per Christum in Deum, op. cit.*

[5] See *Per Christum in Deum*, pp. 116-125, 144-147.

[6] For further details, see W. Thüsing, *Die Johannesbriefe* (Düsseldorf, 1970), especially pp. 141-154. (This work is cited in all footnotes below as *Johannesbriefe*.)

[7] See *Johannesbriefe*, pp. 149-152.

[8] See K. Rahner, 'Love', *Sacramentum Mundi* III, pp. 234-252, especially pp. 248-250.

[9] This certainly applies, despite Rahner's explicit consideration of the Old Testament in his article on this subject in *Sacramentum Mundi* I, pp. 101-108. My opinion is confirmed by Rahner's overemphasis on one aspect of the idea of fulfilment, namely that the covenant is fulfilled in the unity of the two partners in the covenant (God and man) in the one God-man. (See p. 104.) Underlying this idea is a Christology in which the present is clearly stressed and towards which the Old Testa-

ment is thought to point. Rahner's qualification on p. 107, that it is not
easy to say what is still left of the Old Testament, makes no different
to this, as the decisive datum, the promise, is not reflected in the argument supporting this teaching.

[10] Rahner cannot be criticized for denying that the openness of the
event of Christ applies to an absolute future that is still to come. His
emphasis is, however, placed so heavily on a Christology of the present
that there is an even greater danger than usual of reading selectively and
one-sidedly, especially if Rahner's work as a whole is not taken into
consideration.

[11] See *Per Christum in Deum*, pp. 43 ff, 180 ff.

[12] This can be said as a corrective, even when it is recognized that the
term 'irreversible' refers, in Rahner's works, to the event of Christ and
is certainly open to corrections of this kind.

[13] See H.J. Kraus, *Die biblische Theologie* (Neukirchen, 1970), p. 279;
see also C.H. Ratschow, *Der angefochtene Glaube* (Gütersloh, 1957),
p. 86.

[14] It should be borne in mind here that the line of the so-called messi-
anic promises in the Old Testament is very weak and indistinct compared with the strong line of the promises made by Yahweh himself.

[15] See P. Schoonenberg, 'Der Mensch in der Sünde', *Mysterium Salutis*
II (Einsiedeln, 1967), pp. 845-941, especially the fifth section on
'Erbsünde und Sünde der Welt', pp. 928-938; see also K. Rahner,
'Erbsünde', *Sacramentum Mundi* I (Freiburg, 1967), pp. 1104-1117,
especially p. 1109 and 1115 ff.

[16] See K. Rahner, *Zur Theologie des Todes* (Freiburg, 1958), especially
pp. 53-61; ibid., 'Über das christliche Sterben', *Schriften zur Theologie*
VII (Einsiedeln, 1966), pp. 273-280.

[17] This section contains three points, which have been left in the form
of a bare outline here and are developed more fully later in Chapters 5
and 6 below.

[18] See K. Rahner's instructive interview with E. Simons: *Zur Lage der
Theologie* (Düsseldorf, 1969), p. 38.

[19] See K. Rahner, *Schriften zur Theologie* V, pp. 183-221.

[20] What is certain is that a Christology within an evolutionary view of
the world does not mean the same in Rahner's work as what is implied
here by the abbreviated formula 'evolutionary Christology'. All the
same, it is not without value to question his idea of a possible incarnation in the light of the formal pattern of world evolution, reaching its
culmination in God's self-communication (see p. 216).

3. The relationship between the late New Testament Christology and the classical theology

[1] Karl Rahner has said that, in our present situation, we are entitled to regard the late New Testament Christology as having been dealt with in the Church's classical Christology.

[2] This idea can only partly be traced back to the historically conditioned statement in Jn 16. 28 ('I came from the Father . . . I am going to the Father'). The theocentric implications of Jn 17 as well as Jn 14 and 15 have to be taken into considerations in this text.

4. The theology of the death and resurrection of Jesus

[1] See W. Thüsing, 'Erhöhungsvorstellung und Parusieerwartung in der ältesten nachösterlichen Christologie', SBS 42 (Stuttgart, 1970), for a fuller treatment of the material in this chapter. (This work is cited in all footnotes below as Älteste Christologie.)

5. Christology and theology: the Christologically determined theology of the New Testament

[1] I am convinced that a thorough study of the relationship between Jesus and God is the most important pre-condition for any New Testament approach to Christology. This is what I have attempted to provide in this long central chapter. This important chapter, then, forms the basis for the following Chapter 6, which contains a number of theses for such New Testament approaches.

[2] W. Pannenberg, Grundzüge der Christologie (Gütersloh, [2] 1966), p. 13. (This work is cited in all the footnotes below as W. Pannenberg, Christologie.)

[3] op. cit., p. 14.

[4] See R. Schäfer, Jesus und der Gottesglaube. Ein christologischer Entwurf (Tübingen, 1970), pp. 30ff, 93ff, 98.

[5] See R. Schäfer, op. cit.

[6] According to W. Bousset, Kyrios Christos (Göttingen, [2] 1921), p. 150, the fact that Paul saw the Kyrios Christ alongside God added a complication to the image of God, with the result that Paul's image was less clear than that found in Judaism and with Jesus himself. See Per Christum in Deum, pp. 1-5, 258-261.

[7] R. Schäfer, Jesus und der Gottesglaube, p. 98.

[8] Gerhard Ebeling, Das Wesen des christlichen Glaubens (Munich and Hamburg, [2] 1965), p. 68.

[9] M. Buber, Zwei Glaubensweisen (Zürich, 1950). This work is also

published in M. Buber, *Werke* I, *Schriften zur Philosophie* (Munich, 1962), pp. 651-782.

[10] *op. cit.*, p. 33. This statement refers to the theology of John, but it also applies to Paul, who, Buber believed, was the 'real author of the Christian conception of faith' (p. 42), and to the theology of the synoptics.

[11] For this problem, see J. Blank, *Paulus und Jesus. Eine theologische Grundlegung* (Munich, 1968), pp. 111-123, especially p. 122.

[12] R. Schäfer, *op. cit.*, p. 31 ff.

[13] *op. cit.*, p. 30.

[14] This section does not contain all these amplifications. Others will be found in 5. IV.

[15] D. Bonhoeffer, *Widerstand und Ergebung* (Munich and Hamburg [3] 1966), p. 191 ff. ET: *Letters and Papers from Prison* (London, [3] 1967).

[16] *Zwei Glaubensweisen*, p. 45 ff.

[17] In this context, we do not have to establish the extent to which Hellenistic or mystic thinking influenced the response to questions in the religious environment.

[18] This question is dealt with in much greater detail in my *Per Christum in Deum*.

[19] The permanence of the cross implies, in the light of 1 Cor 1-3, that Christ is of God.

[20] In his use of the Aramaic word 'Abba', Paul is clearly referring to the tradition of Jesus' earthly life.

[21] According to I. Hermann, *Kyrios und Pneuma* (Munich, 1961), p. 50 ff, this is an 'explanatory identification, by means of which Paul traces the experiences reality (the Pneuma) back to the origin behind what is experienced (that is, Christ). In a sense, then, it is an identification from outside and from within the same matter'. What Hermann means by this 'explanatory identification' is that the Pneuma expresses the 'dynamic presence of the Kyrios' in his community. This is clearer than Hermann's first statement above, which is open to misunderstanding.

[22] The risen Christ lives orientated towards God (verse 10). Christians ought therefore to regard themselves as those who are, because of their community with Christ ('in Christ Jesus'), living orientated towards God (verse 11).

[23] Rom 5. 2: the translation 'leading towards' for *prosagoge* is better than the usual translation ('gaining access'). See *Per Christum in Deum*, p. 187 ff.

[24] For this question and the following comments in this section, see W. Thüsing, *Die Erhöhung und Verherrlichung Jesu im Johannesevangelium* (Münster, ² 1970). (This work is cited in all footnotes below as *Erhöhung und Verherrlichung*.)

[25] See the word 'looking (up) to' Jesus in this verse (*aphorontes*); this points to Jesus' exaltation. See also Heb 3. 1.

[26] See the word *hupostasis* in Heb 11. 1, which is interpreted correctly by E. Grässer, in *Der Glaube im Hebräerbrief* (Marburg, 1965), pp. 99-102, as 'holding on to in the sense of constant persistence . . . to what is hoped for'.

[27] See also the texts in Hebrews referring to the orientation of the high priest towards God in his sacrifice (Heb. 7. 27; 9. 14, 28, for example) or his way to the heavenly sanctuary (Heb 9, 24, for example).

[28] 'Gotteserfahrung heute', *Schriften zur Theologie*, IX, pp. 161-176, especially pp. 166 and 168.

[29] See K. Rahner, *Einübung priesterlicher Existenz* (Freiburg, 1970), p. 19.

[30] K. Rahner, *Gotteserfahrung heute, op. cit.*, p. 171 ff.

[31] K. Rahner, *op. cit.*, p. 175 ff.

[32] See, for example, Heb 12. 2: Jesus as the 'pioneer and perfecter of our faith'.

[33] See in this context the dynamic element in Paul's theology. Extremely simplified, this is the theology of the overcoming of death. An answer to the urgent Pauline question in Rom 7. 24 is given, for example, in Rom 8. 31-39. See also the question of longing for the sabbath rest in Heb 3-4.

[34] The Paraclete of the farewell discourses in the fourth gospel corresponds to Paul's Pneuma, despite the difference in tradition.

[35] This statement about God is a kind of summary of John's message about the greatness of God.

[36] See the statement that Christians 'have' the high priest Jesus (Heb 4. 14; 8.1; 10. 21). See F.J. Schierse, *Verheissung und Heilsvollendung. Zur theologischen Grundfrage des Hebräerbriefs* (Munich, 1955), p. 159. For the question of 'looking (up) to' Jesus, see p. 159-161.

[37] According to Heb 10. 23-25, the community of Christians and the assembly of this community play an important part in this experience of God.

[38] See P. Benoit, 'Paulinisme et Johannisme', *NTS* IX (1962-1963), pp. 193-207.

[39] For Matthew, see W. Trilling, *Das wahre Israel. Studien zur Theolo-*

gie des Matthäus-Evangeliums (Munich, [3] 1964), especially pp. 21-51. For Mark, see E. Schweizer, *Das Evangelium nach Markus* (Göttingen, 1967), especially p. 7, last paragraph. For Luke, see G. Voss, *Die Christologie der lukanischen Schriften in Grundzügen* (Paris and Bruges, 1965), especially pp. 131-153. For the logia, see W. Thüsing, *Älteste Christologie, op. cit.*, pp. 55-70. For the whole question of the unity of the New Testament, see E. Schweizer, *Jesus Christus im vielfältigen Zeugnis des Neuen Testaments* (Munich and Hamburg, 1968); A. Stock, *Einheit des Neuen Testaments. Erörterung hermeneutischer Grundpositionen der heutigen Theologie* (Einsiedeln, 1969); H. Lubsczyk, *Die Einheit der Schrift* (Stuttgart, 1970).

[40] This is both possible and necessary from the exegetical point of view. See *Per Christum in Deum*, pp. 225-232.

[41] 'Der eine Mittler und die Vielfalt der Vermittlungen', *Schriften zur Theologie* VIII, pp. 218-235, especially p. 223.

[42] See W. Pannenberg, *Christologie, op. cit.*, pp. 121-123.

[42] See W. Pannenberg, *Christologie, op. cit.*, p. 117; for the whole problem, see pp. 114-119.

[43] The word mythologoumenon is used here in the sense of a mythological term that has illegitimately been made independent.

[44] See R. Schäfter, *Jesus und Gottesglaube, op. cit.*, p. 115.

[45] See U. Wilckens, *Die Missionsreden der Apostelgeschichte* (Neukirchen, [2] 1963), p. 210-213, 215 ff.

[46] 'Die ewige Bedeutung der Menschheit Jesu für unser Gottesverhältnis,' *Schriften zur Theologie* III, pp. 47-60, especially p. 48f.

[47] *op. cit.*, p. 115.

[48] This can only be understood if we take as our point of departure not only the man Jesus' understanding of God, but also God's action with regard to Jesus as reflected in the proclamation of the earliest witnesses.

[49] G. Ebeling, *Das Wesen des christlichen Glaubens, op. cit.*, p. 66.

[50] *op. cit.*, pp. 66, 70.

[51] See R. Schnackenburg, *Wer war Jesus von Nazareth?Theologisches Interview Schnackenburg-Schierse*, Düsseldorf, 1970), p. 16 ff.

[52] R. Schnackenburg, *op cit.*, p. 16; see also R. Slenczka, *Geschichtlichkeit und Personsein Jesu Christi. Studien zur christologischen Problematik der historischen Jesusfrage* (Göttingen, 1967), pp. 322-352.

[53] F.J. Schierse, *op. cit.*, p. 11ff, seems to insinuate this.

[54] R. Schnackenburg, *op. cit.*, p. 12, goes on to ask: 'Is that what one does for an ideology'?.

[55] It may perhaps be possible to throw some light on the need to not

only to include the New Testament structures and emphases to which
we have already pointed (and especially the biblical use of dialogue) in
Rahner's ideas, but also to demonstrate how these ideas are inwardly
nourished by these New Testament elements.

[56] See M. Frisch, *Tagebuch 1946-1949* (Frankfurt, 1950), pp. 26-28.
The author says that the love that keeps us in a state of readiness, so
that we can 'follow a person in all his developments' sets everything in
him free 'of every likeness'. On the other hand, however, 'we make a
likeness of ourselves' when we are 'tired' of enduring the 'mystery that
man is'.

[57] See J. Moltmann, *Theologie der Hoffnung* (Munich, 1965), p. 312.
ET: *Theology of Hope* (London, 1967).

[58] O.H. Pesch has called prayer 'speaking faith', even in the title of his
recent book, *Sprechender Glaube. Entwurf einer Theologie des Gebetes*
(Mainz, 1970).

[59] *op. cit.*, pp. 109-116. In this section, I have used a dash twice in the
heading instead of the word 'or'. This shows that the question as to
whether there is an alternative must remain open.

[60] R. Schäfer has concluded that this is 'not possible' (*op. cit.*, p. 114;
here related to praying to Jesus). He does not revoke this decision in
the qualification that follows or in his attempt to understand the facts
that emerge from the history of dogma and the liturgy and to trace
them back to a 'proximity to Jesus' prayer' (p. 115 ff).

[61] *op. cit.*, p. 112; cf. G. Ebeling, *Das Wesen des christlichen Glaubens,
op. cit.*, p. 71.

[62] *op. cit.*, p. 113.

[63] *ibid.*; R. Schäfer regards the idea of faith in Jesus and Jesus' divinity
as in many cases 'quite harmless' and would like to exclude them from
theology 'for the sake of clarity', because he regards the complex use of
the term 'faith' in the New Testament as 'confusing and ambiguous'
(p. 114). According to Schäfer, the Christological debate about the
relationship with Jesus is not concerned with faith that is identical with
the relationship with God. This is only correct in Schäfer's narrow idea
of faith. It is not correct in the New Testament sense.

[64] *op. cit.*, pp. 114-116; for similar arguments, applied to the question
of faith, see p. 113.

[65] 1 Cor 16. 22 and Didache 10. 6 in the Aramaic form, in the Greek
translation Acts 22. 20. In the context preceding Didache 10. 6, it is
possible to read 'may be Kyrios come' instead of 'may grace come'; see
R. Bultmann, *Theologie des Neuen Testaments* (Tübingen, [4]1961), p.

219, note 1.

[66] This can be justified by the Johannine view (see, for example, Jn 14, 9ff: 'He who has seen me has seen the Father'). In the same way, a similar address can also be found in the fourth gospel (Jn 20. 28: 'My Kyrios and my God', which is clearly a reflection of the prayer of the Johannine communities).

[67] 'If anyone has no love for the Kyrios, let him be accursed'. As the immediately following 'Maranatha' and the preceding admonition of the 'holy kiss' (1 Cor 16. 20) show, this is clearly a call or acclamation from the liturgy of the Lord's Supper. See G. Bornkamm, 'Das Anathema in der urchristlichen Abendmahlsliturgie', *Das Ende des Gesetzes*, Aufsätze I (Munich, 1961), pp. 123-132. It is worth noting that admission to the Lord's Supper and therefore full membership of the community is not dependent here on the confession of a person, made in a doctrinal formula, but on that person's love for the exalted Kyrios.

[68] Rahner demonstrates in *Ich glaube an Jesus Christus* (Einsiedeln, 1968), pp. 55-65, especially pp. 58, 60-63, that prayer to Jesus can be traced back to love for Jesus.

[69] Rahner's argument — in 'Gotteserfahrung heute', *Schriften zur Theologie* IX, p. 174 and other articles — in which the idea of address is dominant, which are determined by transcendental anthropological thinking and which certainly go to the heart of the matter might lead to a narrowing of vision in readers who fail to consider the whole theological context.

[70] R. Schäfer, *op. cit.*, p. 116; see also p. 113.

[71] My work, *Erhöhungsvorstellung und Parusieerwartung in der ältesten nachösterlichen Christologie, op. cit.*, is an attempt to apply this claim to the Christological theo-logy of the earliest post-paschal period.

[72] This tradition was developed theologically in Luke's gospel. See W. Ott, *Gebet und Heil. Die Bedeutung der Gebetsparänese in der lukanischen Theologie* (Munich, 1965), pp. 94-99.

[73] This is quite clear from the testimony of the New Testament. In Mark, for example, the cross and the imitation of the cross are the source of strength for service of others. The three passages following the three prophecies of the Passion in Mark's gospel (Mk 8. 34ff; 9. 33-42; 10. 35-45) are clear examples of this. Mark interprets the logia in the light of the tradition of the Lord's Supper. Mk 10. 45, for example, should be compared with the passages about who among the disciples was to be the greatest and with Lk 22. 24-27. (It should be

noted that, in Luke, the dispute about who was to be the greatest is in the context of the Lord's Supper.) In the logia, the radical demand of love is only apparently not connected with the radical demand of imitation.

[74] Or to an imitation of the cross; see Mk. 8, 34: 'let him . . . take up his cross'.

[75] See A. Vögtle, *Das öffentliche Wirken Jesu auf dem Hintergrund der Qumranbewegung* (Freiburg, 1958), pp. 6-10 or 13. Vögtle refers to a 'religious principle of separation' at the time of Jesus, consisting of 'attempts, by means of human effort, to create the true people of God, that is, a pure community, by following the path of active piety and denying the real intention of the Mosaic law'. See also the author who drew attention to this fact even before the Qumran texts were known: J. Jeremias, 'Der Gedanke des "Heiligen Restes" ', *Abba. Studien zur neutestamentlichen Theologie und Zeitgeschichte* (Göttingen, 1966), pp. 121-132. This article first appeared in *ZNW* 42 (1949), pp. 184-194.

[76] A. Vögtle, *op. cit.*, p. 13.

[77] See J. Jeremias, 'Der Gedanke des "Heiligen Restes" ', *op. cit.*, pp. 129-132; *ibid.*, *Die Gleichnisse Jesu* (Göttingen, [6]1962), pp. 221-224, 124-145; A. Vögtle, *op. cit.*, pp. 12-16.

[78] A. Vögtle, *op. cit.*, p. 16.

[79] See H. Schürmann, *Worte des Herrn* (Leipzig, [3]1960), pp. 195-197.

[80] U. Wilckens, article on *hupokrinomai ktl.*, *ThWNT* VIII, p. 564 ff: '*hupokrisis* is a kind of sacrilege. It is not used to describe an appearance of piety, hiding the true state of sacrilege. The translation 'hypocrisy' is therefore quite unsatisfactory. The word points above all to the deception which characterizes sacrilege as a falling away from or denial of God'.

[81] In Luke this appears as 'merciful' (Lk 6. 36).

[82] The possibility of an experience of God by Jesus' disciples is implied in their service as a whole of the Basileia. This background to a mediation of the experience of God is of great importance in the New Testament and should always be borne in mind. See also the Matthaean interpretation of discipleship (Mt 23. 8-12), as contrasted with the attitude of the pharisees (Mt 23. 16, 19, 24; cf. Lk. 6, 39) and the Lucan passage about unworthy servants (Lk 17. 7-10; cf. Lk 14. 7-11: the 'lowest place' at table.

[83] See A. Vögtle, 'Zeit und Zeitüberlegenheit im biblischen Verständnis', *Zeit und Zeitlichkeit* (Freiburg, 1961), p. 99-116, here p. 113: 'Luke 11. 20 can undoubtedly be traced back to the *ipsissima vox* of

Jesus, who was speaking of the thrust of the kingdom of God as an active power on the generation that experienced him, but also as something that belonged essentially to the future'. On p. 114, Vögtle also says that Luke 11. 20 points to 'a kind of thrust forward of the dynamic power of the kingdom of God, a kind of extension of God's eschatological activity into this era'.

[84] See A. Vögtle, 'Exegetische Erwägungen über das Wissen und Selbstbewusstsein Jesu', *Gott in Welt*, Festgabe für Karl Rahner (Freiburg, 1964), I. pp. 608-667, here p. 647: 'Mark 9, 1 ff can be explained as an early extension of the primitive logion of Mark 13. 30, which refers to the destruction of the temple'. For Vögtle's comment on Mk 13. 30, see p. 650 ff, where he says that this logion is a word of consolation, which incorporates Jesus' saying in Mt 10. 14 par ('If anyone will not receive you . . . leave that house or town') and the promise of the coming of the Son of Man, but 'originated as a whole in Palestinian Christianity'.

[85] I do not use the term 'mathematical point' here in the sense in which it is used by the school of Bultmann.

[86] See H. Schürmann, *Das Gebet des Herrn* (Leipzig and Freiburg, 1958): 'The end must come so that God's holiness will be made manifest. Where God is made visible as God, the world is not only affirmed, but also questioned. Taking God completely seriously demands an eschatological fulfilment, which at the same time signifies destruction and new creation'.

[87] This ought to be possible within the framework of the consequence resulting from the imminent proclamation, which is discussed in the following section (5. IV 4 b iii). H. Schürmann's term 'constant expectation', which is very easily misunderstood, can be verified only in this context.

[88] See A.P. Polag, *Die Christologie der Logienquelle* (type-written dissertation, Trier, 1968), p. 122.

[89] See the saying about saving and losing one's life (Mk 8. 35) and its parallels (for example, Mk 9. 42-47).

[90] See H. Schürmann, 'Eschatologie und Liebesdienst in der Verkündigung Jesu', *Ursprung und Gestalt* (Düsseldorf, 1970), pp. 279-298.

[91] See W. Thüsing, 'Die Vision des "neuen Jerusalem" (Apk 21, 1-22, 5) als Verheissung und Gottesverkündigung', *TThZ* 77 (1968), pp. 17-34, especially pp. 30-34.

[92] The universal nature of this law of salvation must also be presupposed, according to the content and meaning, if not according to the

literal words, even in the synoptic tradition. See the tradition of the Lord's Supper, which, in my opinion, goes back to Jesus himself, with its 'for the many' or 'for all'.

[93] See K. Rahner, 'Die Christologie innerhalb einer evolutiven Weltanschauung', *Schriften zur Theologie*, V, p. 183: the quesion of the suitability of an evolving view of the world in Christology is 'a possible and even better and more radical question'. (*Theol. Inv.*, vol. V).

[94] Insofar as Jesus' consciousness of his mission was orientated towards the validation of the promise of the Basileia in the future, an arrow could be included in this Scheme B II from the 'mission' ('having been sent') of Scheme B I, that is the point at the top, representing the present, connecting with the arrow pointing from the Old Testament (and the 'abundance of promises') to the future. The same could be done in the case of the 'response' shown in Scheme B I. These arrows would correspond in Scheme B II to the dotted lines in Scheme B III, but they would also indicate more clearly Jesus' acceptance of the Old Testament promise.

[95] See J. Moltmann, *Theologie der Hoffnung, op. cit.*, p. 127 (ET: *Theology of Hope*). See also Rev 1. 4, 8; 4. 8, where God is described as the 'one who is to come'.

[96] See Rom 8. 11: God will raise . . . through his Pneuma which dwells in you'; see also Rom 8. 23-28.

[97] See H. Schürmann, 'Das hermeneutische Hauptproblem der Verkündigung Jesu. Eschato-logie und Theo-logie im gegenseitige Verhältnis', *Gott in Welt I, op. cit.*, pp. 579-607, especially pp. 604-607.

[98] A.P. Polag, *Die Christologie der Logienquelle, op. cit.*, p. 54 ff, 80, 106.

[99] What is meant here is 'the Son' in the absolute sense, as opposed to the 'Son of God', where the 'Son' is determined by the genitive 'of God'. The two forms should be kept distinct in the history of traditions. F. Hahn, in his *Christologische Hoheitstitel* (Göttingen, 1963), pp. 319-333, regards the word 'Son' in this sense as a very early usage, based on 'conditions imposed by the early tradition of the Palestinian community' (see p. 329) and possibly going back to Jesus himself In my opinion, however, there is not convincing evidence that this should be traced back to Jesus himself (see Lk 10. 22 par Mt; Mk 13. 32 par Mt).

[100] 'Kirchliche Autorität im Anspruch der Freiheitsgeschichte', J.B. Metz, J. Moltmann and W. Oelmüller, *Kirche im Prozess der Aufklärung* (Munich and Mainz, 1970), pp. 53-90, especially pp. 74-79.

[101] *Jesus und der Gottesglaube, op. cit.*, p. 64 ff.

[102] See E. Grässer, *Der Glaube im Hebräerbrief, op. cit.*, pp. 46-62, especially pp. 48, 60.

[103] See Heb 12. 2b: despite his unique soteriological function, Jesus is placed in parallel with those whose archegos he is to be. This, Grässer *believes (op. cit.*, p. 60), is so insofar as he 'proves the value of *stasis* in enduring contestation and shame'.

[104] E. Grässer, *op. cit.*, pp. 57-62, especially p. 60; p. 60, note 280.

[105] The addition of the words 'and fasting' in Mk 9. 29 is secondary from the point of view of textual criticism and should therefore not be taken into account in considering the theological meaning of the text.

[106] Within the framework of the story of the cursing of the fig-tree by Jesus, what is of primary importance here — certainly in the sense of Mark's editing — is Jesus' own faith in prayer. In my opinion, in linking together the statement about the faith that moves mountains and the story of the fig-tree, the evangelist has given emphasis to the primary Christological meaning which was at least implicit in the very early version of the statement about the faith that moves mountains.

[107] Paul's formula of a sacrifice of one's living existence, as a response to God's saving activity in Christ (Rom 12. 1 ff) expresses very well what is meant here by prayer as a total expression of life and what is, according to the content and meaning (though not, of course, in the history of traditions), is also constitutive for the synoptic faith in prayer.

[108] Mk 9. 23 is interpreted differently by many exegetes. This is because this text is often seen in the light of the Matthaean interpretation of the pericope and of the parallel miracle stories in the synoptics, in which only the faith of the one making the petition is called into question. This variety of exegetical interpretations is above all due, however, to insufficient attention (or none at all) being given to the relationship between Mk 9. 23 and Mk 9. 29 (and 11. 22 ff). See, for example, G. Ebeling, 'Jesus und Glaube', *Wort und Glaube* (Tübingen, [3]1967), pp. 203-254, especially p. 240 ff.

[109] See H. Schürmann, *Jesu Abschiedsrede Lk 22, 21-39* (Münster, 1957), pp. 36-43, especially p. 39 ff, who regards this text a pre-Lucan and traditional. Despite the author's interest in the *perasmoi*, however, it is unlikely that Luke tried to shape the text. This is clear from his fashioning of the Gethsemane scene (Lk 22. 39-46), which does not stress Jesus' agony, as Mark does, but tones it down and presents it as a lonely test of faith. The important verse in this connection is Lk

22. 43, which can be taken together with verse 44. Despite the textual evidence cited, not entirely convincingly, by W. Grundmann, *Das Evangelium nach Lukas* (Berlin, [2]1961), p. 410 ff, verse 43 can be regarded as having belonged originally to the Lucan passage.

[110] For the interpretation of Jesus' *perasmoi*, see the story of the temptations (Lk 4. 1-13 par Mt) which is derived from the logia. This passage contains a narrative expansion of a single situation of temptation, that of Jesus' sojourn in the desert (cf. Mk 1. 12 ff) and provides, in this narrative, an interpretation of what happened in the life of Jesus in many different situations as well as an interpretation of his activity as a whole and his movement towards ultimate catastrophe. This interpretation is, moreover, given in the form of a summary.

[111] In the sense of the Hebrew *tamîm* and *salêm*, both of which are rendered in the Septuagint by *teleios*, meaning undamaged, undivided, complete, whole or sound. They are used with reference to the undivided service of the people of God and the undivided orientation of the individual's heart towards Yahweh and his will. See G. Delling, article on *teleios, ThWNT* VIII, pp. 72-78, especially pp. 72-75.

[112] K. Rahner, 'Dogmatische Erwägungen über das Wissen und Selbstbewusstsein Christi', *Schriften zur Theologie* V, pp. 222-245, especially pp. 236-239. (Cf. *Theological Investigations,* vol. V).

[113] The wider basis of my thesis will be grasped if the statements about anxiety and storing treasures (Lk 12. 22-34 par Mt; see also the parallels in content, if not in words, among which Lk 9. 57 ff is relevant from the Christological point of view) are borne in mind.

[114] See W. Trilling, *Das wahre Israel, op. cit.*, especially p. 213, lines 14 ff.

[115] The strongly emphasized aspect of knowing about the unity with God in the statement made in Jesus' prayer (Jn 11. 41 ff) and generally in the Johannine portrait of Jesus can only be misunderstood if it is isolated from the rest of John's theology. The high priestly prayer of Jesus (Jn 17) is the clearest indication of the Johannine re-interpretation of Jesus' faith in prayer. Both the radical theocentricity and the unique quality of this prayer are expressed in Jn 17 and connected with Jesus' work, the culmination of his obedience in death (the completion of his work; see Jn 17. 4, together with 19. 30 and 4. 34; see also 17. 17-19) and the finality of his work (that is, faith or the salvation of the world; see Jn 17. 20-26). It is only if we recognize the Johannine re-interpretation of the tradition of Jesus and the fundamental kerygma and its distinctive theological quality (that is, as a combination of Jesus'

NOTES

work on earth and the exalted Jesus' activity that we shall avoid playing
off the Johannine emphasis on Jesus' sovereign knowledge and power
against a continuity with the earlier tradition of Jesus. I am convinced
of this, unlike E. Käsemann, *Jesu letzter Wille nach Johannes 17*
(Tübingen, 1966) and G. Dautzenberg, *Christusdogma ohne Basis?*
Rückfragen an das Neue Testament (Essen, 1971), pp. 32-35.

[116] See, for example, Peter Lombard, *Sent. lib.* III, dist. 26, cap. 4;
Thomas Aquinas, *Summa Theologiae* III. q. 7, art. 3. See also the quotations in G. Ebeling, 'Jesus und Glaube', *Wort und Glaube, op. cit.*,
p. 240 ff, note 92.

[117] Paul may also have succeeded in doing this too, in a different way,
by combining the *pistis Christi* and being in Christ. For parallels to this
faith of Jesus, see D. Wiederkehr, 'Entwurf einer systematischen Christologie', *Mysterium Salutis* III/1 (Einsiedeln, 1970), pp. 477-648,
especially pp. 626-629; G. Ebeling, 'Jesus und Glaube', *Wort und
Glaube, op. cit.*, and *Das Wesen des christlichen Glaubens, op. cit.*, pp.
40-52; Hans Urs von Balthasar, 'Fides Christi', *Sponsa Verbi* (Einsiedeln,
1961), pp. 45-79.

[118] Paul uses the concept of *pistis*, in the vast majority of cases, in an
absolute sense or in connection with a subjective genitive. When he
wants to speak about faith in Christ, he uses the verb *pisteuein*. It is
only possible to decide from the context whether the genitive *Christou*,
in the rare expression *pistis Christou* — it is only used, apart from Rom
3, 21 ff, 26, in Gal 2. 16, 20; 3. 22; Phil. 3. 9; see also Gal 3. 26 (*pistis
en Christo*) — is used as an objective or a subjective genitive. In any
case, the statements about *pisteuein* in Jesus and the few places in
which *pistis Christou* may indicate faith in Christ are not an adequate
basis for arguing that *pistis Christou* can only have this meaning in Paul.
They are not enough to invalidate the arguments in favour of the interpretation 'the faith of Christ' in Rom 3, 21 ff, 26.

[119] The *apistia* of 'some' Jews cannot make the *pistis* (that is, his faithfulness to the promise or covenant) of God ineffective. See also Rom.
1. 17; 1 Cor 1. 9:; 2 Cor 1. 18; 1 Thess 5. 24: God as *pistis* means that
he is faithful to his promise.

[120] This revelation takes place as the dynamic expression of the proclamation of the gospel; see especially Gal 1. 16; Rom 1. 3, 9; 1 Cor 1. 9;
2 Cor 1. 19. See also Per Christum in Deum, pp. 144-147.

[121] See, for example, Heb 10. 19 ff together with Heb 9. 11-14. See also
W. Thüsing, ' "Lasst uns hinzutreten . . ." (Hebr 10. 22). Zur Frage
nach dem Sinn der Kulttheologie im Hebräerbrief', *BZ*, new series 9

(1965), pp. 1-17, here p. 8 ff.

[122] *Das Wesen des christlichen Glaubens, op. cit.*, p. 57.

[123] See especially Jn 17. 22: the *doxa* which Jesus gives to hiw own, like the *doxa* that he has received from the Father, is to be seen as the power and radiance of his unity in love with the Father. See *Erhöhung und Verherrlichung, op. cit.*, pp. 181-186. See also Jn 17. 26.

[124] It would be interesting to compare the view of Jesus as the one to whom faith is directed — the view reflected in the classical Christology and in Rahner's re-interpretation, which is, of course, partly determined by the Chalcedonian definition — with Ebeling's view of the 'witness to faith, who became the ground of faith' (op. cit., p. 57). It could perhaps be demonstrated that Ebeling's approach — and that of his pupil Schäfer — is closer to the New Testament datum, but that Rahner's total conception, despite the corrections that ought to be made on the basis of the New Testament, may be closer to the Christological foundation of the New Testament, insofar as any limitation to the Jesus of history, which is less obvious in Ebeling's work than in Schäfer's, is completely excluded by Rahner.

[125] See 1 Jn 2. 8; 2 Cor 5. 17. Neither of these texts contains an explicitly Christological statement, but the new element to which they refer is based in the newness of Jesus himself. In 1 Jn 2. 8, the 'new commandment' can be proclaimed because 'the true light is already shining', that is, the light of the absolute *agape* revealed by Jesus. In 2 Cor 5. 17, Christians are the 'new creation', because they are 'in Christ', who, as the 'first fruits of those who have fallen asleep' (1 Cor 15. 20), is the original new creation of God.

[126] See *Per Christum in Deum, op. cit.*, p. 260 ff.

[127] See A. Diessler, 'Gottes Selbstoffenbarung im Alten Testament,' *Mysterium Salutis* II, pp. 226-269, especially pp. 243 ff and 244-248 (the name of Yahweh as the revelation of the old covenant). On p. 247, Deissler says that God wanted to reveal 'every structure of his existence' in the name of Yahweh 'which he, as an absolutely free person, disposing entirely of himself, had given to himself by deciding to turn his face towards man — in this case, man is Israel — and to unite himself with mankind (in the first place Israel) in a personal relationship known as the covenant'.

[128] See the promise of Joel 3. 1 ff; Ezek 36. 26 ff; Jer 31. 33 ff, which was universally fulfilled or was to be universally fulfilled, at least according to the New Testament kerygma.

[129] The author of the gospel according to Matthew was particularly well

aware of the danger of phariseeism which threatened the disciples, but showed, in the directive given in Mt 23. 8-12, which he deliberately added to his composition of anti-pharisaical statements as a key to their understanding, the extent to which this danger can be overcome.

[130] M. Buber uses these terms in his *Zwei Glaubensweisen, op. cit.*, p. 6 ff.; the contact is primarily that of the Old Testament *'emûnah* and the acceptance is primarily the New Testament *pistis*.

[131] In the light of Old Testament Semitic ideas, Jesus can only be understood, in his soteriological function, as a 'corporative personality'. This is indicated by the parallels between Adam and Christ in Romans and other texts. See the theme of the Son and the sons, for example, in Rom 8. 29 and Heb 2. 10-12.

[132] Perhaps because of his Chassidic background, M. Buber certainly had a premonition of what the cross of Jesus meant for Christians. See, for example, his 'Nachahmung Gottes', *Werke* II, Schriften zur Bibel, pp. 1053-1065; 'Der Glaube der Propheten', *op. cit.*, pp. 231-481, especially the last chapter on the God of the suffering, pp. 400-481, where he refers at one point explicitly to the effects of the image of the suffering Messiah on Chasidism.

[133] *Zwei Glaubensweisen, op. cit.*, pp. 15-19.

6. Theses for new approaches to a contemporary Christology based on the New Testament

[1] My suggested new approaches to a New Testament Christology are contained in a concentrated form in the sixteen theses in this chapter. Each of these theses was subjected to intensive discussion and the results of these discussions appear in this chapter as commentary on the individual theses or elucidations.

[2] These official doctrines of the Church will be found in H. Denzinger and A. Schönmetzer, *Enchiridion Symbolorum, Definitionum et Declarationum de rebus fidei et morum* (Barcelona, Freiburg, Rome and New York, [34] 1967).

[3] The main corrective function of the Church's doctrines cannot easily be shown in a diagram. The Church's definitions of dogma are not the source, but rather the stone surrounding which prevents the water from running away into the desert sand and which can from time to time be improved or renewed.

[4] For the tradition-historical origins of the idea of pre-existence, see F. Hahn, *Christologische Hoheitstitel, op. cit.*, pp. 315-319; E. Schweizer, 'Zur Herkunft der Präexistenzvorstellung bei Paulus', *Neotestamentica*

(Zürich and Stuttgart, 1963), pp. 105-109; *ibid.*, 'Aufnahme und Korrektur jüdischer Sophiatheologie im Neuen Testament', *Neotestamentica, op. cit.*, pp. 110-121.

[5] See E. Schweizer, *Jesus Christus, op. cit.*, pp. 68-91. For the special position of Phil 2. 6-8 see *ibid.*, p. 87, note 43; p. 89 ff.

[6] By this, I mean the view that Jesus pre-existed as the Son. For the positive sense of this view, see W. Pannenberg, Christologie, *op. cit.*, p. 152 ff.

[7] See E. Schweizer, 'Zum religionsgeschichtlichen Hintergrund der "Sendungsformel" Gal 4, 4f; Röm 8, 3f; Joh 3, 16f; Joh 4, 9', *Beiträge zur Theologie des Neuen Testaments* (Zürich, 1970), pp. 83-95.

[8] For a more detailed discussion of the way in which the fourth gospel broke through the gnostic pattern of thought, see *Erhöhung und Verherrlichung, op. cit.*, p. 293 (the connection between the theology of the revealer and that of going to the Father); p. 224; the terminology of the change of place; the gnostic pattern of Jn 16. 28 is an expression of the fact that, despite Jesus' unity with the Father — see Jn 14. 10; 10. 30; unity as a unique inner nearness — what is expressed here is the concept of outward distance; p. 335: the evangelist did not have the intention of presenting Jesus, in contrast to the consciousness of faith that had existed up to his time in the early Church, as 'God walking on earth' (see E. Käsemann, *Jesu letzter Wille nach Johannes 17, op. cit.*, pp. 22, 29), but of looking at the traditional kerygma of the saving significance of Jesus' death and resurrection in a new way and connecting it with the tradition of Jesus' earthly activity. For the importance of the orientation of Jesus' incarnation towards his exaltation and glorification in John (or the line importance of the line running from Jn 1. 14 to Jn 6. 51c and 19. 34 f), see *Erhöhung und Verherrlichung*, p. 326 (and *passim*, for example, p. 226 ff).

[9] For this functional Christology, see Schemes B I-III, in which the structure of relationships of the objectivization of Jesus' relationship with God is indicated in such a way that the essential structure of the synoptic tradition is clearly revealed.

[10] *Eikon* means the 'appearance of the inner essence of a matter'; see H. Kleinknecht, *ThWNT* II, p. 386. In this case, then, it means the appearance of the essential content of the concepts 'Son of God' (Rom 8. 29) and 'God' (2 Cor 4. 4). See *Per Christum in Deum, op. cit.*, pp. 121-125, especially p. 121.

[11] I am indebted to W. Breuning for stimulating these ideas.

[12] See F.J. Steinmetz, *Protologische Heils-Zuversicht. Die Strukturen*

des soteriologischen und christologischen Denkens im Kolosser- und Epheserbrief (Frankfurt a. M., 1969), pp. 11, 76 ff.

[13] See *Erhöhung und Verherrlichung, op. cit.,* pp. 159-165, 311 ff, 322 ff, 324-326.

[14] A combination of the two views is possible on the basis of statements made in Jn 1. 1 ff about the theology of creation. These are now, however, representative of the Johannine theology, since they are at the service of the Logos hymn that the evangelist took over and his Christology of the revealer. There are also similar statements to those made in 1 Jn and the gospel of John about God's revelation of his love in Paul (see especially Rom 5. 5, 8; 8. 31-39).

[15] See W. Pannenberg, *Christologie, op. cit.,* pp. 406-413.

[16] We are referring here to what the evangelist has taken from the Old Testament and the Old Testament and late Jewish wisdom literature in his concept of the Logos- revealer.

[17] See *Per Christum in Deum, op. cit.,* pp. 122-125; 126-134; 143 ff. See also J. Jervell, *Imago Dei. Gn 1, 26 f im Spätjudentum, in der Gnosis und in den paulinischen Briefen* (Göttingen, 1960), pp. 171-336, especially pp. 256-284.

[18] It also means that it must be related to the whole of mankind. In this, it must be safeguarded against individual misunderstanding and the individual must not be lost in the collectivity.

[19] The hope of resurrection on the part of all mankind can be combined here with the experience of Jesus' resurrection. The point of departure for the development of Christology is to be found in the statements with an explicit orientation towards the future which were at that time very much in the foreground, although the orientation towards the present of the later Christology of the exaltation was implicit.

[20] It is not possible to eliminate a proclamation of this dynamism of God towards an absolute fulfilment or new creation from the New Testament, especially if the apocalyptic and other related material in the New Testament is taken into consideration.

[21] The evolutionary view has to be supplemented by the law of salvation expressed in Jn 12. 24. In other words, the principle of the cross must be recognized here.

[22] See F.J. Steinmetz, *Protologische Heils-Zuversicht, op. cit.,* pp. 113-130.

[23] See W. Pannenberg, *Christologie, op. cit.,* pp. 15-22; ibid., article 'Christologie II. Dogmengeschichtlich', *RGG* I, p. 1775. See also the same author's article 'Christologie III. Dogmatisch', *op. cit.,* pp. 1780-1784.

[24] This kind of statement does not contradict the Christology of pre-existence. Looking theo-logically at the Jesus who is living now, in other words, recognizing that this Jesus who is living now is with God, it is possible to accept, in the light of the New Testament concept of God, the statement about pre-existence, which safeguards the unique aspect of this one man as the absolute bringer of salvation, as a sub-structure, at least in the abstract sense.

[25] See F. Diekamp, *Katholische Dogmatik nach den Grundsätzen des heiligen Thomas* II (Münster, [9] 1939), pp. 246-250, especially p. 247. I have chosen Diekamp because his work is typical of the Christology that was dominant in the Catholic Church for so long and is still dominant in some circles. As late as 1952, a new (tenth) edition of Diekamp's work appeared, revised and brought up to date by K. Jüssen. (Further editions appeared in 1958.)

[26] See R. Schnackenburg, 'Episkopos und Hirtenamt. Zu Apg 20, 28', *Schriften zum Neuen Testament* (Munich, 1971), pp. 247-267, especially p. 252 ff and 253, notes 13 and 14. See also G. Voss, *Christologie der lukanischen Schriften, op. cit.*, p. 122.

[27] In the sense of Jn 14. 9 ff ('He who has seen me has seen the Father', in other words, the Son, as the revealer, is completely transparent to God) in the context of the combination of the immanence of the believer in Jesus and the immanence of Jesus in the Father (see Jn 15. 9 ff; 14. 23).

[28] See *Per Christum in Deum, op. cit.*, pp. 147-150 (in the second edition, p. 151).

[29] See the missionary theology of Paul, especially the central statement made in Rom 1. 16 ff (the gospel as the 'power of God for salvation'). See also the typical post-Pauline statement made in 2 Thess 3. 1.

[30] We only know about the immanent Trinity through the economic Trinity; see K. Rahner, 'Bemerkungen zum dogmatischen Traktat "De Trinitate" ', *Schriften zur Theologie* IV, pp. 103-133. See also Rahner's comment, *op. cit.*, p. 123: 'The economic Trinity *is* the immanent Trinity'. The first part of the thesis 6. II 7 can also be justified from the gnoseological point of view.

[31] See I. Hermann, *Kyrios und Pneuma, op. cit.*, pp. 135 ff, 138 ff. 'Any attempt to hypostasize the Pneuma in the direction of an inde-pendent third person of the Trinity' is out of the question in interpre-ting Paul's theology. See especially R. Schnackenburg's review in *BZ*, New Series 7 (1963), pp. 302-305.

[32] See 'Exegese und Dogmatik', *Schriften zur Theologie* v, pp. 82-111,

especially p. 89.

[33] I Hermann, *op. cit.*, p. 50.

[34] See the concept of *doxa* in the context of 2 Cor 3. 17 (3. 7 − 4. 6).

[35] See the concept of *dunamis*, which is closely associated with *pneuma* (for example, in Rom 15. 13, 19) and the combination of *pneuma* and *agape* in Rom 5. 5.

[36] This image of the sun and its rays is very similar to an early comparison between the activity of the Trinity and the sun and its effects in the theology of the Church Fathers. In the third verse of F. von Spee's hymn to the Trinity, there is a clear reflection of this patristic imagery: 'God the Father, thou art the sun; thy Son the brightness and thou, O Holy Ghost, thou art the warmth and fillst the world with life'.

[37] See E. Sjöberg's article on Pneuma, C III, *ThWNT* VI, p. 386. According to Sjöberg, the Jews thought of the Spirit as a 'reality . . . coming from God to man, to some extent representing God's presence, but not identical with God'.

[38] The lines running through I. Chr. correspond to the theological datum which Paul expressed in his formula 'through Christ'.

[39] See K. Rahner's article on the Trinity in *Sacramentum Mundi* IV, pp. 1013-1016, and his article on the theology of the Trinity, *op. cit.*, p. 1030 ff.

[40] For a justification of this New Testament approach, see J. Ratzinger, 'Bemerkungen zur Frage der Charismen in der Kirche', *Die Zeit Jesu. Festschrft für H. Schlier* (Freiburg, 1970), pp. 257-272, especially pp. 260 ff. On p. 261, Ratzinger says: 'It is possible to say that the Christological re-interpretation of pneumatology provides the real point of departure for a doctrine of the Trinity, in which the Holy Spirit is no longer seen as the third person who has been added more or less by chance, but as the point of departure'.

[41] See *Per Christum in Deum, op. cit.*, p. 154 ff.

[42] J. Moltmann, *Umkehr zur Zukunft* (Munich and Hamburg, 1970), pp. 133-147, especially p. 146. Moltmann's point of departure is Jesus' cry from the cross (Mk 15. 37) or the 'appropriate interpretation' in Mk 15. 34 (see p. 136 ff). See also E. Jüngel, *Gottes Sein ist im Werden* (Tübingen, ²1967), pp. 97-103, especially p. 101; R. Prenter, 'Der Gott, der Liebe ist. Das Verhältnis der Gotteslehre zur Christologie', *ThLZ* 96 (1971), pp. 401-413, especially pp. 411, 413.

[43] See *Per Christum in Deum, op. cit.*, pp. 13-20. See also, in 1 Cor 15, 35-44, the dying of what is sown.

[44] It should be added here: also if the cross is also taken into considera-

tion as making *sumpaschein* possible, with the aim of *sundoxasthenai* (which is, of course, the fulfilled *huiothesia*).

[45] It cannot be denied that the late theologies of the editors of the gospels of Matthew and Luke (together with Acts), possibly including the gospel of Mark, have the function of mediation here. I have not considered this question mainly for reasons of space, but they are in any case not so instructive for our purpose as the theologies of Paul and John.

[46] Moltmann said this in a lecture at the University of Münster on 21 January 1971; see also *ibid.*, *Umkehr zur Zukunft, op. cit.*, pp. 181-187; *ibid.*, *Theologie der Hoffnung, op. cit.*, pp. 140-155; *ibid.*, 'Die "Rose im Kreuz der Gegenwart" ', *Perspektiven der Theologie* (Munich and Mainz, 1968), pp. 212-231.

[47] See W. Thüsing, 'Die Botschaft des Neuen Testaments — Hemmnis oder Triebkraft der gesellschaftlichen Entwicklung?' *GuL* 43 (1970), pp. 136-148, especially p. 145.

[48] See K. Rahner, 'Der eine Mittler und die Vielfalt der Vermittlungen', *Schriften zur Theologie* VIII, pp. 218-235.

[49] See *Erhöhung und Verherrlichung, op. cit.*, pp. 174-192, 224.

[50] See J. Kürzinger's article on Rom 8. 29, *BZ* New Series 2 (1958), pp. 294-299. See also *Per Christum in Deum, op. cit.*, p. 121 ff.

[51] See H.E. Tödt, *Der Menschensohn in der synoptischen Überlieferung* (Gütersloh, [2]1963), who has elaborated this idea in the logia; see especially pp. 231-241, 276-282. See also *ibid.*, *Älteste Christologie, op. cit.*, pp. 74-78.

[52] A.P. Polag, *Christologie der Logienquelle, op. cit.*, pp. 41-43, 107 ff.

[53] This analogy, which has been shown to exist in the synoptic tradition (for example, Lk 10. 16 par Mt), is clarified in the fourth gospel (see, for example, Jn 13, 20 and 17. 18).

[54] See Lk 12. 49-53; not peace, but 'division' (Lk 12. 51 par Mt 10. 34). The confessing community with Jesus is primarily intended in Lk 12. 51-53, but the confessing community only becomes radical in nature in the serving community. Evidence of this can be found in the instructions for Jesus' messengers in Lk 9. 1-5 Mk and Lk 10. 3-12 par Mt. See also the three sayings in Lk 9. 57-62, of which Lk 9. 60 and 62 are related in the Lucan editing to the proclamation of the Basileia and can therefore be interpreted as pointing to the serving community.

[55] See W. Trilling, *Das wahre Israel, op. cit.*, pp. 28-32, 213.

[56] See W. Thüsing, 'Aufgabe der Kirche und Dienst in der Kirche', *Bibel und Leben* 10 (1969), pp. 65-80. Jesus' intention was to remain open

first to God and then, on the basis of his openness to God, to his fellow men.

[57] See W. Thüsing, *op. cit*., p. 72 ff.

[58] *Sacramentum Mundi* III, pp. 548-551. See also the article on Church membership in *Sacramentum Mundi* II, pp. 1209-1215 and *LThK* VI, pp. 223-225. I have chosen the article on mission and implicit Christianity here, because the missionary aspect, which is so important from the New Testament point of view and which is more implicit in the articles on Church membership, is taken more explicitly into account in the article in *Sacramentum Mundi* III.

[59] Volume I (Freiburg, [2]1970), pp. 121-246, 356-377. See also K. Rahner, 'Die Gliedschaft in der Kirche nach der Lehre der Enzyklika Pius XII: "Mystici Corporis Christi" ', *Schriften zur Theologie*, II, pp. 7-94; see also Rahner's articles headed 'Beiträge zur Ekklesiologie', *Schriften zur Theologie* VI, pp. 301-554; ibid., 'Das neue Bild der Kirche', *Schriften zur Theologie* VIII, pp. 329-354; 'Kirche, Kirchen und Religionen', *op. cit.*, pp. 355-373. The article 'Der eine Mittler und die Vielfalt der Vermittlungen', *op. cit.*, pp. 218-235, is also valuable in the context of the relationship between Christology and ecclesiology. (Cf. articles on the Church in *Theological Investigations*, vols. II, VI, VIII).

[60] *Sacramentum Mundi* III, p. 548.

[61] *op. cit.*, p. 548 ff.

[62] *op. cit.*, p. 549.

[63] *op. cit.*, p. 548.

[64] See K. Rahner, 'Über den Begriff des Geheimnisses in der katholischen Theologie', *Schriften zur Theologie* IV, pp. 51-99. (*Theol. Inv.*, vol. IV).

[65] See his 'Reflexionen zur Problematik einer Kurzformel des Glaubens', *Schriften zur Theologie* IX, pp. 242-256. (*Theol. Inv.*, vol. IX).

[66] 1 Cor 16. 22 contains the idea of *philein ton Kurion*, or consenting to the Lord Jesus as an expression of a loving response to him, as a condition of admission to the Lord's Supper. It is probably taken from the liturgy of the Lord's Supper.

[67] Jesus calls for a decision in favour of the kingdom of God which is already thrusting into this era. He also makes this decision possible by giving community with himself.

New Testament Index

238